PASSPORT TO
EXOTIC
REAL ESTATE

**BUYING U.S. AND FOREIGN
PROPERTY IN BREATHTAKING,
BEAUTIFUL, FARAWAY LANDS**

Steve Bergsman

WILEY

John Wiley & Sons, Inc.

Published by John Wiley & Sons, Inc., Hoboken, New Jersey.
Published simultaneously in Canada.

For general information on our other products and services or for technical support, please contact our Customer Care Department within the United States at (800) 762-2974, outside the United States at (317) 572-3993 or fax (317) 572-4002.

Wiley also publishes its books in a variety of electronic formats. Some content that appears in print may not be available in electronic books. For more information about Wiley products, visit our web site at www.wiley.com.

Library of Congress Cataloging-in-Publication Data:

Bergsman, Steve.
    Passport to exotic real estate : buying U.S. and foreign property in breathtaking, beautiful, faraway lands/Steve Bergsman.
        p.   cm.
    ISBN 978-0-470-17330-5 (cloth)
        1. Real property—United States.   2. Second homes—United States.
    3. Real property—Foreign ownership.   4. Americans—Foreign countries.
    I. Title.
    HD259.B483   2008
    333.33'8—dc22

                                                            2008006123

Printed in the United States of America.
10 9 8 7 6 5 4 3 2 1

CONTENTS

Acknowledgments   v

About the Author   vii

Introduction   viii

Chapter 1   American History: The Evolution and
             Migration of Second Home Investments   1

Chapter 2   Hawaii: Condo Demand Ebbs and Flows Like
             Strong Ocean Tides; Southern California
             Real Estate Good Market Indicator   15

Chapter 3   Alaska: The Beauty of Summer Here Is
             Unequal to Anything Else; It's Not All
             Remote Cabins As Golf Homes and
             Ski Condos Attract Folks from Lower 48   33

Chapter 4   Puerto Rico: Skyrocketing Housing Market
             Comes to Abrupt Halt; Bank Problems Mean
             More Scrutiny, Time in Mortgage Process   51

Chapter 5   Virgin Islands: Popular Second Home Market
             for East Coast Investors; Crime Issues
             Worrisome but Certainly No Deterrent   67

Chapter 6   Guam: Military Buildup Rolls Back Real Estate
             Depression; Take a Second Home Here and
             Travel to Asia and Other Pacific Islands   85

Chapter 7 Saipan: The Last Real Estate Bargain under the Stars & Stripes; Federalization, Leasehold Law Liberalization May Be Needed to Save this Economy   101

Chapter 8 American Samoa: Storied Tropical Paradise in the Heart of the South Pacific; Communal Property Ownership a Real Impediment to Development   117

Chapter 9 Mexico: Reverse Migration as Americans Head South across the Border; Ownership Regulations Complicated but Trustworthy   131

Chapter 10 Costa Rica: Salubrious Climate, Beautiful Topography Creates Countrywide Market; Lack of Regulation Means Buyer Beware   145

Chapter 11 Panama: High-Rise Condominium Market in the Tropics; Cheap Living, Senior Discounts Attract Retirees   165

Chapter 12 Honduras: The Island of Roatan Boasts Caribbean Lifestyle; Investors Enjoy Full Ownership Rights to Beachfront Property   181

Chapter 13 Dominican Republic: Punta Cana Second Home Market Hot, Hot, Hot; Prices Remain Moderate except in Upscale Projects Like Cap Cana   197

Chapter 14 Newfoundland: An Unlikely Canadian Success Story; Europeans Rediscover New World and Create a Second Home Market on Shores of Mountain Lakes   213

Notes   **228**

ACKNOWLEDGMENTS

I would never have been able to write this book if it wasn't for the cooperation of real estate developers, project guides, brokers and agents, resort operators, homeowners, attorneys, and the various other professionals I visited in lands stretching from the Caribbean and Central America to the islands of the Northern Pacific.

Before a journey, my modus operandi was to research a country's real estate market online, call or e-mail sources, and, hopefully, induce them to meet me while I was visiting their country. So many people were so generous with their time. Everywhere I went, sources would not only sit and talk, but there were many who spent hours driving me around, showing me their local real estate markets.

Not only were there lunches, dinners, and drinking beers at expat bars, but I was invited into homes, taken to association meetings, and introduced to government officials. So I lift my glass to all the wonderful people who befriended, guided, and instructed me on local real estate practices. And as to the question that was always asked, "Will you be buying a second home here?" The answer is yes, but I don't know where yet.

Thanks to all: Karl Lober, Patricia Martinez, Rico Pester, Dana Dominguez, Dean Brown, Emma Espinal Inoa, Justine Mis, Bill Otto, Rosemary Sauter-Frett, Marsha Maynes, Merry Nash, Wally Leopold, Jorge Zabala, Molly Assad, Elena Munoz, Douglas Marsters, Suzanne Dechter, Jim Galasso, Mike Clewer, Margaret Budgell, Lisa Anthony, David Gillard, Chris Brothers, Mel Tessier, Wayne Smith, Phillip Schrage, Matthew Schrage, Nicholas Captain, Ramon Puangco, Suki Nicole Sul, Liz Duenas, Anthony Godwin, Donna Ysrael, Ron Hodges, Roy Alexander, Mustafa Shakir, Tom Drabble, Henry Kappel, Steven Watson, Edwin Sanchez, Alvaro Riba, Alfredo Benchoam, Scott Oliver,

Terry Mills, Jeffrey Hickcox, Chris Simmons, Karen England, Marcel Segui, Juan Francisco Pardini, Casey Halloran, Rebecca Tyre, Steve Hasz, John Edwards, Jamie Stathis, Duane Thoreson, Barb Wastart, Jessica Cerrato, Brian Porter, Giovanna Mosqueda Aldana, Vernon Penner, Christine Chin, Valerie Brown, Ross Brown, Jennifer Perell, Sharon Keating, Harvey Shapiro, Michael Sklarz, Darlene Nagatani, Jon Mann, Skip Minder, Jennifer Overcast, Brittney and Matt Abbott, Dennis Illies, Casey Steinau, Jim Crawford and Larry Maulden.

I've tried to include on this page everyone I interviewed, but if I've forgotten someone, please forgive me. It was only a foolish oversight.

ABOUT THE AUTHOR

Steve Bergsman is a nationally recognized financial and real estate writer. For more than 25 years, he has contributed to a wide range of magazines, newspapers, and wire services, including the *New York Times,* the *Wall Street Journal Sunday, Executive Decision, Investment Dealer's Digest,* and Reuters News Service. He has been a regular contributor to the "Ground Floor" real estate column in Barron's and has written for all of the leading real estate industry publications, including *National Real Estate Investor, Real Estate Portfolio, Shopping Center World, Mortgage Banking,* and *Urban Land.* In addition to all the business journalism, Bergsman has been a very active travel writer, contributing to Copley News Service among other outlets and visiting 125 countries around the world. Bergsman is the author of *Maverick Real Estate Investing* and *Maverick Real Estate Financing,* also published by Wiley.

INTRODUCTION

An April 2006 article in Barron's noted, "real estate consultants and brokers report a sharp spike in retirees looking for foreign havens." The article cited one foreign real estate consultant, based in Boston, who reported inquiries from people in the 40- to 60-year-old age bracket exploded from a typical 5,000 inquiries a year to about 8,000 in 2006.

The talk at cocktail parties and business lunches these days? It's a lot less about the condo market in Aspen or retirement properties in Naples, Florida, than the villa in Costa Rica or the beach property in Honduras.

Many potential second home and retirement home buyers have been priced out of North America, and so they have turned their attention to markets that just a decade ago might never have been a consideration. And for good reason! Croatia, which was once the scene of a protracted civil war following the breakup of Yugoslavia, now sits on the radar as a hot second home market. With its Adriatic beaches and endearing ancient villages of whitewashed walls and red-tiled roofs, it certainly sounds enticing. (With any luck, there will be no more martial conflict in its future.) Buenos Aires is another location that gets mentioned often. It's cheap and the city is beautiful, but the current leadership is increasingly leftist, chummy with Venezuela's Hugo Chavez and sometimes anti-American.

If there is one problem with investing in properties overseas, it's uncertainty. One never knows when regimes will change, if basic services will be available, if ownership rights can be protected, when bouts of anti-Americanism will flair up, and how secure anyone's legal position is. Nevertheless, it's hard to turn away from that villa in Tuscany or a cliffside house in Malta.

For the adventurous second homebuyer, there are a number of options to reduce risk. Certain locations around the globe offer beauty and a measure of security, while others are, in fact, located on American-owned soil. Guam and the Virgin Islands are exotic, but American.

Adventurous yet risk-adverse, second home buyers are target readers for *Passport to Exotic Real Estate: Buying U.S. and Foreign Property in Breathtaking, Beautiful, Faraway Lands.* This unique real estate book will explore the possibilities, necessities, costs, availability of services, and the adventure factor in acquiring real estate overseas—in foreign countries and on American soil.

Factors driving Americans over the border include globalization of the housing market, dollar exchange rates, cheap prices overseas, a retiring population that is comfortable with travel and, most of all, the high cost of property in the United States.

A booming second home market in the United States has relentlessly driven pricing northward—beyond the ability of most middle-class folks to buy into the extended version of the American dream. There were 1.07 million vacation home sales in the United States in 2006, up 4.76 percent from the year before, according to a report by the National Association of Realtors (NAR). The median price for a vacation home peaked in 2005 at $204,100, but following the general residential real estate market declined slightly in 2006 to $200,000. The drop in median price resulted from investors shifting away from pricier markets like Florida, Nevada, and Arizona to affordable locations in New Mexico, Idaho, Utah, and the Carolinas.

"The baby boom generation is driving second home sales. They're at the peak of their earnings, interest rates remain historically low, and boomers want to diversify investments," explained David Lereah, NAR's chief economist.

The profile of the typical vacation homebuyer is a 52-year-old with earned income of $82,800. With that kind of budget, it's no wonder an investor looking to buy a second home might disregard that $750,000 condominium in West Palm Beach, opting instead for a $40,000 plot of land on a Honduran island. But while it's true that an investor who buys land in Honduras will probably pay less to get the manse built and less for services, there's always the problem of getting basics: food, power, water, and other necessities.

Escapehomes.com, recognizing the fact that Americans have been looking further afield in regard to second homes, devised a quick checklist of things to worry about:

- Are foreigners welcome?
- What visas are required?

- Can foreigners own property?
- Are loans available?
- What are the tax implications?
- Is there a language barrier?
- Is there a favorable exchange rate?
- Is the currency stable?
- Are there restrictions on moving currency?
- Are medical services nearby?
- What is the cost of travel in and out?
- What is the cost of local travel?

Passport to Exotic Real Estate: Buying U.S. and Foreign Property in Breathtaking, Beautiful, Faraway Lands will answer all these questions and more by taking readers on a virtual tour of potential properties from the Pacific Ocean to the Caribbean Sea.

The book is divided into two sections: U.S. properties around the globe and hot spots of second home markets in North America.

Of the two states and territories not in the contiguous 48, only one, Alaska, would be both an excellent winter and summer destination. That's one reason why people like a second home. They're winter sports enthusiasts—skiing or snowboarding—and they like to have a place near the slopes. And because these homes are generally in truly gorgeous locations, the owner might also be inclined to spend summer months there as well. Probably the most desirable second homes and retirement homes, however, are in communities near the sea. This is exactly where the American empire can be bountiful. Most landmasses controlled by the United States are islands, either in the sunny Caribbean or the balmy Pacific.

Of the five overseas U.S. territories, two are in the Caribbean: Puerto Rico and U.S. Virgin Islands. Out in the Pacific, one can find our 49th state, Hawaii; the territories of American Samoa, Guam, and the Commonwealth of Northern Mariana Islands.

In regard to North American territories, the book looks at the most popular second home locations in North America including Mexico, Panama, Dominican Republic, Costa Rica, and Roatan Island off the coast of Honduras. Then, it explores one major second home market in Canada: Newfoundland.

After visiting a western Pacific beach home or a villa in the Caribbean, the traditional U.S. locations of Florida, Cape Cod, or the Carolina beaches may no longer look so enticing.

AMERICAN HISTORY

THE EVOLUTION AND MIGRATION OF SECOND HOME INVESTMENTS

On a beautiful autumn day in the Valley of the Sun, the evocative name for the Phoenix metropolitan area, I drove the 20 miles from my house in Mesa to the Arizona Biltmore Resort & Spa in central Phoenix for a mortgage technology conference. Many of the people attending the conference had arrived from cold weather locations and for the two days in Arizona, they thought they were in paradise. I was coming to the conference to interview one of the presenters for a business magazine, but I stayed on through the handsome luncheon. When the folks at my table learned I was a local, they asked a few questions about the surrounding area, just in case they had time to do some local exploring.

I suppose because I was partial to the building, I gave them this small bit of introduction, telling them that if they just stepped out of the conference center and looked up at the top of the hill just in front of them, they would see a large white building. While it is now called the Mansion Club, it was originally a second home of chewing gum magnate, William Wrigley Jr. Actually, it was one of five Wrigley homes, but this one was built as a 50th wedding anniversary gift for Wrigley's wife, Ada.

Now this was a true second home, or vacation home, as defined by standards of American life from the mid-nineteenth century through the early part of the twentieth century. Whereas in Europe and elsewhere around the world, royalty of one sort or another generally boasted of other homes, either in the countryside or on the coast; in the United States, the great second homes were constructed by and for the emperors of business and their families. Thus arose Newport, Rhode Island, the greatest second home market in the United States during the Gilded Age (from 1865 to 1901), where the great financiers and industrialists built their summer mansions. Many of these can still be visited, such as The Breakers, a 70-room summer residence built by Cornelius Vanderbilt II, at a cost of a then wildly extravagant $7 million.

Newport wasn't the only famous colony for the wealthy. Between the middle of the 1800s and the start of World War I, Long Branch, New Jersey, attracted not only the rich, but the famous as well. Jay Gould, infamous stock manipulator and railroad magnate built four cottages in this coastal community, while George F. Baker, banking chieftain, constructed two. Also regular vacationers in Long Branch were two of the most famous actors of their time, Edwin Booth and Oliver Dowd Byron.[1]

By the early twentieth century, a number of smaller second home markets for the less-than-incredibly wealthy began to develop in places such as Lake George, New York. Elsewhere, the American Southwest opened up to travelers and artistic types with the inclination to visit or live close to wide vistas of mountainous desert regions. Santa Fe and Taos, New Mexico, attracted the likes of everyone from writer D.H. Lawrence to artist Georgia O'Keefe, the latter of whom visited seasonally starting around 1930 before moving there as a permanent resident.

Nevertheless, because of two world wars and an economic depression sandwiched between, the business of second homes continued to be the business of industrial and financial barons through most of the twentieth century.

Phoenix, the capital of Arizona, was still a relatively small city (its population didn't exceed 50,000 until after World War II), but it, too, was beginning to attract seasonal visitors. The Biltmore, then simply the Arizona Biltmore Hotel, opened in February 1929. The Wrigley Mansion, originally known as La Colina Solana (sunny hill), was finished in 1931. It boasted 16,850 square feet of living space, 24 rooms, and 12 bathrooms. With all that, it was the smallest of the Wrigley homes and only used sparingly, maybe four to eight weeks of the year.

The area around the Wrigley home and Biltmore Hotel was sparsely populated and guests still felt the sense of nature, untamed desert, and Wild West. Today, the Mansion Club and Biltmore sit in the very heart of Phoenix, which by itself, boasts a population of more than 1 million.

Phoenix's astronomical growth really began after World War II, and the cities comprising the Valley of the Sun, including Scottsdale, Mesa, Tempe, Glendale, and a few others, all grew up together. With population expansion in the 1950s and 1960s, the first large wave of seasonal visitors started arriving, northerners who rented or built a wide variety of residential structures, from mobile homes to small, single-family residences. This was a market for the middle class from cold climates, including Canada.

Phoenix mirrored other warm weather locations, attracting a small, but growing number of middle-class families that came south for the sun and started buying homes to be used occasionally.

In the United States, second homes as a middle-class phenom-enon was a post-World War II development, when a strong economy, a greater amount of excess family capital, entrepreneurial real estate development, and the creation of new roadways and airplane travel all helped redefine vacation travel.

Taking a peek at popular second home locations around the country, we find the middle class heading to Cape Cod beginning in the 1960s. As *The Boston Globe* noted, "During the 1960s, 1970s, and early 1980s, the Cape was a retreat for a middle class who could afford the modestly priced vacation homes being developed then."[2]

Down in South Carolina, the development of Hilton Head Island really got started in 1956 when two things happened: The James F. Byrnes Bridge was constructed, opening the island to direct auto-mobile traffic from the mainland; and Charles Fraser bought his father's interest in Hilton Head Company and began developing it into Sea Pines Plantation. By 1958, the first deed to a lot in Sea Pines was signed. Beachfronts initially sold for $5,350, but it didn't take long for demand and appreciation to set in; four years later beachfronts were selling for $9,600. Part of the reason for the bigger price tag was that the island's first golf course, Ocean Course, opened in 1959.

It wasn't only beach areas that began attracting the middle class for seasonal residency; skiing had just begun to catch on in the United

States before World War II, but the war threw ski development plans into a hiatus. Finally, at the end of the 1940s, some of the country's major ski resorts began to take shape. As an example, the Aspen Skiing Corporation was founded in 1946, and the Aspen, Colorado, area very quickly caught on with skiers. Just 12 years later, the popularity of skiing was growing so quickly, Aspen opened two more ski areas, Buttermilk and Aspen Highlands. Expansion continued with the opening of Snowmass in 1969.

Vail, Aspen's big competitor for the high-end skier and cross-state rival, is a younger development. Construction on its ski resort didn't start until 1962 and the town itself wasn't incorporated until 1966. Interestingly, in 2006, the *Vail Daily* newspaper ran a story about the local residential market and it began by featuring Gary Lebo, the owner of a company called Alpenglow Property Management. A key point in Gary's career history was that he began in the 1970s by selling second homes.

The event that really put skiing on the map for most Americans was the Winter Olympics of 1960, which took place at Squaw Valley in the Lake Tahoe region, which sits on the border of California and Nevada in the Sierra Nevadas.

For the first half of the twentieth century, development around Lake Tahoe consisted of a few vacation homes, but the Olympics, and most importantly, completion of the interstate highway through the region in preparation for the Olympics, opened up Tahoe to development. Here's the telling statistic: Over the 20-year period from 1960 to 1980, the permanent resident population increased from 10,000 to 50,000, while the seasonal population jumped from 10,000 to 90,000.

When I moved to Mesa, a suburb of Phoenix, in 1976, there was already in my town a large swath of RV parks, residential developments, and over-55 communities that catered to the seasonal visitor. The word "snowbird," to connote residents of cold weather climes who traveled south for the winter months, was already used extensively. In my early years in Mesa, it used to amuse me to identify license plates from the various states of the union and provinces of Canada. At the end of my first year in Arizona, I had developed a theory that east of Chicago, snowbirds migrated to Florida, but from the Windy City west, they came to Arizona. (Mesa is the spring training home of the Chicago Cubs—an underappreciated rationale for second home selection is where the home baseball team goes for spring training.)

While the sunshine, beach, and ski second home markets for the middle class began to build in the 1960s, '70s, and '80s, it should be noted for as long as there has been a United States, there has always been a fairly low-end, niche market in this sector for hunters and fishermen, who often owned cabins, camps, lodges, or other rudimentary structures that were used almost exclusively for these outdoor activities. As William Faulkner wrote about the annual hunting trip in mythical Yoknapatawpha County in *Go Down, Moses:* "It had already begun on that day when he first wrote his age in two ciphers and his cousin McCaslin brought him for the first time to the camp, the big woods, to earn for himself the name and state of hunter provided he in his turn was humble and enduring enough."

This part of the market still exists; some of it has gone upscale, and depending on where the cabin is located, consistent appreciation has been a side benefit to the good hunt.

The 1990s

Consistent appreciation, a traditional hallmark of most second home markets, ended in the 1990s. Instead, the value of vacation homes began to accelerate dramatically. The reason for this was due to a confluence of factors: financial, economic, and demographic.

In 2004, I wrote one of the first major articles on the vast appreciation being experienced in second home venues for *Barron's* magazine. At the time, markets were peaking. Within a year, prices would begin to plateau, finally dropping into a slight decline by 2006.

My favorite location in the story was Nantucket, Massachusetts, which was, and still is, a playground for the corporate elite, the twenty-first century's equivalent of Newport in the Gilded Age. Before he moved his primary residence to the federal prison system, Dennis Kozlowski of Tyco International summered on Nantucket, rubbing shoulders with Lou Gerstner (IBM), Jack Welch (General Electric), Lawrence Bossidy (United Technologies), and many others. Gerstner had paid $12 million for 1.6 acres on Nantucket.

Well, when Corporate America wants in, that can only mean one thing: Prices are going to skyrocket and Nantucket experienced its own little bubble. Along the harbor, home values in Brant Point and Monomoy were appreciating at a sizzling 10 to 12 percent a month when I wrote my story. Even in the less ritzy mid-island section, homes values jumped about 40 percent annually.

The National Association of Realtors (NAR) first surveyed the second home market in 1989. At the time, it reported there were 288,000 sales of second homes in the country and the median price was $99,200. Ten years later, sales volume had risen to 377,000 and the median price jumped to $127,800.

By 2005, the NAR would report that 12.2 percent of all homes bought that year were vacation residences. Investment home sales were also very high, and the NAR lumped both categories together, reporting 3.34 million second home sales that year, up 16 percent from the year before. Separating out just vacation homes, sales were a record 1.02 million, up 16.9 percent from the previous year's 872,000 sales figure and a long way from 377,000 sales in 1999.

According to the *Christian Science Monitor,* the number of secondary residences steadily climbed in the last decade of the twentieth century, from 5.5 million in 1990 to 6.4 million in 2000, and by 2010, the newspaper predicts sales will reach 9.8 million.[3]

The question is: Why was there so much sudden interest in second homes on the part of the American middle class? The answer begins with demographics. Like many post-World War II phenomena, this one is being driven by the 80 million strong baby boomers.

In the year 2000, the leading edge of baby boomers began to hit 55 years of age. This is not only the optimum time in life when people become interested in second homes, says David Lereah, chief economist of the NAR, but they are at the peak of their earnings. Indeed, at 55 years, some baby boomers in the upper middle-class range are already retired or planning to retire within five to seven years. Real estate is now a key feature in retirement planning, either because of the possibility of retirement in warmer environs or avoiding the cold winters by spending part of the year in those warmer places.

"Vacation home sales will remain strong for the foreseeable future given the fact that baby boomers are favorably positioned in terms of affordability, as well as being at the stage in life when people are most interested in making that kind of lifestyle purchase," says Lereah.[4]

It's not only earnings power that is driving the second home decisions of the baby boomers but their inheritance potential as well. The parents of the baby boomers, who beginning in the 1950s overcame economic barriers to storm into the middle class or better, often amassed considerable assets, which they passed on to their children. As a means of diversifying their assets, financially astute baby boomers have used that inherited capital to invest in real estate, often the second home.

The single largest transfer of wealth in U.S. history is occurring with the baby boomer generation, notes David Hehman, president of EscapeHomes.com. "Baby boomers are inheriting a lot of money from their parents. They are prioritizing their lifestyle and recreational interests and what follows is a second home purchase."

The baby boomers have been lucky in regard to the second home markets because both government-induced and free market turns have been in their favor.

The first boom for the second home market occurred in 1997 when tax law changes allowed most sellers to exclude up to $500,000 in capital gains from taxation (for a couple who lived in a home for two out of the five previous years). The tax change allowed people to make decisions based on needs and desires rather than simply trying to avoid a tax hit. Under the old law, the incentive was to always buy a more expensive home to avoid a tax penalty. Now people could trade down to a smaller, luxury condo and then go out and purchase a second home.

The second boom occurred after the year 2000, when the Alan Greenspan-led Federal Reserve pursued a low interest rate policy, with the rates falling to as low as 1 percent for federal funds in 2003, which was a benchmark not seen since the Eisenhower administration in the 1950s.

With a recession on the horizon following the collapse of the stock market at the close the of previous decade, Greenspan quickly pushed for lower interest rates. By 2001, the effect on just one sector of the economy, housing, was like a lightning bolt. The low interest rates gave (by keeping monthly payments down) first-time home buyers entry into the market, induced many existing homeowners to trade up to bigger homes, and made the acquisition of a second home a possibility. By 2001, newspapers such as *USA Today*, were reporting that the low rates stoked the housing market so strongly, they kept the nation out of a recession.

A survey by Centex Destination Properties reported in June 2004 that 25 percent of affluent households expressed an interest in second home ownership over the next two years. The respondents had a median age of 45 years, 78 percent were married, and 87 percent already owned their own homes. The most desirable locations sought by respondents were those offering year-round temperate climates, with the top five most popular destinations being: Naples/ Marco Island, Florida; southern New Jersey and Delaware coasts; the Florida Keys; the South Carolina coast; and Maui.[5]

Investment sectors often experience a kind of hysteria that is often labeled a "bubble." The genesis of these bubbles is usually the result of the bursting of some previous bubble. For example, an exuberant real estate market in the 1980s collapsed at the end of the decade, which left many investors, who remained whole, looking for places to park capital. Eventually, in the 1990s, this money began to flow into the stock market, in particular to the innovative and often revolutionizing technology companies that seemed to be like starbursts in the new economy. At the start of the next decade, the technology bubble burst, flattening the effervescent stock market. It was time for free investment capital to find a new home, and it was once again real estate that was back on everyone's tip list. However, whereas the boom in the 1980s was led by commercial real estate, at the turn of the new millennium, it was residential.

The low interest rate environment combined with this massive flow of investment capital into real estate inflated a new housing bubble, which itself began to collapse around 2006.

While it lasted, the movement of free investment capital absolutely stoked the second home market already benefiting from demographics and government economic policies.

With all that demand, prices rose accordingly. The median price of a vacation home in 2005 hit $204,100, up 7.4 percent from the year before and a considerable improvement over the $127,800 in 1999. These numbers temper the fact that in most of the country's most desirable second homes markets, there was probably little to be had for under $350,000 at best, and one would have to go to seven figures to get into Aspen, Colorado; Sea Island, Georgia; or Palm Beach, Florida.

After the turn of the millennium, the vacation home market, particularly the condominium sector, got juiced. The rapid appreciation began to attract not just soon-to-be retirees, but investors, people who had no intention of living in their secondary homes, and their shady counterparts, speculators. The difference in the two is simply a matter of "hold." Investors get in for the long run, but speculators want to turn properties as quickly as possible; in effect, they want to flip the real estate.

Beginning in the 1990s, investor activity in secondary homes became so strong that the NAR had to recognize it as a subset of the second home market. Indeed, while second homes as a percentage of total home sales rose 40 percent, so did the percentage as investments. In 2005, 27.7 percent of all home purchases were investments (up from 23 percent in 2004), reported the NAR. That number easily swamped the percentage that was bought as vacation homes: 12.2 percent in 2005.

"Vacation homes once constituted the majority of second home purchases, but the soaring real estate market has attracted more Americans to real estate investing," observed NAR's Lereah.[6]

Perhaps no sector of the second home market attracted more speculation than condominiums.

In November 2006, a small blurb of a news story about condos appeared in the *Wall Street Journal*. The story related how six luxury condo developers building in South Florida, including Donald Trump and Related Group (Time-Warner Center in New York) executives, hosted a cocktail party in Manhattan for prospective buyers. The story quoted one developer, who was selling units for as much as $6 million as saying, "For people who have that kind of money, it's not an investment. It's a lifestyle."[7]

Obviously, there are condominium units being marketed for seven figures, but generally, condos sell for less than single-family homes. They are also easier to rent and more subject to flipping. As a result, condo markets often exhibit a lot more price movement, going up and, unfortunately, going down.

In that same *Wall Street Journal* story, one broker was quoted as saying, "It's a known fact the [condo] market is in a downturn."[8]

Back in 2005, I did a story for the Urban Land Institute's *Multifamily Trends* magazine about what I saw as a condo bubble that was ripe for bursting, which turned out to be accurate. At the time, I quoted two economists. Celia Chen, director of housing economics at Economy.com, told me, "Condo prices tend to be more volatile than prices for single-family homes. They go up higher and they fall down further." Echoing those sentiments, David Stiff, a senior economist with Fiserv CSW, added, "There is usually more fluff in the condo market because people are trying to speculate on new development. Speculators target condos simply because they are easier to construct and cheaper to flip."

For a while, everyone was making money in real estate. In the summer of 2004, a close friend of my son and other members of his family took their place in line for the opening of sales at a condominium complex in Edgewater, New Jersey. After waiting on line through the night, the next morning, my son's friend and his family acquired a number of condos selling at just over $300,000. After a year, they were reselling the units at an average profit of $100,000 each.

In 2005, investment home prices jumped an amazing 24 percent over the year before to a median cost of $183,500. This spiral of inflation came to an end in 2006 with the collapse of the residential housing bubble, but the damage had already been done. Investment and vacation homes had leveled off at such a high plateau, buyers were already looking at the next frontier, cheaper real estate overseas.

Turn of the Century

Sometime at the end of the 1990s, I found myself, on separate trips, on the Mediterranean islands of Cyprus and Malta. As I journeyed around the respective islands I noticed some new home construction. Inquiring, I learned that they were retirement homes for British citizens. I wasn't sure if the British who were retiring to the Mediterranean were permanently leaving Manchester or London or Cornwall and heading south or simply coming down for the winter. Nevertheless, the explanation made sense because the British had a long history on both islands.

Middle-class Europeans, especially those from the cold countries, have a long history of owning second homes around the Mediterranean from Greece to Spain. In addition, certain European states have had a long colonial history, and a certain amount of second home movement occurs between the old colonial power and the modern, independent state that emerged from that legacy.

Around the turn of the twenty-first century, with the euro and British pound attaining a position of strength against the dollar, many Europeans took advantage of the difference to buy second home properties in the United States, especially in Florida. In the cold lands of Churchill, Manitoba, I was hiking into the tundra to spot polar bears with three Germans who had flown up from Naples, Florida, where one of them owned a vacation home. It was where they all came every winter, except for little adventures in North America, such as this one to Churchill.

Over in the United States, Americans never had a colonial legacy to explore, nor the inclination to even consider establishing a residence abroad, especially when there was such sunshine-dappled bounty within the country. When the American middle class began to dive into the world of second homes, it came south to places like Florida, South Carolina, Arizona, and California.

However, everything changed in the new century.

The last time the U.S. State Department did a survey of Americans living abroad was in 2000. At the time, the government concluded 4 million Americans were living outside the United States, but that included dual citizenship individuals and people who registered with a particular agency.

The next time the State Department does a similar survey won't be until 2010, and by then it will probably have to change its methodology because over this 10-year period, Americans have been buying vacation homes in random places around the world in greater numbers. Many of these individuals might live in their second homes for just three months of the year, so how would the government include those people in the survey?

In 2005, a United Features Syndicate survey quoted a Londoner who had a vacation home in Cape Town, South Africa, as saying, "You never used to hear an American accent in Cape Town. Now you hear it all the time. They're all over the place." Closer to home, the same story interviewed a director of sales for a gated community on Grand Bahama Island, who boasted that Americans were interested in the Bahamas because, "there are no property taxes, inheritance taxes, or capital gains taxes."[9]

The first rush of stories about Americans seeking vacation shelters in foreign ports occurred in 2005. The press often catches up to trends after the trend has already been established and is flourishing, and then numerous publications all begin to report different variations of the same story. So, if the press started to write about Americans buying vacation homes in 2005, the actual rush of home buying overseas probably first began in 2003 and 2004, which is significant because that's about the time when residential real estate in the United States began to plateau. National median existing single-family home prices finally peaked around the third quarter of 2005.

More importantly, for those interested in vacation homes, the price of residential property of any type along the ocean shore or in mountain resort areas, rose to a point where it was essentially out of reach of the American middle class. Just a decade earlier, a condo on the beach was a pricey consideration but certainly attainable for a family with excess capital. That wasn't the case by the new millennium. So Americans with a strong desire to have a sunshine-filled retirement or to spend three months of winter on the beach began to look at places around the globe where the dollar could buy a lot more than within the confines of the continental United States.

"Vacation home prices have gone through the roof," exclaims Jeffrey Hornberger, manager of international business development at NAR. "Appreciation in the last couple of years has been unprecedented. As a result, it has been very difficult to touch second home properties in the prime beach or mountain locations. They are out of reach for the typical, middle-class American. Whereas the previous generation could afford a condo on the beach, this generation cannot. That is why Americans began to look even further south, in Latin America and the Caribbean."

While the high cost of real estate was certainly a primary factor in the internationalization of the vacation home market from an American perspective, a secondary cause was the evolution of the travel industry.

First, baby boomers began traveling overseas as young adults in the 1960s and 1970s and even if they stopped doing so (or did so intermittently) during their career-building and baby-rearing years, when they approached the empty-nester time of life, they started to travel again. Middle-class baby boomers had a comfort level with international travel.

Second, through the last half of the twentieth century, the global travel industry created a vast infrastructure of hotels, resorts, cruise lines, and travel routes to make international travel easier and when possible, risk free. At the same time, an ever-expanding airline industry could bring travelers to every part of the globe at reasonable prices.

Third, the Internet not only made travel easier, but it helped create the internationalization of real estate by allowing anyone around the globe to search for information, agents, local listings, local conditions, and selling prices for just about any place on earth.

"With the Internet, information is at your fingertips," Hornberger notes. "People can find out about buying property in Nicaragua or Panama in a short amount of time. They can get a grip on how much beachfront property costs, how long it takes to get there, and how strong the local currency is compared to the dollar. This is all coveted information. People are doing the research online then getting on a plane."

Fourth, many countries that Americans are now considering as potential second home locations have gone from politically unstable to stable, democratic governments. Manuel Noriega is long gone from Panama, and today Panama is a hot real estate market for Americans.

A *New York Times* article in 2005 told the tale of an Aspen, Colorado, married couple who bought a half-acre of land in Altos del Maria, a second home community about 90 minutes from Panama City for $54,000. The magazine interviewed the husband, who told the reporter they were considering installing an infinity pool. He was quoted as saying: "Labor here is very cheap. High-end construction is about $65 a foot. In Aspen, the norm is $400." Another formerly unstable country, Croatia, is booming with second home buyers from other parts of Europe and the United States. The same article quoted a Brooklyn man who was looking overseas for a second home and chose Croatia's Dalmatian coast. "It's the new Riveria," the man exclaimed. "Croatia is still relatively undeveloped. And relatively cheap."[10]

Finally, Americans have gotten more comfortable buying overseas because so many U.S. real estate and financial companies are now global. Names are familiar and practices are standardized, all of which heightens that comfort level. If, for example, a couple from New Jersey has used Century 21 to help them buy their last two homes, the odds are the couple could find a Century 21 agent in many of the foreign places they would look to buy a second home. If the couple liked gated communities, it would be no problem in most second home markets worldwide. And if they needed to deal with a bank, Citicorp has probably gotten to wherever they may want to go first.

In 2006, many U.S. real estate markets turned tepid. Interest rates climbed, the stock market bulls came out roaring, and over-building occurred in a number of communities. None of this affected the trend line for buyers of vacation homes overseas. "The fact is," says Hornberger, "the real estate slowdown in the United States has not quieted the international marketplace. Americans are just getting started abroad."

CHAPTER

HAWAII

CONDO DEMAND EBBS AND FLOWS LIKE STRONG OCEAN TIDES; SOUTHERN CALIFORNIA REAL ESTATE GOOD MARKET INDICATOR

P eople come to Hawaii to find their own little bit of paradise.

Valerie Brown did. The friendly Ontario native, who is one half of a husband-wife Realtor team, was working as a registered nurse when she moved to Oahu in 1998. In the parking lot of a hospital, while looking for her car, she met Ross Brown, who was also looking for his car. They fell in love, got married, and she soon joined him in the pursuit of selling real estate.

In the almost eight years since she's been in Oahu, Valerie Brown only once returned home to the Toronto area. She recalls the trip with dread. "It was in March," she told me, "and it was so cold."

She had lived most of her life in Ontario, and it was a jolt to return after so much time in Hawaii, where the weather is consistently sunny and pleasant and where business attire for men generally consists of a brightly flowered shirt and khakis. The cold weather was her most searing memory of that journey back to her childhood home.

Ross, her husband and business partner, moved around quite a bit while growing up. One stop of many was a sojourn to the Kailua area of Oahu, or as people in Honolulu say, the windward side of the island. It must have been a unique memory because he eventually moved back to Windward Oahu, where he entered the local real estate world. When I was visiting the islands in the summer 2006, the Browns, who always work together, showed me three properties in and about the Kailua area.

Although the distance between Kailua and Honolulu is not great (today the driving time is about 30 minutes), in ancient times people living in either area may never have known of each other's existence because a steep, jagged mountain range separates the two places. There is a coastal road, but it was only with the creation of the Pali Highway, including two tunnels through the mountain, that commuting between the locations became easy.

And it's not just the mountains that separate Kailua and Honolulu, there's a different mindset between the two places, as well. Honolulu is a dense, urban cosmopolitan city, but Kailua has the look and feel of a small town in the 1960s. That divergence could have gone differently. Back in the 1970s there was a scheme to develop Kailua into the next Waikiki—a high-rise jungle at the edge of the ocean—but townsfolk for the most part beat back development schemes. Now all that remains of that dream are a couple of mid-rise condo buildings in the center of town.

These weren't the condos that Ross and Valerie showed me. The three places I saw were typical Sunbelt-style developments, a series of one- or two-story buildings, some of which were built around a golf course. All three projects were erected in the 1970s, and all were built in a townhouse style. Their design was a bit old-fashioned, but each unit had a wonderful lanai, or patio, which I'm told is important because there is no central air-conditioning in many houses and condos. The cooling trade winds blow across the islands and one simply opens the windows to catch the crosscurrents.

Any of the condos could have been mine for a price of $625,000 to $799,000. Sure, that seems like a lot by mainland standards but not for Hawaii, and I have to say, you get plenty of space for your dollar—interior space ranged from about 1,600 to 2,000 square feet. Anything like that in Waikiki would certainly be in the seven-figure range to start.

I could have been lured to any of these projects if I had been looking for quiet in my life. In fact, I begin my story about condo living in Hawaii, not in Waikiki, which is essentially the epicenter of condo living in the state, but outside of the metropolitan area in sleepy Kailua. The degree of quietude and attitude toward the modern world is both the attraction and distraction that drives people to seek out a second residence outside the mainland U.S., and eventually sends them home.

Although it is our 49th state and the capital city of Honolulu is an urbane metro, Hawaii is a series of islands in a temperate climate. And if there is one generalization that can be made about living in any tropical island paradise anywhere in the world, it is that there is a certain pace and attitude that is slower than what we expect in Chicago, Indianapolis, Dallas, or even Des Moines.

Ross Brown believes in Kailua, where he lives and works, and after spending a day with him, he would have you believe in the place as well. He only spent a few years of his youth in Hawaii, the rest of his growing up took place back on the East Coast of the Lower 48, and he knows what sets Hawaii apart: "A slower pace, a more relaxed view," he said diplomatically.

Valerie summed it up this way: "I was told when I moved here that if I had a list of things to accomplish, I would probably only accomplish one a day, compared to the mainland, where you do seven or eight things a day. Any renovations that need to be done take longer and can be more challenging. Getting a contractor is a challenge as they are usually doubling up on jobs."

"Just try to get some help when the surf's up," Ross laughed.

I was thinking the "surf's up" line had to be some kind of local cliché, especially today in a modern Hawaii. But the next day I was talking with Jennifer Perell, a relatively new real estate agent who also worked primarily in the Kailua area, and she agreed that yes, when the surf's up nothing gets accomplished on the island.

She was telling me how she lured her boyfriend to Hawaii from the mainland, where he was working in construction. "There is a huge opportunity for construction right now," she said. "Contractors are in high demand. It is a benefit that my boyfriend has a good work ethic. That's not to say that other people here don't, but if the surf's up . . ."

A "surf's up" lifestyle can't be blamed for everything. Although homes are expensive in Hawaii (average sale price of more than $775,000 for a single-family home at mid-year 2006), much of the stock is old. The value is actually in the land, not the structure, says Ross Brown. So when new buyers move in, they really do need to upgrade the dwellings. As the island's residential real estate markets have boomed in the past few years, so has the need for additions and alterations. In 2004, the total value of homeowner improvements hit a record $286 million for the state and then nearly doubled to $408.5 million in 2005.

There always has been the complaint that there are not enough contractors in Hawaii, but in 2006 the situation grew ridiculous. In August of that year, *The Honolulu Advertiser* ran a story called, "Wait Line Grows for Renovations: Backed-Up Contractors Enjoying a 4-Year Boom in Demand for Home Remodeling." The article laid out all sorts of horror stories, but the one that impressed me was the tale of a high-end swimming pool builder, who told the paper anyone wanting a pool would have to wait two years. It didn't make a difference as to the specific renovation need—be it for roofers, tile companies, or custom remodelers. Everyone was short on labor. "If you have a small job, you might as well forget about it because you'll never get anyone to come out," Valerie Brown said. Apparently, it is not much different for big jobs.

"My boyfriend would probably like to do something else, as construction is hard work and he's working all the time," Jennifer Perell told me.

Perell, 27, the youngest real estate agent I spoke with in Hawaii, was just three years into the business. After graduating with a degree in psychology from the University of Colorado in Boulder, one of the great party schools, Perell continued doing what she did at college—essentially, partying. She made a living as a bartender moving from Southern California to Surfer's Paradise in Australia. Her parents had moved to Hawaii and enticed her to Oahu with the promise of one year's free rent. Oddly, coming to Hawaii had a settling effect on her.

She decided to sell real estate and because she really did have an engaging personality, Perell turned out to be quite good at it. Like Ross and Valerie Brown, whom she knew, Perell worked for Coldwell Banker. Perell sold her first property after about a month at her job, and when I met her in the summer of 2006 she had recently sold a $4.5 million property. With the earnings from that sale, she bought her first house.

Perell hadn't handled very many condos, but she thought that might change in the future because there was a stretch of dilapidated multifamily housing near downtown Kailua slated to be torn down; in its place a series of high-end condo projects was to be erected. There was already one mid-rise in the area and it had done well.

A check with the Honolulu Board of Realtors data showed that in the first seven months of 2006, 89 condos were sold at a median price of $420,000 in the Kailua-Waimanalo region, which was up smartly from the same time period the year before, when 80 condos were sold at a median price of $382,500. That was a 9.8 percent price jump, which came on top of a 30.4 percent price jump in 2005. Clearly there was a demand for condo development in the Kailua area, and this new construction to replace the derelict housing would be the first intensive condo development in this quiet town since the 1970s.

In an infinitesimal way, this is really the story of the entire condo market in Hawaii.

Building Booms

From my hotel on the 12th floor of the Holiday Inn in Waikiki, I have a clear view of the city stretching west and toward the interior of the island. Since I was still on mainland time, I would wake up early and the first thing I would do is look at the world from my window, where I would notice a consistent set of phenomena. The first was natural. At daybreak, one could see heavy, ominous clouds settling over the mountains outside the city. Rain for sure, I thought that first morning. But I was wrong. The clouds, no matter how potent, were for the most part snared by the mountain peaks and never managed to drift into the city, thus ensuring perfect weather for the beaches every day that I was there.

The second phenomenon was the hint of a construction boom: I could see new towers and at least a half dozen high-rise cranes indicating a whole new set of buildings would be opening sometime in the next year. The new high-rises were not just offices but condo towers as well. In 2006, condo building and development was a big business again in Honolulu. Even Donald Trump had entered the fray, with plans to build a superluxury hotel-condo in Waikiki. The $400 million project would boast 460 condo units, to be sold at prices from roughly $500,000 to more than $6 million.

Although there were a number of condo projects in various stages of development while I was visiting Honolulu, Trump's proposal was unique for a couple of reasons. Most of the new development was in the central business district area, where land was becoming available. Trump found a location in Waikiki, which was difficult because the famed Honolulu neighborhood is densely urban. Older or low-rise buildings would have to come down to make room for another project. Second, Trump's project was considered by the local press to be superluxury, and that kind of condo development was still fairly new to Honolulu.

Sharon Keating, a delightfully informative real estate agent for Century 21 in Honolulu, was kind enough to hand me a press clipping from July 25, with the screaming headline: "Baby Boomers Fueling Run on Luxury Condos in Hawaii." The high point of the story was the mention that a three-bedroom condo in the city listed at $6 million went into escrow. The writer had a sense of humor about it all and opened the story with this witty intro: "In Hawaii, million-dollar homes are as common as coconuts. But a $6 million condominium?" The article listed a number of new condo projects throughout the islands where the sticker price was decidedly over $1 million. I expected this new building boom would be at the higher end.

It was time the condo market caught up with the trend lines.

I met with Harvey Shapiro, the research economist at the Honolulu Board of Realtors and the island's residential housing guru, at a Starbucks in Hawaii Kai, a residential area east of Honolulu proper but still in the metro area. Shapiro had walked over to the coffee shop from his condo, which he had bought decades before. When I asked him if he was now property rich, he only smiled. Since the median price for a Hawaii Kai condo had passed the $575,000 mark, I assumed the smile was for good reason.

Hawaii Kai, from Shapiro's own numbers, is really the high-end market for Honolulu-area condominiums, and the numbers were up there, more than 20 percent from July 2005 to July 2006. Hawaii Kai wasn't an isolated market turn; the median sales price for island condos during the same period rose from $250,000 to $310,000, or 24 percent. That should be considered the wider context of a 29 percent rise for all of 2005.

The important numbers are these: In all of Hawaii, there are more condos sold than single-family homes every year. During 2005 in Oahu, as an example, 7,990 condos and 4,617 single-family residences were sold.

The Mother of All Condo Markets

The beginnings of that unique trend line (more condos sold than houses) and the reason why the Hawaii condo market is so important is that the state experienced the first real condo boom in the United States. From the mid-1990s through the turn of the millennium, the Lower 48 entered a period of tremendous condominium growth—without precedent in the country. The reasons were myriad: low interest rates, interest in second homes, baby boomers growing old, baby boomers inheriting from parents. All this was old hat to Hawaii, in particular Honolulu, which experienced the first, over-the-top condo boom ever in the late 1960s through the 1970s.

Sharon Keating walked with me from my hotel to the huge Hilton Hawaiian Village complex. As we crossed to the east side of Ala Moana Boulevard, she stopped to point out an old, mid-rise condo surrounded by other condos and hotel towers. The building where she first stayed when she made her initial journey to Honolulu in 1970 stood right where that mid-rise now sat. Her room was the top floor of a three-story building, and she recalls standing on her lanai and counting 70 building cranes in her view.

Ala Moana smoothly curves at the appearance of the Hilton and flows just two more blocks until it hits Kalakaua Avenue, the main road through Waikiki. Just before the curve, sitting between Ala Moana and the Ala Wai Yacht Harbor is a large Y-shaped building, which Keating pointed out was the Ilikai. With its splotches of aquamarine and odd shape, it looked like the usual bad architecture of the 1960s. A day after we met, Keating sent me an e-mail, noting the building was constructed in 1965. Bad architecture or not, it was now a classic and costly to buy into.

Keating, doing a little research on my behalf, also noted in her e-mail: "There were quite a few high-rise apartments built in the 1950s, mostly along the Gold Coast (by Diamond Head), but they were all cooperatives. Some are still cooperatives although many have gone condo. It was not until after statehood in 1959 that Hawaii passed a condo law (originally known as the Horizontal Property Regime but now called the Condominium Property Regime) and that the building boom began in earnest."

Hawaii was the first state to adopt a condominium law back in 1961, and that was mostly because of the shortage of useable land and higher construction costs, a recognizable problem 50 years ago. Prior to statehood, most of the commercial and rental structures in Honolulu were considered low-rise buildings. Any multifamily units would have been rentals, with a few pioneering efforts at joint ownership through a cooperative (buyers purchase shares in a corporation that owns the building). The condominium law, Keating explained, was partly instituted to regulate the development and construction of high-rise buildings, plus "the condo law helped protect buyers, making it easier to get a mortgage and regulating land use. Creation, sale, and management of condos were covered in the law."

Keating was born and spent her early years in Cape Breton, Nova Scotia, before her family moved to, of all places, Brooklyn, New York. Having just visited Nova Scotia a few months before, I thought it would have been an unbelievably difficult adjustment to the crazy urban life represented by the densely populated Brooklyn. She shrugged. Her family, she explained, would move again. Perhaps this is the reason

Keating, when she found her place, stayed put. She came to Hawaii for a short visit with a cousin, went back to the mainland for about six months, and then decided Hawaii was where she wanted to be. Keating has been living in the state for more than 35 years.

Of all the agents I talked to in Honolulu, she had been in the business the longest, 18 years, having toiled for a long time in the hospitality industry before that. Keating worked the city area, so most of her clients were condo buyers and sellers. She was extremely knowledgeable about the market, and if there was something she didn't know, she knew where to find the answer.

Keating's dream was to retire and live in a Waikiki condo, where she could be close to everything the city had to offer, from shopping to culture to restaurants to the beach. She owned a home, but sheepishly admitted that it was the first she had ever owned and that she had bought it only six years prior. Before that, she tried to explain, "My rental situation was too good to leave."

The first time I learned about Hawaii's importance in the development of the U.S. condominium market was when I sat down with Michael Sklarz, an acquaintance from news stories I had written in the past. I had met Sklarz at a mortgage-technology conference in Newport Beach, California. At the time, he was a senior vice president and head of analytics at Fidelity National Financial and a specialist in automated valuation models (AVM), which are computer programs that provide real estate market analysis and estimates of value. When I saw him in Honolulu he was about to embark on pioneering AVM efforts in Japan. Before all that however, Sklarz was the original residential-market data guru for Honolulu and Hawaii. It was all by accident.

As a kid growing up in New Jersey, he was one of a dedicated group of young men that surfed the Atlantic Coast. So after graduating from Columbia University he decided to go to grad school in Hawaii where he could resume his passion in a surfing paradise. His major was ocean engineering and, he received a Ph.D. in the discipline, doing research in the technical field of tsunami modeling.

Oddly, it was a real estate company that hired him and it did so for his technology skills. The company wanted to develop and organize market data in regard to the real estate industry, so as to affect objective analysis. Sklarz did that for 20 years, thus becoming the island's first real estate market authority.

The origins of the Hawaiian condo market, Sklarz explained, had its roots in statehood, jet travel, evolution of the tourist industry, and the state's limited geography. The other interesting thing about Hawaii is that it had virtually no apartment construction for about 25 years, as rents were never high enough to justify building. Essentially, the condo market was the replacement for apartments.

"Our condo market was really one of the first in the country," he said. While it might seem like boasting, the comment makes perfect sense. If you think about residential housing in the 1960s and even into the 1970s, it was either apartment living or single-family home ownership. The concept of owning an apartment, except in cities like New York, which preferred the cooperative model, really didn't exist to a large extent anywhere, not even in Florida.

Sklarz's tip for anyone who wants to speculate in Hawaiian real estate: follow the Southern California market. "Over the last 30 years, we closely tracked Southern California, with a lag time of 6 to 24 months. Watch what is going on in Orange County, as it is an excellent predictor of what to expect here."

Cycles

Like Sklarz, Harvey Shapiro became the local residential housing guru by accident. Having grown up in Pennsylvania, Shapiro decided as a teenager that he was going to move to a place where it was warm and sunny. Unfortunately, the place he ended up was Michigan. Finally, in 1986, he escaped to Hawaii. Being a techie of sorts, Shapiro started looking for a job in computers or engineering and finally ended up at the Board of Realtors, helping implement a computer system. While at the board he helped the research person accumulate and organize data. That person left and Shapiro inherited the position.

Working for the Board of Realtors, one has to be very much an optimist about the local real estate market. It's the job of all members of the Board of Realtors to avoid controversy and always be upbeat. Even if you end up as the numbers guru like Shapiro did, you still must project enthusiasm.

"Today, there is less demand and less pressure on prices to move up, but I think there is sufficient demand to keep prices at least at the levels they are now," Shapiro said. "If history repeats itself that is exactly what will happen."

Shapiro was very generous in regard to data and forthcoming in conversation. Nevertheless, I didn't totally agree with his interpretations. Hawaii's most recent real estate boom began about 2000 and after five years it finally ran out of steam. I had seen Shapiro quoted in a news story from earlier that summer, which reported: "Hawaii home prices are still generally on an upward trend, despite a falloff in the rate of growth," and Shapiro described the sharp decline in prices in the mid-1990s as a rare event. "Our prices are more like a staircase where they go up sharply and then they level for a few years and then they go up sharply again. Even if you buy a property in that level period, it will appreciate at the next upward period."

The stair metaphor tripped me up.

Hawaii is a very small market, with only about 1.2 million people in the whole state, of which 72 percent, or just under 900,000 people, reside in Honolulu County. Small states don't have layers of economic diversity to buffer prices when individual market drivers go south. This is a problem with Hawaii's residential real estate sector; it historically suffers extreme market swings. When Hawaii's residential market is on a roll, it is a great place to invest. However, when the cycle turns, things get very, very grim and I'm not talking about a leveling-off period.

For all practical purposes, the first great real estate boom for Hawaii in the 1970s was fueled by a construction-generating condo craze. About a decade later, a period of Japanese economic expansion created a buying frenzy on the island as yen-rich investors from Tokyo, Osaka, and beyond madly rushed into Hawaii, buying up anything that wasn't nailed down. When the Japanese economy turned sour, these same investors pulled their capital out of Honolulu's real estate markets. This happened just as the United States and other global markets fell into a deep real estate recession of their own. As noted, in such a small market as Hawaii, such a phenomenon creates an economic tsunami.

Using Shapiro's data, which only begins in the year 1985, we can interpret the severity of the downturn through the numbers. Over the four years from 1985 through 1988, residential sales climbed from 5,150 to 9,572. Then the market stalled, and the number of sales started to drift downward until three years later when residential sales fell off the cliff, dropping 37.9 percent in 1991. It took another five years to reach the bottom, when home sales finally leveled off at 3,739.

What happens to pricing when sales start to decline? Nothing. At least not at the start of a real estate downturn. Sellers do not want to lose the equity they've earned from the market, so invariably they hold out for top dollar as long as possible. This creates a lag time between a drop-off in sales and sellers finally accepting reality, or the inflection point when prices start to decline. In Hawaii, sales volume peaked in 1988, while home prices continued to climb for the next five years. Then the market just flat out collapsed. In 1992, condo prices peaked at a median price of $193,000, held steady for one year, and continued to deflate until a bottom was reached in 2000, with the median price at $125,000.

With real estate booming worldwide after the turn of the millennium, Hawaii's residential market solidified and began to make up lost ground quickly. Still, it took until 2004—11 years—before the median sales price finally surpassed the previous peak in 1993.

In 1997, residential sales in Hawaii began to pick up, and the winning streak of increased sales volume continued for the next nine years. These were astounding years for Oahu real estate, with sales volume quadrupling over that period of time. Unfortunately all good things have to come to an end, and in 2005 sales volume declined almost 2 percent. The July 2006 numbers revealed that, compared with the same month the year before, sales volume had dropped 12.8 percent.

Again, there is a lag time before a drop in sales begins to affect pricing. When I visited Shapiro in the summer of 2006, we were in that halcyon period, with prices still climbing. For condominiums, the median sales price jumped 29 percent in 2005, and for the July 2005 to July 2006 time frame, median sale prices rose 24 percent. When I checked the data a year later, sale prices from July 2006 to July 2007 had declined 3 percent for all single-family homes in Honolulu; and for the condominium market as a separate entity, sale prices absolutely flattened, up a mere 1.8 percent.

While I was wandering about Waikiki, gauging the happiness of the high-rise condo market, I had a sense that an impending pricing bust up wasn't going to take five years to happen as it did in the 1990s. Perhaps it was something a Honolulu agent named Darlene Nagatani had said to me: "Buyers have become savvier about prices, offering less than the listed price. Sellers are putting down their guard and negotiating." Some of her clients were already readily chopping prices. Because the average sale price on an Oahu condominium had jumped more than 40 percent over the previous three years, buyers had done so well on their investment that many figured if they dropped the sale price by $20,000 or $30,000, it wouldn't make a big difference, as they had already made $300,000 in three years.

Add into the equation the fact that Hawaiian real estate has a tendency to swing to the extremes, construction projects left over from the banquet years were in full blossom, and no real estate boom ever ends quietly. All this told me there was no reason to be sanguine about the condo market in the near future.

How to Buy Property in Hawaii

I was hoping to meet Jon Mann while sojourning in Waikiki but never did. I first came across his web site, which was not only informative and comprehensive, but literally spoke to me as well. That was fitting considering Mann bills himself as "Hawaii's High-Tech Real Estate Agent." When I called to introduce myself and arrange an interview in Hawaii, he told me, "I don't meet people unless I'm making money." A telephone interview was okay, though.

After working for "a large petrochemical company" in Houston, Mann moved to Hawaii in 2003. A year later he was full-time into real estate. In 2005, he did 12 deals, a good run for an agent in Oahu.

As it turned out, Mann was an exciting interview mostly because he didn't hold back. While he really enjoyed the switch to real estate, there were a few quirks in the island's real estate business that got under his skin, the most damning of which were the leasehold laws.

"Stay away from leasehold properties," he bellowed. "You can talk to 15 real estate agents and I'm the only one who will tell you that. I won't sell them."

On the mainland, almost all real estate deals are fee simple, or fee simple absolute. That means the buyer acquires ownership of a whole property, including land and buildings; it is the most complete form of ownership.

In addition to fee simple, Hawaii also has something called the "leasehold," which means the buyer of a residential property does not own the land and must pay ground rent, in addition, the use of the land is limited to the remaining years covered by the lease. In effect, the buyer is only acquiring the right to use a property for a period of time. After the contractual period ends, the land returns to the lessor—the "reversion." Typical leasehold provisions run for 55 years with the rent fixed for approximately 30 years. New rates may be based on the current market value of the land. The state limits the lease rent.

In Hawaii, much of the land is owned by trusts, dating from the time when the islands were a monarchy and a few large estates owned the land. After statehood, these trusts retained the ownership of the land. Remember, the first building boom occurred in the 1960s and 1970s, so 30 years later the fixed rent of many of these leasehold properties began coming due. This exposed the weakness in the leasehold system because the lessor could pump up the rates, leaving you, as the owner of a property but not the land, in a vulnerable situation. Back in the early 1990s, little old ladies were appearing on television crying that they were going to be put out of their Hawaiian homes.

On the other side of the coin, much of the income from the leaseholds goes to native Hawaiian trusts, which have established foundations and charitable organizations. Also, buying a leasehold was much cheaper than buying the same property in fee simple format. I visited a condo for sale at a development called Yacht Club Knolls, located in Kaneohe on the windward side. It was a spacious, townhouse-style condo with a great view of Kaneohe Bay and the mountains beyond. The price was $470,000 for the condo. However, in this situation, the buyer could actually acquire the leasehold for $154,000, making the price $624,000.

In 1991, the Honolulu City council passed a law to help leasehold owner-occupants gain title to the land under their units. Basically, the law allowed these owner-occupants to petition the city to compel a landowner to sell the fee interests on their units at prices determined by a third party. This law was repealed in 2005. After the city council voted to get rid of the controversial law, repeal supporters, including representatives of charitable trusts, small landowners, charter school students and teachers, and native Hawaiian activists, applauded the action.

The market, however, often misuses good intentions, and when explaining all this to me, Jon Mann began to rant. "At one point leasehold properties represented about 20 to 25 percent of all properties available, and at this time represent closer to 7 percent because there was a law on the books forcing moves to fee simple. But last summer, the Honolulu city council reversed that law in the face of lobbying by the nine trusts. Seven of the nine trusts are fine, but two I would not trust as far as I can throw them."

He continued, "I will not sell leasehold properties to any client because I have seen too many people lose their shirts. What happens is, you find a real nice property for $350,000, which is an incredible price. Then you realize it is not fee simple, because if it was it would price at $950,000. As a leasehold all you have to do is pay for the mortgage and interest and the monthly ground rent, which is essentially the lease. What people don't understand is that every three to five years that ground rent comes up for renewal and the lessor is allowed to increase rents willy-nilly. Most of the time the increases are reasonable, but two of the nine trusts will increase rates exorbitantly. The lessees can't make the payments and give up the properties. The lessor doesn't mind because it gets to sell the property again at a higher price, and then three to five years later it does the same thing. It's a scam."

When it comes to leaseholds, suffice it to say: Let the buyer beware.

One of the nicest people I met while in Honolulu was Darlene Nagatani, a true native of Honolulu. She arranged to meet me at the Wailana Coffee Shop, about a block from my hotel, and I when I arrived at 10 A.M. there was a line out the door. I never could quite figure out the attraction. Wailana was essentially a diner, complete with chatty, gum-chewing waitresses. However, between the hours of about 9 A.M. and 2 P.M. there were always lines. My guess was that the Wailana offered an inexpensive alternative to folks staying at the Hilton Village and the other surrounding hotels.

Nagatani had been in the real estate business for over 25 years but only since 2003 as a Realtor. Before that she had been selling timeshares and was an escrow secretary. "When I started seeing mediocre agents getting big commission checks, I went to my boss and said I want to do this," she said.

Though a bit late, she apparently made the right decision, winning a trophy from her company for selling $4.3 million worth of real estate in 2005, which was good considering she worked solely the Honolulu market and much of the product she represented was condos. Nagatani had a lot of cautions to offer investors.

The thing most investors didn't realize, she told me, was that there are strict zoning regulations in regard to the renting of condos. Many building associations don't allow short-term rentals. Those decisions are local; one side of the street can be zoned for "resort," which means short-term rentals are allowed, but the other side of the street may not be. That's an important point because so many buyers in Hawaii are either speculators or second-home investors, who perhaps have been counting on renting their units to vacationers when they are not in Hawaii. Indeed, investors (for whom the units are not the primary residence) make up more than 60 percent of the condo owners on Oahu, and more than 80 percent in Waikiki and Leeward Oahu.

The second most important caution is the structure itself, Nagatani says. The first massive building boom in Hawaii was during the 1970s, and when the real estate market went bust a decade later, there was little new construction until recently. As a result, much of the condo product in Honolulu is old, which means maintenance is continual and that translates into higher maintenance fees. It's not unusual to find monthly maintenance fees in the four-digit range.

The other problem that shocks people is parking. When the Browns showed me a condo townhouse in Kailua, they stressed one of the unique features of the place, called Kukilakila, was that it had a two-car garage. This was a 1970s structure and assuredly almost anything built afterward, anywhere in Oahu, was one-car, if that. In the Waikiki area, which is dense with high-rise condos, street parking is almost nonexistent—it's like living in Manhattan. Parking remains a major consideration and a major problem in regard to Honolulu condo living.

Finally, potential buyers need to consider the weather factor, especially if investing in a condo outside of Waikiki. Although Oahu is geographically small, the island is cut by precipitous mountain ranges, and that changes weather patterns. Temperature, wind, and precipitation vary greatly in relatively short distances.

This also affects that great Hawaiian architectural feature, the lanai. When I returned to the Lower 48, Keating was kind enough to send me a column written by an associate of hers. The author wrote: "Unless a building is fully air-conditioned (older buildings are not), the orientation of the windows and lanais toward the trade winds is crucial! Some condos have windows only on one side. Unless those windows receive adequate air flow, you could be sweltering in the doldrums for most of the year."

Owning a condo toward the top of a high-rise comes with its own set of cautions. If the lanai and windows are facing northeast, beware the wind tunnel effect, where lightweight patio furniture suddenly becomes airborne.

When condo shopping on a quiet, windless day in Hawaii, the world is an illusion of paradise. Three months later, when the wind is whistling madly through your air-conditionerless apartment and patio chairs are whipping dangerously around the lanai, you'll understand that in Oahu, you don't have to be a weather forecaster to know which way the wind blows.

10 Things to Know about the Hawaii Condo Market

1. Island living is either an attraction or a distraction; you live there because of the quiet lifestyle, or you have to leave because it drives you crazy.
2. Renovations take time—a lot of time.
3. A lot of condo product is 30 to 40 years old; maintenance could be an expensive problem.
4. New condo construction tends to be in the luxury category, which puts it out of range of many buyers.
5. Condo prices have appreciated greatly since the turn of the century, but the boom is over.
6. Hawaii real estate goes through intensive boom and bust periods.
7. Not all condos can be rented to short-term vacationers.
8. Be careful of leasehold properties.
9. Weather is a key factor when choosing a location.
10. The lanai is an important feature in Hawaiian architecture, but it has to be facing the right direction to catch the cooling winds.

CHAPTER

ALASKA

THE BEAUTY OF SUMMER HERE IS UNEQUAL TO ANYTHING ELSE; IT'S NOT ALL REMOTE CABINS AS GOLF HOMES AND SKI CONDOS ATTRACT FOLKS FROM LOWER 48

My hotel could be found just beyond the perimeter of the Anchorage Airport and when Jim Crawford picked me up to go to lunch, he took me all of about 50 yards down the road to another hotel. But, this hotel was different. It was called the Millennium Alaskan Hotel and printed in letters as big as the hotel brand were the words, "Iditarod Race Headquarters."

Later that evening, I walked back to the Millennium to check it out. While on the outside it looked like a large, nondescript roadside venue, the lobby rooms were decorated in pure Alaska—representative game animals were stuffed, mounted, and installed as if the place was the Museum of Natural History in New York. I loved it and spent a long time staring at creatures like the 360-pound halibut caught in Resurrection Bay and the musk ox shot on Nunivak Island, but my favorite was the wolverine, lounging naturally on a glimmering rock surrounded by faux snow. The plaque identified the mounted weasel as a winner in the 1986 World Taxidermy Championship.

Crawford didn't pick the Millennium for the décor but for its restaurant, picturesquely called The Fancy Moose. I was a little disappointed in the eatery because I couldn't even get a mooseburger—despite its name. Yet it was a great selection due to the fact that it showcased outdoor seating, and the late August day that Crawford and I met to discuss the second home market was absolutely gorgeous. The sun peeked in and out of billowy clouds, the temperature rose to 75 degrees, and the air was crisply clean. Coming from triple-digit temperatures in Arizona, I was happy as a ptarmigan in a secluded Alaska valley.

The only downside to the restaurant was that it was situated on the edge of a sailport (the largest in the country I'm told) and every few minutes a small plane, after cruising over the surface of the lake waters, would lift off with a roar. I eventually had to put my tape recorders away. We would conclude business at his office in downtown Anchorage.

Crawford was a former banker who now toiled in real estate. He had his own little company, called Exit Realty Alaska, and as he told me, he could sell me a property, do my mortgage, and if it was a commercial project, would probably invest as well. Crawford was a man of large girth, not so unusual in Alaska. That same night I would eat at a popular spot not far from the airport called Gwennie's Old Alaska Restaurant, where I ordered the local halibut, breaded and fried and served with three different kinds of starches. Weight gain can come easily in our northernmost state.

The thing about Crawford was he was smart, interesting, and a real family man. He apparently was also a Republican of good standing because when I went to his office, I saw pictures of him with the first President Bush and President Reagan. Crawford also did his homework. When I visited his office to talk second homes, he had already researched the market and pulled up on his computer second homes for sale from one end of the state to the other. He had gotten so excited by his research, he decided for the first time in his life that he was going to buy a second home.

In a sense, Crawford was already a part owner of a secondary residence. Well, not exactly a home, but a shack, basically a 20-foot by 20-foot structure where he and his son would reside when hunting or fishing. It sat on leased land and Crawford hadn't been there in 10 years. His son grew into a talented football player—all-state lineman—and I guess football season overlapped with hunting season and one had to go.

Well, that's okay, because Crawford was ready for a real second home. And I was to get my introduction to the market.

As Crawford sees it, Alaska's most enticing second home market is along the Kenai River, which he exclaimed, "is the most beautiful river you have ever seen, and it has the biggest king salmon you will ever see, in fact, it has all five varieties of salmon."

Homes along the Kenai, he continued, are generally on a half acre to an acre lot, but he assured me, "this is no subdivision type thing; it is the opposite."

So what would it cost to own a place along the Kenai? Crawford estimates the cheapest properties would cost $250,000 to $300,000 and with that would come 1 to 1.3 acres of land with a ranch style home. A dock for a boat would cost extra. He warned that sometimes these homes sit 40 feet to 100 feet above the river so you will get plenty of good exercise just walking down to the water's edge.

Crawford senses the second home market in Alaska is on the verge of being discovered by folks down in the Lower 48. When asked why, he noted that a handful of celebrities have started making the trip north. "Tom Selleck has a place down in Homer," he said, "and Steven Segal has been up here a bunch of times."

Later, Crawford and I went back to his office where he had prescreened vacation homes for sale in the Anchorage region. He sorted the screening in different ways and it was my first peek at the listings; there were not just a few homes, in total there could have been a hundred homes. They were of every shape, type, and location. One printout he gave me had 20 homes listed, ranging in price from $125,000 to $1.5 million. The least expensive one could be found along the Deshka River and it was just 1,176 square feet. The $1.5 million property appeared to be in a development and was 6,188 square feet.

I had a vision of a classic Alaskan second home as being a log cabin built in a remote area, so I asked Crawford if his listings had anything like that. There were plenty and he printed out three flyers.

- The first log cabin home was on Crawford's beloved Kenai River and it was selling for $525,000. The descriptive remarks read: Beautiful dwelling overlooking the Kenai River, approximately 110 feet of river frontage, currently operated as a very well established lodge, almost 3,000-square-foot main lodge plus three smaller log cabins used as rentals.
- The second log cabin home was near Haines in southeast Alaska and it was selling for $650,000. The cabin, itself, was very small, just 1,200 square feet, but the landholding was extensive. The size of the lot was listed as 6.7 million square feet. The descriptive remarks read: remote homestead and great mountain views.
- The third log cabin home was near Talkeetna, in the heart of Alaska's central valley, and it was selling for $489,500. The home had 4 bedrooms and was 2,600 square feet. The lot was large at 217,800 square feet. The property was described as "remote," and indeed the directions read: fly in, approximately eight miles from Talkeetna, or use an ATV trail from the Talkeetna Bluff trail.

The cost of cabins depends on the degree of remoteness, laughed Crawford. "If someone wants a Jack London lifestyle, to be out in the boonies and live off the land, I can find them an inexpensive five acres so they can build a cabin. But, I have $2 million cabins listed as well."

Golf in the Wilderness

During the Vietnam War years, Larry Maulden had the good fortune to be stationed in Alaska. First, he was out of harm's way, and second, it was hard not to love the state's beautiful scenery, even if the winters were long and harsh. When his term of service ended, Maulden remained in Alaska, trying his hand at a number of jobs before going to work as a real estate agent with a small company called Jack White. That was 38 years ago and Prudential Jack White/Vista Real Estate is now a much bigger company with hundreds of agents throughout the state. Of all of them, Maulden has the longest tenure.

I met Maulden in the town of Wasilla, about a 45-minute ride north of Anchorage. For those of you who have never made the cruise to Alaska, Anchorage sits on the Cook Inlet where it divides into the Turnagain and Knik arms. Follow the Knik Arm north for about 45 minutes and you will eventually come to the Wasilla area near the quaint community of Palmer. The area is called Mat-Su, short for Matanuska-Susitna, a large valley that someone described to me as the playground for folks living in Anchorage. I was also told the valley was about the size of Oregon. I suppose that could have been an exaggeration, but then again, everything is big in Alaska.

The Wasilla-Palmer region is one of the fastest growth areas in the state and a lot of that is due to the cheaper real estate as compared with Anchorage. Also, there's plenty of natural beauty, and it is a relatively short ride from Anchorage for someone looking for a second home. Other investors from the Lower 48 have discovered Wasilla-Palmer as well. In fact, says Maulden, there is a tiny but growing collection of reverse snowbirds living there. They fly up for the summer and then retreat south to the Lower 48 for the winter.

I wanted to meet with Maulden, not only because he was an experienced real estate agent, but he was also an investor in something new and different for Alaska, a luxury home community surrounding a golf course. There are a thousand different kinds and sizes of recreational homes in Alaska, from hunting shacks to cabins, from log houses to vast lodges, from mountain estates to river- and lakefront properties, but there was never a golf course community before the development of Settlers Bay outside of Wasilla.

Now, Settlers Bay wasn't contrived by Maulden and his coterie of investors. A Lower 48 company had built the golf course and sold homesites there. However, that company had plunged into financial difficulty and Maulden was able to unite a group of investors to buy the property in 2002.

"The original front nine was built about 28 years ago and the back nine constructed in 1996. We are the third owner," Maulden told me. "We bought 640 acres."

Maulden's group not only purchased the golf course but also property fronting 16 of the 18 fairways. During their five years of ownership, the group built homes on another three fairways and Maulden said they still have 350 acres to develop. (Some of the land is tidewater property and a salmon stream runs through other parts, so not all the land is developable.)

The original owners sold half-acre lots that attracted middle-class buyers who built homes and these now sell in a range from $160,000 to $320,000. Considering the original homes might have sold for $50,000 or $60,000, this isn't bad appreciation over a 20-year period.

However, much of that appreciation has come in recent years. "When we purchased the property there were still 300 lots without houses in the first phase of development," "That's not the case anymore because from the day the new investors came in, we built 100 homes a year for three years running. These were inexpensive lots in good locations and building really went fast," Maulden said.

Maulden's group is looking to take Settlers Bay more upscale and the newer homes will be built on larger plots. For example, Maulden showed me one home under construction on a fairway that was 2,200 square feet with a three-car garage. The precompletion price was $550,000. A beautiful, palatial log cabin sitting on a bluff over a fairway was almost complete with its 4,000 square feet of space. Maulden estimated the home would sell for $750,000 to $800,000.

He expects build out at Settlers Bay will take another 15 years.

Maulden, himself, lives on the 18th fairway.

By the way, if you are wondering how long the golf season is in Alaska, Maulden put it this way, "If you are an ardent golfer, you go from the end of April to the end of October." He did, of course, stress the word, "ardent."

Hot Venue in a Cold State

I was standing around the lobby of the Coldwell Banker offices in Wasilla waiting for Brittney Abbott, who was going to show me some second home properties in the Mat-Su area. After about five minutes of shifting about and looking at brochures, a very pretty, very young woman arrived and much to my surprise introduced herself as Brittney Abbott. I have to admit I was a little shocked because the woman standing before me seemed so young. She was actually 24 years of age, but most of the agents around the globe that I had been interviewing for this book were at least in their 40s, and many were older and had been in the business a long time.

Abbott was a rookie. She first worked in the title business, then was an office person at Coldwell Banker before deciding to go full-time as a real estate broker. In between all that, Abbott gave birth to her first child, who I was soon to meet, as the seven-month-old baby was cooing away in her truck just outside the door. Sitting with the baby was her husband, Matt, who was going to be our driver for the day as Abbott was to sit in the backseat doing double duty as a mother and real estate broker.

One of my first questions was for Matt, who worked on the North Slope oil fields in the northernmost region of Alaska. His schedule was two weeks at the oil fields and two weeks off. "So," I said to Matt, "how do you feel about your wife being a real estate broker?" Matt, who first dated Brittney when they were in junior high school, answered carefully. "She's made more money working as a broker in the last three months than she made at her 40-hour-a-week job."

As a rookie Realtor in 2007, Abbott already had four sales under her belt by the summer, which was very good considering the Alaska real estate market, mirroring the Lower 48, was quickly losing steam.

"When you called me this morning," she said while entertaining her baby, "I was working with buyers from Kodiak who were looking for a second home in the Mat-Su. They own a business down there. The wife is native Alaskan and it is hard for her to leave the small community. Also, it rains pretty much all summer and winter in Kodiak, and the valley is more temperate."

In the summer, the temperature in the valley gets up to 70 or 80 degrees. "We have three or more months of good weather," she continued. "People don't realize how nice the summers are until they come. I get calls all the time from people in the Lower 48 who ask if we live in an igloo and outside, it's 80 degrees."

After spending a day with Abbott, I could understand how she started so quickly as agent. First, she was a native of Wasilla and knew the area extremely well, second, she was personable, and finally and most important, she was well prepared.

For my visit, she had researched the market ahead of time so as to be able to show me the best examples of second homes at different price tiers in the area. And what I found extremely helpful—after months of visiting second homes around the world—she was one of the few if not the only person who aggregated local housing and home sales data for me.

Wasilla-Palmer has been the fastest growth area of Alaska for two reasons: It is a bedroom community for Anchorage and an area of such beauty that it is also a popular second home market. The data that Abbott pulled was for the "Wasilla Core Commute Area," so this didn't include the wider Mat-Su Valley, which extends all the way to the Denali National Park, about a five- to six-hour drive to the north.

Here's the key data point. In 2004, the average residential/condominium sale price was $186,771. Over the next two years, the average sale price climbed quickly to $227,302. That all changed in 2007. Through the first eight months of the year, the average sale price had dipped to $226,353, which Abbott said was the first year prices had dropped since the 1980s.

Abbott's research also delineated individual markets in the Mat-Su area for single-family residential properties (excluding condos and mobile homes) on a comparative basis over the past two years. So, this not only included the townships such as Wasilla, Palmer, and Houston, but also Big Lake, a combined primary and secondary home area, as well as remote regions. In Big Lake, for example, home sales from 2006 to 2007 were off 31 percent, while the average sale price was essentially flat, up just 1 percent.

Abbott showed me a home she was representing in Big Lake. It wasn't on the lake, which usually means the prices are lower and in this case it was true. The two-bedroom chalet was selling for $175,000. While not large, it was nicely appointed, plus it boasted a large loft, sauna, jetted tub, front deck, and detached two-car garage.

Obviously, in the remote regions of Mat-Su, homesites are rare and sales are fewer, just in single digits, but trend lines are still striking. In "remote NE Mat-Su," there were more homes listed in 2007 than in 2006, but just one sale, at a price point of $55,900. There was only one sale in this area in 2006, and that home sold for $72,300. The busiest outlying region was "remote SW Mat-Su," which had four sales in 2007 as compared with seven in 2006; the average sale price in 2007 was $75,750 compared with $114,857 in 2006.

The largest home Abbott showed me was not in a truly remote area as surrounding lands were sparsely settled. It sat on a knoll beyond the town of Houston. To call it a log cabin, which it is, belittles it, because the absolutely gorgeous residence was 4,800 square feet with three bedrooms, a loft, and four baths. The lot wasn't small at 439,520 square feet and the view from the front over a cleared, grass yard was terrific.

Most log cabins are constructed from kits created by individual manufacturers. This one was a Gastineau Log Home, but the builder, who was a Gastineau sales representative, put so much custom work into it, one couldn't tell. For example, the outdoor block facia on the ground floor was all hand-picked rock from a local stream. Inside, the builder, Dennis Illies, decorated the home with his hunting trophies. The price for the property was $952,000.

Abbott was a Wasilla enthusiast, as befitting a sixth-generation Alaskan living in the area, but her husband, a hunter and outdoorsman, told me if he had a choice he would live in the Talkeetna area, about an hour to the north, because it was getting so built-up in Wasilla. Talkeetna, on the road to Denali and Fairbanks, has become a very popular location (a two-hour drive to Anchorage). Indeed, although the general Alaska residential market has softened, Talkeetna sales volume jumped. Again, we're not talking about a major home market. The number of properties sold in the area was just seven in 2006, but during the tougher sales climate of 2007, the volume popped to 20 homes, and average sale prices vaulted from $96,129 in 2006 to $140,380.

The oddity of Talkeetna was that the number of home sales in the first eight months of 2007 was the same as in Big Lake, which is considered one of the primary second home regions in the state.

Earlier that same day, the very generous Abbott handed me off. Instead of trying to do it all in terms of showing me properties, she had found a good example of a Big Lake second home and passed me along to a friend, who had the listing for that particular home.

Casey Steinau, a Midwesterner, had come to Alaska on a visit and simply fell in love with the state and decided this was where she wanted to live.

"It was instantaneous," she laughed. "I just love Alaska. It is the most picturesque place you can ever imagine."

She also fell in love, but that's a whole other story. Anyway, Steinau, who had been selling homes in Alaska for the past six years, was to be my guide to a home that was for sale on the shores of Big Lake.

The Big Lake community covers nearly 138 square miles at the west end of the Mat-Su Valley. It boasts 2,000 full-time residents including local celebrity, Martin Buser, three-time Iditarod champion. Yet, 58 percent of the area's housing is considered recreational. Of the 138 square miles, the lake itself covers 12.9 square miles and many of the residences can only be reached by boat or floatplane.

The home Steinau was going to show me was considered boat-access only, but when Steinau got the listing she realized it was near a friend's cabin, which was accessible by a rugged back road. Steinau drove into the Big Lake wilderness as close as she could to the home and then we took a pleasant, short stroll down to the house. The 1,128-square-foot home on a 21,780-square-foot lot was selling for $249,900. It was actually a little compound as there was a shower/sauna building on the grounds as well as a few other small structures. The home was built on a beautiful little cove and since it was technically a boat-access only home, there was a very large dock on the property as well.

"This was a vacation home," Steinau said. "The owners live in Anchorage the rest of the year. They bought this as a shell and built out everything."

We were standing on the dock looking at some islands in Big Lake that were dotted with summer homes. The only access was by water, either float in or fly in. The prior winter, Steinau had sold another home in the area, this one at Echo Lake. It was also small, about 1,200 square feet with two bedrooms, two baths and a one-car garage. Because it was on a road, it sold for $325,000.

She pointed to the house we were visiting, and commented, "If you could drive to the home, it would add another $75,000 to the price tag."

Girdwood

As noted, between 2006 and 2007, Alaska residential prices began to soften except in small, individual locations like Talkeetna. There were other pockets of strength as well, in particular, in a very unusual market to the south of Anchorage.

About three years before my 2007 visit to Anchorage to research the vacation home market, I flew to Alaska in the dead of winter to try the state's famous ski location, Alyeska Resort, which was located in the Girdwood area about a 45-minute drive (or less depending on the weather) from downtown Anchorage. Alyeska boasted a small but terrific ski mountain with outstanding views. Before beginning the schuss downward, one only had to look out to see Turnagain Arm glimmering at the base of snow-capped mountains. There was also a large, first-class hotel at the foot of the ski mountain.

The whole complex—mountain and hotel—was owned by a Japanese company going through some financial turmoil and frankly everything was suffering. The hotel needed refurbishing and service was terrible. In December 2006, Cirque Property L.C., headed by Utah investor and outdoorsman John Byrne, acquired the property and has been rapidly investing in the infrastructure to bring the mountain and hotel back to top-of-the-line resort standards.

The investment by Byrne reinvigorated Girdwood, basically a picturesque canyon winding from Route 1 to the ski mountain. Ancillary developments including upscale condominiums were being built when I was there, and a host of new projects were already planned. More land under government control was to be released for development and a general plan was to be introduced by the Girdwood region to outline future development needs.

Skip Minder, a principal of Alyeska Real Estate, and one of his new brokers, Jennifer Overcast, who had been a Realtor in Jackson Hole, Wyoming, met me in Girdwood to give me a tour of the area.

Minder, who was from Montana, had come to Anchorage in 1971, and as he says, "never went home."

About four years ago, he built a cabin in Girdwood and a few years later decided to concentrate his real estate brokerage business in his home area. "Anchorage got too big for me," he said.

The same thing could happen in Girdwood. "Compared to Anchorage and the Mat-Su Valley, we are in our own bubble," Minder said. "There's a lot of new ownership here, a limited amount of land, and home prices are still rising."

Although there had been steady migration to Girdwood for a number of years, the market seemed to catch on with Anchorage residents and a few out-of-staters as both a primary and secondary market after the change of ski mountain ownership. "Since John Byrne came in, the mentality of the place changed. He's making the ski mountain more friendly, and he will be developing 80 acres at the base of the mountain for retail, restaurants, and ski-in/ski-out condos," said Minder.

Beyond the mountain, more condominiums and restaurants are being built in the area. Minder estimates about 6,500 residences are now in Girdwood of which 2,300 belong to full-timers. In 15 years, Minder said he could see 15,000 people living in the area.

He showed me a grouping of condominiums being built by private developers near one of the ski lifts, but not on Alyeska Ski Resort property. The units range in size from 1,400 to 1,800 square feet and sell for $600,000 to $800,000. There are some older units here that sold four to five years ago for around $320,000. "This is as close as you are going to get to ski-in/ski-out outside of Alyeska, which accounts for the higher prices," Minder said.

He paid $55,000 for the mountain lot he built his cabin on, and comparable lots in the summer of 2007 were going for $180,000 to $190,000. "I have one lot for sale at $160,000 and I'm surprised it hasn't sold yet," he said.

Minder drove me around his mountain neighborhood showing me homes that have sold or are for sale. "That home we just sold for $638,000, but it was first listed at $649,000," he pointed out.

The day before when I met with Crawford, he pulled me a list of 10 homes for sale in Girdwood. They ranged in size from 1,634 square feet to 4,000 square feet, and they were all in the $500,000 to $700,000 range.

Overcast says home values have increased so much that many existing residents in the area are reinvesting in their homes and, indeed, there were a number of homes being renovated and having additions put on.

Near downtown Girdwood—yes, there is a downtown—which would take all of five minutes to walk, Overcast showed me a major condo project that was being built. The first two buildings had sold out quickly, she said, and there were only 12 units left in the third building when I was there. "The original prices in the first building were $229,000 to $290,000, but in the third building, units were selling at $281,000 to $350,000," she said. The individual units were two bedroom/two bath but of average size at about 1,100 square feet.

"The buyers are mostly second home purchasers from Anchorage and a few from other places," she said. "There are a number of people from the Lower 48 buying here."

Minder, who has a real affection for Girdwood, says he equates the place with Bozeman, Montana. "When I lived in Bozeman there was a population of 7,500. Now it has 43,000," he said. "Give Girdwood another 10 years."

How to Buy Property in Alaska

No Listings. Alaska is a nondisclosure state. When a home is purchased in most states, the price of the transaction is published, or listed publicly, but Steinau told me that in Alaska there is no obligation to report the selling price. That, of course, means the MLS (multiple listing service) cannot access sale prices. Instead, they use assessors, but as Steinau noted, "in the Mat-Su borough there are four assessors and Mat-Su alone is bigger than many states. So imagine just four people trying to figure out what all these properties are worth and how much things are selling for."

Supplies and Services. Alaska vacation homes in developments, on the fringe of society, or in remote locations require a lot of upkeep and sometimes the creation of homegrown utilities. In other words, the property won't be connected to municipal sewer lines or water pipes and therefore wells need to be dug or septic tanks built. The home has to be heated, so wood, oil, or propane has to be brought in. All this means logistics are a major factor.

"Septic tanks are a big issue," Maulden said. "The ground conditions vary. Just because you have big trees on your property doesn't mean the land can handle a septic tank. Also, a septic tank cannot be any closer than 100 feet from any existing well. If you are around a lake or river, you might have a small holding tank that would have to be pumped out at some time, which is expensive." Water wells can also be iffy and expensive to drill. "I sold homes on hillsides where the first three homes had wells that were 150 feet deep, but the next three homes had wells 650 feet deep," Maulden said. "When you pay $30 to $35 a foot for a well, it can get expensive."

Those homes sitting on the side of a mountain with gorgeous views? Well, when winter comes, the winds howling across the mountain can easily reach 40 miles an hour creating windchills of 30 below zero. It's going to be mighty cold up there.

Finally, if the home is not going to be used in the winter, it has to be winterized. A lot of things can go wrong when the temperature hits 30 below.

Log Homes. My first choice for a second home in Alaska would definitely be a log home. As noted, most are built from plans and designs created by companies that specialize in log home construction. These companies often will sell the materials to construct the home as well. None of it is cheap.

Oddly, although Alaska is rich in lumber, many of the logs for these kinds of homes come from the Lower 48 and are part of log homebuilder kits. As Maulden explained to me, the smaller the logs, the cheaper they are. A minimum price for the skinnier logs from the Lower 48 would be about $150 to $160 a square foot. Bigger logs from Alaska would cost $225 a square foot. The huge logs that are used to build lodges can run $400 to $500 a square foot.

Finally, in the first few years after a log home is constructed, there is a continuous settling of the wood as it expands and contracts in different weather conditions, so readjustments have to be made. The huge home that Dennis Illies built using the Gastineau game plan actually came with levers built-in to key support structures so additional adjustments can be made later. The home was not even a year old and Illies pointed out to me some molding in a bathroom that was uneven due to the settling of the logs.

Small Plane Commutes. The state of Alaska is so vast, over twice the size of Texas, that once you pass through the population centers, mostly stretching from the Kenai Peninsula to Fairbanks, there are few if any paved roads. For coastal cities, access can be by boat during the warm months, but for those who chose to live or have recreation homes in the vast interior of the state, the only way in is by plane, more often than not a floatplane.

"There are two varieties of cabins in Alaska," Crawford said, "one is on the road system and the other is not." And when it's not, accessing the property must be done by alternate means. One of the most popular is the fly-in.

For many Alaskans, even for part-timers, a small plane is a primary means of transportation. A common sight in Alaska is a home with a floatplane or two tethered to the dock sitting behind the house. I was told that some folk living in the Big Lake area simply fly to work in Anchorage every morning. (In winter, the floats come off as the planes land and take off on the frozen waterways.)

As a result of the small plane commutation, access to runways or plane-docking residences are popular selling points. When I was at the Coldwell Banker offices in Wasilla, I pulled a flyer on a local residence for sale: a five-acre, two-home property was selling for $400,000. The promotion read that the Big Lake airstrip was within walking distance.

Exit Realty was offering a small cabin, just over 1,000 square feet, which sat on the shoreline of a place called Caribou Lake. The list price was $229,000 and although the land was only 152,000 square feet, a second lot with a 12-foot by 16-foot guest cabin was included in the price. Here were the other selling points: Jacuzzi tub, vaulted ceilings, and a dock for floatplane and boat access.

Finally, while I was visiting the Prudential Jack White offices, I happened upon a flyer in the office that was for a Mat-Su property of 4,500 square feet sitting on 4.84 acres of land. The most prominent promotion on the flyer was that the property included a 2,000-foot grass airstrip and that the slab was complete for a hangar. The price for all that was just $540,000.

Earthquakes. One of the most unusual sights I came across on my visit to Alaska came courtesy of Larry Maulden, who was giving me a tour of his Settlers Bay property. The undeveloped land was still heavily wooded except where it reached out to an arm of the Cook Inlet. Here, the forest suddenly gave way to a tidewater meadow that was quite extensive, at some points almost a mile wide.

We were still in deep forest but I could see the almost treeless meadow was just ahead. Before the topographic break, Maulden stopped our cart next to a very large rusting structure almost completely tangled in vines and vegetation. On closer inspection, I saw it was a boat. I looked around and although I couldn't see the coast, my guess was we were about three-quarters of mile from water.

Why was there a large boat sitting there rusting away in the woods? Maulden explained: On Good Friday in March 1964,

Alaska was smacked with one of the most powerful earthquakes ever to hit North America, measuring 9.2 on the Richter scale. Although the epicenter of the quake was deemed to be in Prince William Sound 78 miles east of Anchorage, the city was heavily damaged. The original Girdwood was completely destroyed and was later relocated a few miles inland.

Far upstream from Anchorage, a tidal wave flowed so strongly and widely against the current that it lifted this poor boat and washed it inland to where we were standing. Obviously, the state experiences occasional and ferocious seismic activity.

Forest Fires. More recurrent natural disasters can also be worrisome.

I have to admit I have bias about Alaska. I find the state fascinating and strikingly beautiful. Between 2004 and 2007, my wife and I took four trips to the state and one of the more unusual journeys was a loop we made from Whitehorse to Dawson City, Yukon, then west past Chicken, Alaska, south to Tetlin Junction, and then east again to the Yukon.

The year we made that loop, the forests of eastern Alaska were ablaze and when we arrived in Chicken, we inquired as to whether it was safe to continue our journey. "Sure," "Go ahead," "What's the problem?" were the responses, so we drove on. Fortunately, we seemed to be a step behind the fast-moving forest fire, because for the most part we were driving past a smoking, smoldering landscape. There were some dicey moments when fires were burning on both sides of the road and we continued through smoke and heat. Yet we kept going, not seeing a fire crew until we were near Tetlin on the Alaska Highway.

The state is so huge that when forest fires occur in the remote regions, they are left to burn. If you have a cabin somewhere out there in those woods, no one is going to attempt to save it. It will be gone.

On my last trip researching this book, Abbott was telling me that her husband's family, the Millers, owned thousands of acres in the Wasilla-Houston-Big Lake area. Back in 1996, when a wildfire struck here, it carried the family name. In June of that year, the Miller's Reach fire destroyed 37,500 acres in the Big Lake and Houston areas, taking out 433 buildings and homes valued at $8.9 million. This was in the heart of Anchorage's recreational and second home market and not in remote Alaska. Forest fires can definitely be an issue in Alaska.

It should be noted, a good fire can create opportunities for buyers. About four years ago, Steinau acquired 11 acres of land that had burned up in the Miller's Reach fire for $28,500. Today she reckons the property is worth about $75,000. "I got it at the low end of the market," she said.

Obviously, there are a couple of factors to note when acquiring land that experienced a forest fire. First, aesthetically, it is not a pleasing sight, and second, at some point if you intend to develop the land, the burned trees will have be pulled down with heavy equipment. On the other hand, I noticed that 11 years after the Miller's Reach fire, a substantial number of young trees and shrubs had revegetated and were already creating a thick, new forest.

Critters. As a recreational homeowner in Alaska, there is one other element of nature that you must consider, and depending on your point of view, it is a blessing or a curse. That is, the sharing of the land with wild animals, particularly bears.

On my last trip to Alaska, I picked up the *Anchorage Daily News* one morning to read on the front page the tabloid-style headline, "Crimes Against Bears." As the article explained, a number of bear carcasses had been found in the settled areas south of Anchorage, just before Girdwood. The bears had been shot and the bodies left to rot. My initial reaction was what a terrible thing this was and could something be done to control this crime. Then I read the story about a plague of bears in the area; some 250 black bears and 60 grizzly bears live in relative proximity to Anchorage. The article quoted one woman who reported with dramatic exasperation that she had seven grizzly bears in her yard over a two-week period. She exclaimed, "This place is like infested. My windows are covered in bear slobber. The last two years have been a nightmare. They were sleeping beside my car; right beside my car, this year."

That reminded me of a story Steinau told me. She was the agent on remote property near the town of Willow, about 75 miles north of Anchorage. The land totaled 40 acres and somewhere on it was a small, one-story cabin with a loft and a barn. About the only way to access the cabin was to hike in along a half-mile trail. "The challenge," Steinau said, "was that on the property there was not only moose, which could kill you, but also grizzly bears. So, when I scheduled an appointment with a Realtor I would always ask if they had a gun and this being Alaska most did. One day, I showed the property to a Realtor and her client, a woman. The Realtor didn't have a gun but the woman was packing."

The client liked the property so much she bought the 40 acres for $100,000—cash.

10 Things to Know about Buying Property in Alaska

1. Whether the location is riverfront, on the shore of a lake or the side of a mountain, there's almost no limit to extraordinarily beautiful homesites.
2. The most popular vacation home spots are found in the state's central valley, stretching from the Anchorage metro area north to Fairbanks, although the state is so huge a cabin can be built almost anywhere.
3. There are few main roads in Alaska, but that shouldn't be a concern as many people float in or fly in to their second homes.
4. Don't fear the loss of civilization. Many vacation home locations are within driving distance from Anchorage and that includes the lands along the popular Kenai River, which Alaskans claim is the best salmon fishing river in the world.
5. Alaska boasts a very good ski mountain called the Alyeska Ski Resort and new ownership has created a burgeoning condominium market.
6. Large tracts of land can be acquired at very reasonable prices. Road access, water access, vistas, and so forth all affect pricing.
7. There is only one major golf community in Alaska. The season is short, but the course is gorgeous.
8. The acquisition price of a home doesn't have to be made public.
9. The more remote the location, the more important it is to consider the logistics of supplying the property and providing for necessities such as running water and disposal of waste.
10. One needs to learn to live with the local wildlife.

PUERTO RICO

SKYROCKETING HOUSING MARKET COMES TO ABRUPT HALT; BANK PROBLEMS MEAN MORE SCRUTINY, TIME IN MORTGAGE PROCESS

W hen I'm not writing about business, finance, or real estate, I have the unique pleasure of writing about travel. What I tell people is that I have a secret, alternative life as a travel writer, which is true. I've probably been doing travel writing for about 20 years. In the course of that delicious gig, I often journey to the Caribbean. Indeed, for about a decade I used to make one trip to the Caribbean every year. I can't remember when that began to peter out.

Coming from Phoenix, I usually began my journeys to the Caribbean on American Airlines, which to me had the benefit of having a hub in Puerto Rico. I would land there before changing planes to head to some of the smaller islands in that part of the world. Sometimes, I could not make the transition from one flight to the next on the same day and I would lay over in San Juan, usually at a hotel near the airport. Sadly, that was the extent of the time I spent in Puerto Rico.

When deciding on Puerto Rican locations to consider for this book, after much debate, I finally opted to focus on the country's traditional condominium market in San Juan's beachfront corridor, which stretches from Miramar and Condado near Old San Juan eastward to Isla Verde by the airport. As a result, when I chose a hotel I ended up once again near the airport, just like in the old days when I was a Caribbean regular.

When staying for just one night, I used to stay at the Hampton Inn, located about a half mile beyond the bounds of a runway. When on assignment within the United States for any of my various business publications I usually stay at a Marriott Courtyard, mostly because they are almost always where I have to be—in some business corridor outside a major city. When checking for hotels in San Juan, I noticed a Courtyard near the airport and booked a room.

The good thing about booking rooms regularly with the same chain is you can close your eyes and still figure out where everything is in your room and intuitively know what to expect at the lobby, front desk, or the restaurant. A Courtyard outside Dallas looks like a

Courtyard outside Portland. When I arrived at the Courtyard near the San Juan airport, I saw immediately something was different. There was valet service. It was about 9 P.M. when I arrived at my hotel and the lobby was jammed with people. I looked about to see what was going on and to my surprise I saw the hotel boasted a small casino and a very busy bar. A quick stroll a little later revealed my hotel was actually on the beach. I had no idea when I made my booking.

I was staying at a Marriott Courtyard—dare I say it—that looked like a resort. Who knew there was such a thing? Being a seasoned traveler, I should have realized something was different because the rates at this Courtyard were much dearer than what I would be paying to be near a business park.

My biggest shock came the next morning when I noticed in the lobby of my hotel, the architectural model of an even grander Courtyard with three towers instead of one; the two additional high-rises to be were a condominium and a condo/hotel. Neither, as it turned out, got developed.

The next morning I met with Jorge Zabala, a real estate broker with Coldwell Banker, who had traveled up from Guaynabo to talk property markets with me. The first question I asked him was about the Courtyard towers that looked so prestigious in the model. The problem, he told me, had nothing to do with market demand but conservation. The San Juan beachfront corridor stretches east into Isla Verde and the last major building was the Courtyard. After the hotel, the beach stretches along a coastal area of relatively undeveloped ocean frontage. Local environmentalists apparently said enough was enough, and called for protection of the beach habitats the turtles use to nest in.

It wasn't just here in Isla Verde that beachfront development had stopped but all over the island. As Zabala explained, the current administration had halted all beachfront development in Puerto Rico. Considering that Puerto Rico is an island of considerable size—110 miles long and 35 miles wide—that's a lot of beachfront being preserved. Zabala was not too pleased with the current administration. In his view, the government had gone too far and was impeding development, halting progress, and constricting employment growth, all of which the island needed because, when I arrived in summer 2007, Puerto Rico was limping through a nasty recession.

A lot of it was self-inflicted. In 2006, Governor Anibal Acevedo Vila and the legislature couldn't agree on fiscal and tax reform proposals, so on March 6 of that year the government basically declared itself bankrupt and laid off 95,000 public employees for two weeks.

Zabala remembers the date well because he was close to finalizing three home sales. After the fiscal crisis, locals became timorous and all of Zabala's deals fell through.

Market Meltdown

Zabala came to real estate a little later than most. A native Puerto Rican, Zabala lived in the States for many years before returning to his home island. With an MBA from the University of Puerto Rico, he worked 35 years at Procter & Gamble. For a while during his P&G years he also dabbled in real estate and did so well at it he decided he would retire from the corporate world, get his real estate license, and go about the business of buying and selling properties.

All things were good, at least through 2005. Residential real estate was consistently appreciating at about 6 percent per year. A lot of speculators were in the market, flipping properties and keeping people like Zabala busy. It was a hectic year for Zabala with over 20 home sales. Then, when 2006 rolled around and the government played dead, real estate deal making ground to a halt. Actually, that would have been good; Puerto Rico's property values are retreating. And for Zabala, the glory began to fade. In 2006, his sales volume dropped in half. In summer 2007, when I visited with him, he was just hoping to get back to 2006 levels.

"It's a buyer's market right now," he told me, and prices are beginning to roll back. Near where Zabala lives, a San Juan suburb called Guaynabo, single-family homes usually go for $700,000 to $800,000, but now they are not selling even though some owners have dropped prices by $20,000 to $40,000. Further to the south, in an upscale residential area called Garden Hills, homes are generally in the $1 million to $2 million range, and said Zabala, "they aren't selling either."

Home prices in Puerto Rico have stopped appreciating, Zabala noted, adding, "In 2007, prices have fallen to 2005 levels and are going lower."

One of the more interesting brokers I met in San Juan was Molly Assad.

Assad's family lived in the Virgin Islands until 1989 when they lost everything in Hurricane Hugo. She came to Puerto Rico and eventually took up a career in real estate, doing a considerable bit of investing on her own, with 14 properties stretching from the Caribbean to Florida. Among her other activities, Assad does motivational and inspirational teaching. The two jobs cross paths occasionally. "I'm evangelizing all the time that this is the best of times for a buyer," she chuckled.

I guess you have to laugh in tough times. Like Zabala, Assad's business dropped off severely starting last year. "I had three closings in the first six months of 2007," she said.

The change in the market has a lot to do with owners finally accepting reality. "The ripple effect of the government shutting down was that a lot of people made a mass exodus to Florida," she said. "Sellers are now cutting prices by $40,000 to $50,000 and are accepting offers."

It's not that owners won't make money. There had been so much appreciation in the past few years, that folks who paid $300,000 for a villa on a golf course five years ago and put it back on the market for $550,000 in 2006, are now dropping prices to $499,000. That is not a hardship, only less profit.

San Juan Beachfront

Before my flight to Puerto Rico, I spent a considerable amount of time online researching the island's real estate market. Except for stories about the island's banks, I didn't find a great deal of information, stories, or even market data. I did, however, come across a *Realty Times* story from 2005 that spotlighted Isla Verde.

The author was Blanche Evans, the editor of the publication, and she quoted a couple of local Realtors who told her, "Isla Verde is a metropolitan San Juan beach and play area . . . with luxurious hotels, sea-view apartments, and plenty to do in this nonstop activity area, just north of the airport."

The most interesting comments in the article from the Realtors involved the market: "Isla Verde has no place to go but up! Even though other areas of Puerto Rico slowed down during the recent recount for governor, properties in Isla Verde continued to move at a fast pace. This beautiful area is preferred living for the young and the active. As with most beach areas, home prices are steadily rising. An assortment of luxury and economy apartments still exists, but older apartments are being bought and refurbished at a fast pace. Still, it is one of the best areas to buy in Puerto Rico. Rentals and short-term rentals are in great demand. A few new buildings are in different stages of construction, but their prices are uniformly high."[1]

I walked Isla Verde from one end to the other and it is, indeed, an impressive neighborhood. On the north side—the beachside—of what is mostly Isla Verde Avenue sit most of the high-rise condominiums and high-end hotels, such as the Ritz-Carlton and El San Juan Hotel & Casino. There are some condominiums on the south side of the street, but for most stretches the buildings are low-rise commercial structures and eateries.

Two years after the *Realty Times* article, the best that can be said about Isla Verde is that it is stable. And while it may still have "no place to go but up," I only passed one condominium project in development, a mid-rise building calling Ocean View.

San Juan's condo corridor begins in Condado. The area is analogous to Miami Beach with hotels, expensive shopping, and good restaurants and has held up a little better than other residential markets in the greater San Juan region. In 2007, there was still a good deal of development going on. That's a great contrast to Isla Verde, where, as I mentioned, there was only one condo project being erected. The other difference between the two ends of the corridor is pricing. In the Isla Verde project called Ocean View, a two-bedroom, two-bath condo would cost $325,000—on the 10th floor, probably $350,000. Molly Assad said she represents a chic new project, not on the beach but near it, in Condado. This is a boutique project with a small number of units, all more than 3,000 square feet and selling for $1.75 million each. "It's because you are in Condado," she explained.

"There are two kinds of property in this area," Assad continued. "There are buildings 30 to 40 years old and those less than 10 years, because there was a period when nothing was being constructed. Condos in the older buildings average about $400,000, while those in the new building can cost $700,000 for a two bedroom on the beach."

Assad, who lives in Isla Verde, says the trick there to good prices is to go to one of the newer buildings on the south side of Isla Verde Avenue. Prices drop by 50 percent once you cross the road.

Dorado

I'm standing in front of singer Ricky Martin's home in a secure, gated community called Dorado Beach Resort. For such a stylish singer, the large home, on the exterior, can be faintly praised as nondescript. It could be a rental property for all the thought that has gone into it. All around it, other homeowners have created lush landscapes of flowers, bushes, and shrubbery (just about anything will grow in this tropical climate), but Mr. Livin' la Vida Loca offers nothing ecstatically floral to set off his property—only a flat, boring lawn.

At least Chi Chi Rodriguez, who lives down the road a bit, has taken some interest in his property. I'm not sure how old Chi Chi is, but the gated community I'm in brags a gorgeous golf course, so if he still can swing a club he probably spends a lot more time here than Ricky Martin.

Everything I know about the area called Dorado comes from Elena Munoz, another one of the fascinating personalities selling real estate in Puerto Rico. Munoz was born and raised in Cuba; her family escaped the island in 1960 and ended up in St. Louis. However, Munoz and her husband so missed the Caribbean, they moved to Puerto Rico in 1971. After selling a store in 2001, she decided to sell real estate.

Munoz worked the Dorado area and was kind enough to give me a tour of her stomping grounds. The good thing about Dorado is that you don't really see it. Coming off the main highway and heading north, the land flattens, but coastal vegetation is dense. Eventually, the gates of the communities appear. That's about all you see as the true neighborhoods are hidden beyond.

The Dorado Beach Resort was one of the most expensive neighborhoods I saw with many houses selling in the $5 million to $7 million range, but then again we're talking about 7,000 to 8,000 square feet of space. There are some smaller villas (attached houses) at the Dorado Beach Resort, and Munoz had a two-bedroom listed for $900,000.

I also visited the more affordable communities. For example, Munoz took me to an absolutely gorgeous neighborhood of attached townhouses all built around wonderfully landscaped common areas. The community boasted a small beach club and communal beachfront. A 2,200-square-foot home here sold for $700,000 to $800,000.

For the past decade, Dorado had been one of the island's hottest vacation home markets. Area residents can count five golf courses, four of which are of championship level, said Munoz. There's a good beach, nice developments, and good schools. "Of course, if this is a second home you don't care about schools, but a lot of local people have moved to the area in the past couple of years," she said.

Like everywhere else on the island, the past decade has been very, very good to owners. In 2002, a Dorado deal that Munoz had a hand in was a home that sold for $900,000. The house next door to it, which is almost the same, was on the market when I was there for $1.9 million. The seller is holding out for that price, and the truth is he probably won't get it.

Dorado, like everywhere else on the island, has got the blues. Munoz says this area, too, has become a buyer's market. Part of the problem specific to the Dorado area is that Hyatt Resorts had two properties there and closed them both down. Some of the less expensive properties, in the $350,000 to $700,000 range are selling at the same price levels as they did in 2003. Again, lower values seem painful, but it is really just the greed factor that makes them seem so. Munoz tells me of a property in the Dorado Beach Resort that was listed for $1.35 million, but the owners dropped the price to $1.25 million. The house, she says, was built about 20 years ago at a cost of $300,000.

East Coast

One of just a handful of true vacation home communities can be found on the southeast coast near the town of Humacao. Called Palmas del Mar, the extensive project—2,700 acres—was originally conceived and developed in the 1970s by Charles Fraser, who built Hilton Head's Sea Pines Plantation, but it has gone through a few ownership changes since then. None of those changes, however, has diminished its stature as one of the premier resort/club communities in the Caribbean.

Today, there are about 3,000 homes in the development and it certainly has not reached its potential.

To see how Palmas del Mar was holding up I checked in with Douglas Marsters of Marsters Real Estate Inc., which has been operating in the community since 1981. Marsters Real Estate was founded by Douglas' parents. He claims it is the oldest established independent real estate agency in the community.

Douglas Marsters' father was an engineer hired by Charles Fraser to do civil engineering work for what was to be the new development of Palmas del Mar. Douglas' parents never left—until they retired. Most people retire to Palmas del Mar, but the Marsters decided to move back to North America proper with a winter home in Florida and a summer home in Canada.

"They left me in charge," said Douglas Marsters.

The community was never hard to sell with three and a half miles of golden beach, two 18-hole golf courses, a marina, a casino, restaurants, and a wide variety of land and water sports. Marsters says he usually averages about 30 sales a year.

With such a vast complex being built out over what is now more than 30 years, there are obviously some years where construction activity is rampant, and some years it's so quiet you can hear birds chirping midday in the trees. Until 2006, Puerto Rico was experiencing an exciting real estate market so a number of new developments were conceived at Palmas del Mar. "Developers got the fever," said Marsters, and the result is eight new projects in Palmas del Mar in the summer of 2007.

Projects are conceived in good times, but build out is so extensive they often come to fruition when the cycle has changed. All those feverish developers are now really sick because the local economy is in a bit of a recession and, as noted, the island's real estate market is slumping. "We have not had a major bust, but I see prices leveling off," Marsters said.

Fortunately for Palmas del Mar a lot of buyers are not local, but from the northeast United States, places like Boston and New York, where the economy is still strong. That should keep Palmas del Mar real estate stable.

Historically, homes in Palmas del Mar were as golden as its beach sand. A two-bedroom condo bought 20 years ago would probably sell now for $400,000, says Marsters. "I've had one 1,400-square-foot property that I originally sold for $300,000 15 years ago, then sold it again for $365,000, and now it is on the market for over $400,000."

Most of the original product was conceived as condos with a moderate price range. Newer development came in with pricier product, from $500,000 to more than $1 million and single-family residences for seven figures. "We have a home listed for $3 million at the moment," Marsters said.

Today, Palmas del Mar is a mix of permanent residents and second home folk from elsewhere in North America. Everyone pays a yearly maintenance fee of $700, but there are country club privileges that cost a lot extra. The good news for investors is that home prices have stayed the course with the rest of Puerto Rico; sales in the community peaked in 2005.

If one checks the Palmas del Mar web site, there's still a bit of boasting going on. One single-family, detached-home community called the Views of Palmas offers homes averaging $600,000. According to the web site, 30 homes went in presale and 140 people hopped on a waiting list. Another project with the name of Solarea Beach Residences claims it sold 74 units with an average price tag of $900,000.

According to most Puerto Rican Realtors by midyear 2007, a lot of presale deals have fallen through. Maybe Palmas del Mar avoided the tumult.

Islands

The newest vacation home market can be found on two small islands off the eastern shore of Puerto Rico. The smallest is Culebra Island, while the larger one, which can be seen from the beach at Palmas del Mar, is Vieques Island. Although quite lovely, they remained largely undeveloped because they were controlled by the U.S. Navy, and it's only been in the last couple of years that the Navy—somewhat reluctantly and amidst controversy—agreed to depart and let private enterprise take root.

Suzanne Dechter, a native of Oregon, came to Puerto Rico because she's fluent in Spanish and wanted to live in a Spanish-speaking environment. That was in 2000.

Oddly, for a big country girl, she chose the small island of Culebra to live on. After starting out in property management, she got her real estate license and in May 2003, just as the Navy was quitting Vieques, she moved to the bigger island, eventually starting her own company, Vieques Realty. "Culebra was very small, about 2,500 inhabitants," she old me. "Vieques is also small, but it has about 11,000 inhabitants. The infrastructure here is good, services are available, there is better grocery service, more choices in restaurants, and more flights out."

When Dechter arrived, a very small guest house and the one large hotel, called Martineau Bay Resort, had opened just before the Navy departure. Dechter arrived on the island at the right time.

"As soon as the Navy left, an absolute buying frenzy ensued," she exclaimed. "The Navy's position on Vieques and the protests had generated so much press, that when people heard the Navy was finally leaving they thought that was a good time to buy."

The boom began suddenly—and it only lasted for a short time.

The pioneer investors, almost all from the Northeast Corridor—from Maine to the Mid-Atlantic—came down just at the right moment. They bought at the going rate on the island (local pricing), and within six months their property values doubled, which meant that prices quickly rose to Caribbean vacation home standards. By 2006, the bloom was off and prices began to stabilize.

So, what are prices like on Vieques? When I spoke to Dechter, she had a 1,200-square-foot house on a teeny-tiny lot but with excellent views in an excellent location in the island's little town listed for $399,000. In a 2007 deal, Dechter sold a three-bath, 2,000-square-foot house on a half acre of land for $680,000. Generally speaking, an acre lot would cost about $250,000.

A couple of things to know about Vieques. In 2007, there were still no condos on the island. The beaches are outstanding with absolutely white sand against turquoise waters. The best beaches are where the Navy base existed, and that is now a national fish and wildlife refuge so those are protected areas not for development.

The last wave of buyers to come down paid higher prices and are not getting the same appreciation, Dechter says. "Things are going to continue to appreciate, but you need to be on a five-year plan." That's probably right thinking because many of the buyers have been baby boomers with retirement in their sight lines.

Jim Galasso went from being a policeman on Long Island, New York, to the owner of Culebra Island Realty on Culebra Island, Puerto Rico. "I retired, came here on vacation, and I'm still here 13 years later," he said. At the time, he paid $90,000 for his 1,300-square-foot house that he could now sell himself for $325,000. That's about the cheapest thing you can buy on Culebra.

The Navy used part of Culebra as a bombing range, but it drifted away in the early 1970s long before the Vieques controversy. Not only did the Navy show a good sense of timing in regard to Culebra, but it did one very unique thing before it left. It zoned the island.

Galasso explained, "Over 60 percent of the island still maintains the zoning, which is 25 acres per house. Then there is an area that is five acres per house and two small areas of 45 to 50 lots that is one acre per house until finally one gets to the little town of Dewey, a commercial area of about four blocks by four blocks."

Most of the Caribbean islands were not zoned until they were, in a sense, commercially exploited, but Culebra was zoned before all that could happen.

As Galasso noted, the island boasts four—and I'll use his words—"incredibly beautiful beaches," Flamenco, Resaca, Zoni, and Larga. The last three beaches are home to razorback turtles and protected by the Endangered Species Act—so, no building out there.

Most of the homes are owned by North Americans and can easily cost many millions of dollars. "There was a house on the market for $8 million, but it was too pricey," Galasso said. "It was reduced in price to $6.5 million and it is in contract."

The day in summer 2007 I spoke with Galasso, he was closing on a one-acre lot that was selling for $410,000. Another of the one-acre lots sold in 2006 for $450,000.

There is not a lot of property movement on Culebra, which is why Galasso was the only broker on the island until five days before I spoke to him. Recently, said Galasso, one of the five-acre lots with a spectacular view sold for $900,000, but generally they would sell for $800,000.

A condo/hotel exists on the island with rooms selling for as much as $250,000. It sounded reasonable until Galasso told me, "If someone you know tries to interest you in it, you better redefine the word friend."

Mortgages

It's always been relatively easy to get a mortgage in Puerto Rico as the Commonwealth's financial system is fully integrated with the U.S. banking industry and capital markets. Indeed, there are about 20 commercial banks operating on the island including a slew of local financial institutions plus a scattering of banks from Europe, Canada, and mainland United States.

Suffice to say, a mortgage in Puerto Rico looks very much like a mortgage in Alabama, California, or New York with the same array of products. Unfortunately, in the summer of 2007 it was probably a little harder to get a mortgage in those states than it had been a year or two before, as credit standards tightened in the wake of a subprime mortgage debacle. Whatever was happening in the states that summer, it was already old news to Puerto Rico, which went through a full-blown banking crisis beginning in 2005.

As in the States, in Puerto Rico it had been too easy to get a loan.

At the end of 2003, *Caribbean Business* reported that while Puerto Rico's economy had already entered a difficult slowdown, there was still one part of the island's financial structure running at full speed—it's financial institutions.

As the magazine noted, loans in particular had shown spectacular growth amid a recession, playing a key role in keeping the local economy afloat. In less than four years, since January 2000, domestic commercial banks and mortgage lenders in Puerto Rico had pumped a whopping $54 billion into the island's economy through consumer, mortgage, and commercial/industrial loans. Mortgage lending by the commercial banks had contributed another $16 billion through 100,000 loans.

The article's key point was, "the economic strength and liquidity of local financial institutions have allowed them to extend credit, without which the island's economy couldn't be sustained."[2]

Fast forward two years and suddenly the banking system on the island is in turmoil with three of its major banks, First Bancorp, Doral Financial, and R&G Financial under investigation in regard to their handling of mortgages.

Because the banks were publicly traded companies, the disaster was observed by *The Motley Fool* analyst who noted: "Any way you slice it, this hasn't been a good year for Puerto Rican banks. Doral is in the dock for questionable accounting on interest-only strips and will likely wipe out more than $600 million in shareholder equity. R&G, meanwhile, is restating its results. The Securities and Exchange Commission is also taking a look at what happened with respect to all three companies' accounting and reporting."[3]

"Last year, the federal government came here to check out the bank books, and they found the banks were doing things they were not supposed to like selling each other thousands of mortgages valued at millions of dollars," said Zabala. "Basically, they were just moving mortgages around. Now the banks are paying penalties and readjusting their books."

Things only got worse over the next few years as a securities fraud class action lawsuit was filed against R&G Financial Corp., which was Puerto Rico's second largest mortgage bank. Plus, it had to restate its previously filed financial statements for 2003–2004.[4] First Bancorp settled a shareholder lawsuit for $74.3 million in 2007.[5] As for Doral Financial, having been rocked by accounting scandals, its share price plummeted from a high of almost $50 to just over $1.

A telling note, Doral in the first quarter of 2007 reported loan production of $268.3 million as compared with $875.7 million for the same quarter the year before.

Somehow, Popular Inc., the biggest financial institution in Puerto Rico, managed to avoid that scandal, but was brought down anyway because it was heavily involved in subprime lending. By 2007, it had exited the wholesale nonprime mortgage loan origination business and shut down its wholesale broker, retail, and call center business divisions. The big Puerto Rican bank was restructuring.

What does all this mean in terms of getting a mortgage? Well, almost everyone I spoke with assured me it was still relatively easy to arrange for a mortgage and they still recommended using a local financial institution.

"I won't comment on whether the banks have troubles or not," said Dechter, "but as far as the level of service and efficiency, you might find you get better service and more efficient performance from some of the smaller mortgage companies."

Dechter points out that U.S. banks will not do mortgages in Puerto Rico unless they have branches in the Commonwealth. Still, she added, "it's not necessarily best to use the bank you have at home, even if you bank with Citibank [also in Puerto Rico] in the States. You are probably better off going with a local mortgage company that is more familiar with the territory. It is not going to be leery about financing second homes here for 80 percent to 90 percent loan-to-value."

As far as a homebuyer is concerned, about the only place you will see the Puerto Rico bank blowout affect the home purchase process will be in the time it takes to close a mortgage.

"If your credit is good, you should be able to get a loan relatively easily," observed Marsters. "But the banks are being more careful now in their paperwork. So what used to take three weeks to close is now taking about two months. After getting the hatchet from the Feds, a mortgage is more complicated but not an impossibility."

Munoz agreed: "The banks are very tight now, very selective. It is not easy to get a mortgage through and the process usually takes 45 to 60 days."

How to Buy Property in Puerto Rico

Again, the home buying process in Puerto Rico will look very similar to anything one would go through in the States.

"Once a client finds a property, I have several banks I can introduce that person to, and at that point each bank will offer a package," said Marsters. "There is the matter of getting the paperwork together, doing the title search, and making sure all the legal documents are in order. It's not a drawn out process, but it could take a while to close."

"We have a lot of cases that get drawn out because of documentation," warned Marsters. "Documentation here is harder to get if it deals with a government agency. Things that may have been overlooked in the past are being sharply monitored now. Underwriters who approve loans may not necessarily be from the lender. The process can be more complicated today."

In Puerto Rico, it's recommended an attorney be involved in the process, mainly because a lawyer has to register the deed, which gets done at a local registry. "You need a lawyer," Munoz confirmed. "By law, unless negotiated differently, the buyer has a right to choose the lawyer and the seller pays for the lawyer. That makes it more even. We usually ask the buyer if they have a lawyer who charges by regulations. They can charge 1 percent of the sale price. Nowadays, most of them charge 0.5 percent to 1 percent of the sale price, but there are lawyers willing to charge less."

Fees are also split between buyers and sellers, with the latter paying for deed of sale and stamp tax while the buyer pays for the registration of fees and stamps.

The standard closing costs cover: loan origination fee, points (optional), appraisal fee, credit report, interest payment, and escrow account. In addition, there are tax-related costs for property taxes and transfer taxes and recording fees. Finally, there might be insurance costs as well for homeowner insurance, flood or quake insurance, private mortgage insurance, and title insurance.[6]

What should all that come to?

According to Assad, closing costs in Puerto Rico are at least 100 percent more than in the continental United States especially if there is a mortgage involved. "I closed on a house that sold for $440,000 and the closing charges were $30,000. It's astronomical once you include legal fees, notary fee, and so on," she said.

Also, noted Assad, if you are a nonresident of Puerto Rico and sell your property with the intent of taking the profits back to the United States, you will be charged a 12 percent investment property tax.

Finally, Assad warns, if you are buying a second home and plan on renting it, that is probably not going to work, especially in the beachfront condo towers, because many of the structures have restrictions against short-term rentals. Generally, the buildings have three- to six-month minimum rental clauses.

A few years ago, Assad bought a house in the Dorado area for $440,000. The home has since been put on the market for $550,000, but with the residential housing market collapsing last year, buyers disappeared. Since there were no takers, Assad reduced the price to $499,000. I asked if she would go any lower. She was aghast. "With $30,000 in closing fees; at that price I would about break even."

10 Things to Know about Buying Property in Puerto Rico

1. A troubled economy has brought a robust housing market to its knees.
2. By 2007, property values in most of Puerto Rico flattened or turned negative.
3. San Juan's traditional high-rise, beachfront neighborhoods appear to be weathering the storm better than other formerly popular Puerto Rican markets.
4. The high-end Dorado region is suffering with Hyatt closing two hotels, but Palmas del Mar on the East Coast is stable.
5. You can live near Ricky Martin if you have $7 million to spend on a house.
6. The land rush on the former U.S. Navy-controlled islands of Culebra and Vieques is over.
7. Puerto Rican banks are racked with problems, and the mortgage process takes longer.
8. When buying a property, it's necessary to work with a lawyer.
9. Closing charges are sometimes negotiable with buyer and seller splitting fees.
10. Closing costs in Puerto Rico are very high.

VIRGIN ISLANDS

POPULAR SECOND HOME MARKET FOR EAST COAST INVESTORS; CRIME ISSUES WORRISOME BUT CERTAINLY NO DETERRENT

W hen I picked up my rental car at the airport in St. Thomas, Virgin Islands, I asked for a map. Like any reasonable visitor to a new place, I unfolded the map to see where I was and hopefully to figure out where I was headed. At the top of the map in bold letters embedded in a distinctive arrow were the words "keep left." I had no idea what that meant.

I learned soon enough that in the Virgin Islands traffic flows on the left, not on the right as it does everywhere else in the United States. No, this is not like the United Kingdom or Australia where the driver's seat is on the right side of the automobile; cars in the Virgin Islands are the same as in mainland United States with the steering wheel on the left side of the car.

I'm sure first-time visitors to the islands often wonder why, long ago, someone decided traffic should flow left and not right. And here is the answer. Actually, here are two answers because all the people I asked this question to responded with two explanations. The first is that the island was Danish before it was American, and their traffic flow was on the left side of the road. That was interesting but not as folklorish as the second response, which was that before there were automobiles, people traveled about the islands mostly on donkeys, which for some reason preferred the left side of the road. So, because of the obstinacy of the donkey, traditional Virgin Island traffic always went left.

Three main land masses, St. Thomas, St. John, and St. Croix, make up the bulk of the U.S. Virgin Islands, but there are 68 islands altogether totaling 135 square miles. All of the islands are volcanic in origin, which accounts for the extremely mountainous topography. As if driving on the "wrong" side of the road is not treacherous enough for visitors, there is little flat land. That is why the roads twist and turn so radically. On St. Thomas, the second largest island and the one with the most concentrated population (52,000 residents), the roads are well paved. But outside the main city of Charlotte Amalie they are narrow with no shoulders and often climb (and descend) very steeply, and one can't go too fast because turns are often sharp switchbacks.

In some of the older communities that hug the slopes of one mountain or another, the interior roads are often ridiculously slim with turns so sharp that they can't be navigated in one motion. One has to introduce the car to the turn, back up to gain the right angle, and start again. On my first day on St. Thomas, I took a ride with an experienced Realtor, Justine Mis of Sunhaven Realty LLC, to the hot real estate market on the eastern end of St. Thomas. She wanted to show me a home that was listed at $1.2 million. It was a gorgeous property, but the ride in the development was crazy as the switchback just to get to the driveway was very steep and too radical for her car to make in one fluid movement.

There is one other big of danger on St. Thomas roads: the local drivers. As noted, except in the Charlotte Amalie area, the roads for the most part are just two lanes with a double yellow divide down the center. In other words, the local police don't want any passing. In my first 10 minutes of driving down a two-lane road, I was passed by a car that completely ignored the double yellow line. As it turned out, this was very common on St. Thomas. Since the roads are normally very busy, it is somewhat of a challenge to pull out into traffic, which I guess is why the locals simply go for broke. They pull out of a side street or driveway right into traffic flow, daring you in an oncoming car to stop for them. The locals are always in a hurry to go not very far—the island is only 32 square miles.

That brings me to the final point about the local roads. In most places in the United States if you are looking to buy a home it is not unusual to drive around to see what kind of residences are available, to get a sense of the community, and see what size and style of houses or condos the place has to offer. That's an absolutely useless task in the Virgin Islands as most homes were built not to be seen from the local road. They are protected with gates, foliage, hidden driveways, and so on. In addition, the island is lush and many homes are built vertically on mountainsides, which means if you are lucky enough to see the exterior, it would only be one floor, all else is hidden from view.

Well, suppose you knew an address of a home for sale and wanted to go see it for yourself. That's also a difficulty because the folks who live on St. Thomas don't use road numbers and sometimes not even names. The tourist map you're looking at numbers the main roads, but I didn't talk to one person on St. Thomas who knew the number of a road they may drive every day.

So here's my first tip. If you are looking to buy a home in the Virgin Islands get yourself a good Realtor and let the Realtor drive you about.

Continually Rising Prices

Justine Mis told me this story about how she came to live in the Virgin Islands. Associates sent her to the islands to evaluate a business opportunity for them. She immediately fell in love with the place, went back to Chicago, sold her business, sold her condo, gave away her "furs, leather, and wool," and, as she said, "here I am."

The year was 1990 and real estate was already expensive.

It's hard to pinpoint exactly when people started buying and building second homes in the Virgin Islands—maybe as far back as the 1970s. I met a commercial real estate developer by the name of Bill Otto, who had moved to the islands around 1974 just to get a suntan and hang at the beach. For a while he worked as a beach attendant at a hotel, then got into the diving business before a friend convinced him to go into real estate. That was around 1979, and even then, Otto could see it was a good business.

Looking to get off the beach, Otto borrowed money from his father to help buy a condo in 1979 for $107,000. He sold it three years later for $165,000. Obviously, in those years home prices were already beginning to elevate.

In 1983, Otto came across a funky, three-bedroom, two-bath house near the water in a place on the north shore called Magens Bay, now a very popular location for homes. He paid $130,000 for it and still lives in it today. He recently had it appraised for $1.7 million.

For a while in the 1980s, Otto was buying two-bedroom condominiums for $120,000 to $125,000 and renting them, but the monthly assessments for hurricane insurance were so high, he could not make a profit and he sold.

Hurricanes are devastatingly important factors in the island's real estate marketplace, not only for the destruction they bring but in terms of land values. The worse the storm, the harder it decelerates the cycle of appreciation. This, of course, is a natural reaction as there is destruction that has to be repaired. Some people decide they have had enough and sell off what they own. It does take awhile for life and marketplaces to get back to normal following a devastating storm. Consider New Orleans—that city is not even close to being what it was before Hurricane Katrina.

The individual landmasses that make up the Virgin Islands are not that far apart, but the effect of hurricanes varies widely from storm to storm. In the last 20 years, two major hurricanes struck the islands resulting in tremendous damage. Hurricane Hugo hit in 1989 and the major devastation was on St. John; just three miles away, St. Thomas was relatively unscathed. Hurricane Marilyn came ashore in 1995 with the major damage inflicted on St. Thomas and lesser destruction on St. John.

When I was touring St. Thomas with Mis she took me to a homesite that was recently put on the market. Essentially it was a slab of cement on a hillside, the home itself had been destroyed by Hurricane Marilyn and never repaired.

Obviously, if people leave the market after a severe hurricane, they usually do so quickly and rare deals appear. That was the case for Mis, who bought her first condo at a place called Point Pleasant Resort on the eastern end of the island. It was a one-bedroom acquired for $51,000. When I met with Mis, she had recently put the property on the market—for $230,000.

After Hurricane Marilyn flattened the island of St. Thomas and its real estate markct in 1995, both came roaring back. Real estate on St. Thomas had been on a decade-long tear, from 1996 to 2006. Over those 10 years, there were a couple of incidents and actions that kept the waters churning.

"Back in the late 1980s, the Virgin Islands initiated an economic development program using tax incentives to attract business and hotels," Mis explained. The result was a boom for the housing market. Then the government changed and the program melted away, but in the late 1990s, government attitude altered again and a new economic development program attracted a lot of North Americans. "That was in 1999, and for three years our property prices went crazy," Mis said.

Then came September 11, 2001, and one of the aftereffects of the terrorist attacks was that people looking to buy outside the United States sought security, and the American flag flying over the Virgin Islands was a major attraction. The market lifted off once again.

"I sold a three-bedroom, three-and-a-half-bath house with a nice view in Magens Bay in late 1999 for $750,000," Mis said. "Someone just bought it recently for $2.5 million."

A Pause in the Market

One of the oddest and greatest success stories I came across on St. Thomas involved Rosemary Sauter-Frett. When she was a young woman in the coal-mining country of Pennsylvania, she and her husband created a fantasy life about living on an island. After her husband became sick with Lou Gehrig's disease and before he died, he made Sauter-Frett promise she would pursue the dream after he passed away.

Sauter-Frett, who at the time had never traveled further than New Jersey, packed up the family's belongings, gathered her children, and flew to Bermuda on a one-way ticket. "I was so wet behind the ears, I didn't know you could only stay there for a limited amount of time and then you had to leave," she laughed at the memory. "I explained to the customs people that my plan was to move there but they told me it took 10 years to become a resident and that if I wanted to be in the sun and sand, I should go to St. Thomas. I said, 'where is St. Thomas?'"

Today, Sauter-Frett not only runs an accounting firm on the island, but she owns the Century 21 franchise as well, with three offices—two in St. Thomas and one in St. John. "I am the largest real estate firm on the island," she told me with confidence.

According to most real estate agents on St. Thomas, sales starting slowing down in 2006, and the moderate pace continues through 2007.

"Things are a little slow this year [2007], which is the first time since 9-11," Sauter-Frett said. "January was slow and traditionally that is a really good month. But things picked up a little in February."

Sauter-Frett didn't think there was a long-term shift in the St. Thomas market, and said the slowdown was partially due the unseasonably warm winter of 2006–2007 in the Northeast. Cold weather on the East Coast is a great motivator to buy a home in the Caribbean and traditionally buyers in the Virgin Islands are East Coast dwellers, living anywhere from Maine to Florida.

"After 9-11, appreciation doubled and in some cases tripled down here. If you bought a house for $300,000, you could turn it around and sell it for $600,000 or $900,000 within a few years, but now we are back to where we were prior to 9-11, and that is appreciation of 3 percent to 5 percent annually," said Sauter-Frett.

That's only on St. Thomas. Over on St. John, thinks look a bit bleaker. "When the housing market started to slow down in the United States in 2006, the market started to decline in St. John as well," said Sauter-Frett. "Nothing is happening over there and property prices have dropped 25 percent. And they still could come down another 25 percent."

St. John

The biggest surprise to folks in the Virgin Islands real estate community was the rapid deceleration of the St. John housing market, which has paralleled the other islands but always at higher price points and more value acceleration. If the real estate market in St. Thomas and St. Croix simmered over the past decade, then St. John blazed. So, in 2006 when the property market went ice cold in St. John it was a complete shock to everyone.

"The last time I looked, there were 132 homes listed for sale on St. John and 116 on St. Thomas." This is the first time, historically, such a reversal has happened, said Sauter-Frett, who has an office in St. John. "If you figure only 20 percent of the island can be developed, then it appears every other home on St. John is for sale at this time."

After hearing this, I figured I better get over to St. John and see for myself what was going on. It should have been an easy commute, but I had a dickens of a time getting to the island from St. Thomas.

My instructions were to board the 9 A.M. ferry and someone would meet me at the dock on St. John. Now according to the tourist map and everyone I spoke with, ferries to St. John leave from Charlotte Amalie and Red Hook, the growing city on the eastern end of the island.

Bill Otto told me the ferry ride was only 20 minutes from Red Hook and at least twice as long from Charlotte Amalie and suggested I should make the drive to the eastern end of the island. But I figured my hotel was just 10 minutes from downtown Charlotte Amalie, so I'd take that ferry instead.

Remember my castigation of St. Thomas driving quirks? Well, I have one more. Too many cars inhabit the island and there are not enough parking spots. I knew that when I planned my trip to downtown and left an hour early. It wasn't early enough as there wasn't a spot to be had anywhere in Charlotte Amalie where I could leave my car longer than an hour. Finally, after driving in circles around each and every street, I found the public parking lot and drove into a spot minutes before the lot completely filled. Then I went to the dock where the ferry pulled in. However, this wasn't the public ferry; it was the private one that only went to Caneel Bay Resort on St. John and because I wasn't a guest there, I couldn't board the boat.

So, I rescheduled for later that afternoon and drove to Red Hook, where the parking situation was equally horrendous, but I wasn't worried because I assumed there was parking at the marina where the ferry docked. When I pulled into the parking area, the attendant told me there was no public parking at the marina and I would have to park on the street. I was incredulous because I knew there wasn't a spot to be had in the whole town, so I ended up doing what all the construction people do who work in St. John and have to take the ferry. I drove about a half mile out of town and pulled off the road onto a thin, flat stretch of dirt between the macadam and the bush and left my rental there at the edge of the wilderness. Fortunately for me, it was still sitting where I left it when I returned.

As noted, the Virgin Islands consist of three main islands. Of the three, St. Croix is the largest geographically and has the highest population. On the other hand, it has the slimmest second home market so I didn't end up making that trip.

St. Croix is a flatter, more industrialized, and less dramatic island, Sauter-Frett explained.

This is not to say there aren't homes of value there. Marsha Maynes was the number one RE/MAX broker in the Virgin Islands in 2006 and no doubt part of the reason for that was that she helped sell a St. Croix estate for $9,050,000. Now that was a nice paycheck.

So, after St. Thomas, the island with the biggest vacation home market is St. John. And, although there are only three miles of water between the two islands, they are a world apart in almost all regards including the real estate market.

St. John is just 19 square miles and has the reputation of being the prettiest of the islands that make up the Virgin Islands, but that may just be because most of St. John is a U.S. National Park and its natural beauty will be forever preserved.

The ferry from St. Thomas motored into a small bay filled with bobbing sea craft, sailboats, catamarans, yachts—all manner of floating vessels—and then safely slid into a slip at Cruz Bay dock.

Cruz Bay sits in my mind as the epitome of the Margaritaville Jimmy Buffett has been searching for over a lifetime.

The small town hugs the bay and drifts inward through narrow streets lined with shops, eateries, and rousing places to drink and make merry. There are no McDonald's, Pizza Huts, or Taco Bells. There is just one nod to the fast-food world and that's a Subway. I was told by Merry Nash, the proprietor of Islandia Real Estate and a resident of St. John for the past 30 years, that there was once a Wendy's in Cruz Bay, but folks got tired of the fast-food detritus—cups and wrappers blowing in the wind—left behind by patrons and one day the Wendy's went totally charbroiled. The chain never rebuilt and apparently all fast-food joints have since heeded the lesson.

To say Cruz Bay is charming is a bit of an understatement, but what I should mention is that the folks who reside on St. John just love that little town. Even St. John resident, country-and-western superstar Kenny Chesney, likes it so much that he'll sometimes appear at a local bar to play just for the fun of it.

I don't know what Kenny Chesney's home is worth, but, just to speculate, it has to be valued in the millions, which is not a big deal on St. John. Because 80 percent of the island is undeveloped and will remain so, the remaining 20 percent is very valuable. For the past decade, people who want to live on St. John have paid dearly for that privilege.

Like many others, Maine-bred Nash came to the Virgin Islands looking for sun and fun and ended up an entrepreneur, the owner of Islandia Real Estate.

It took awhile to find her chosen profession, but her timing was right. She entered the real estate business right after Hurricane Marilyn hit in 1995. Over the next 10 years, St. John property really soared. For a while, it didn't seem that prices would ever relent.

"I have been in St. John for 30 years," she said, "and I have never seen prices go down. From 2003 to 2005, real estate prices almost doubled."

Her first deal as a realtor in 1995 was for some land on the far eastern end of the island. The only building on it was a shack made of plywood. A fellow from Minneapolis bought the property for $40,000. He still owns it, said Nash, but now it's worth about $350,000.

She bought her first house on St. John in 1988, paying $40,000 for a home on two-thirds of an acre overlooking Rendezvous Bay on the south shore. "If I sold now I could probably get $700,000 for it. But I'm not selling," she said. "It's perfect for me—a great floor plan, great views, and great breezes."

Nash was kind enough to take me around the Cruz Bay area looking at homes and condominiums. Nothing she showed me was under $1 million and every home had a great view. There is very little flat land on St. John, at least near Cruz Bay, so it is very tough to find a house that doesn't overlook water at some point.

There are a few, Nash said. If someone were really desperate, Nash said she could probably find a one-room studio with no view. Even that would cost a half million though. "A basic starter home is $500,000," she told me with a straight face. "Properties under a million we call low-end selling."

Obviously, there is no top end on St. John.

"The average annual [residential property] appreciation on St. John has been 10 percent a year," Nash said.

That was until 2006, when everything crashed. "That year was one of the worst I've seen," she noted. "What happened was the market in the States took a slide and it frightened people. Quite a few of our buyers are people who sell properties in the States to buy something here. They might sell a ski lodge in Aspen or Aunt Fannie's house that was left to them in a will. Those properties are not selling like hotcakes anymore."

The big hit was in St. John's middle market, which is around the $1 million range. The high end of the market, over $3 million, has stayed consistent. "Those people don't care what the market in the United States is doing, they buy what they want when they want," Nash said.

I asked her about Sauter-Frett's comment about how many properties were on the market in St. John. While she didn't doubt it, she said the odd thing about the St. John market is that few homeowners feel pressure to sell. "If you look at our MLS service, you will see a lot of houses stay on the market for 300 to 360 days," Nash said.

I was looking at a two-page Islandia Real Estate advertisement in a local real estate publication called *Tradewinds House and Home*. Four homes were featured, only one was priced less than a million at $895,000. The others were a "classic St. John home just across the road from beautiful Frank Bay beach" for $2.9 million; a four-bedroom four-bath masonry home with panoramic view from Bordeaux Mountain for $2.1 million; and a two-bedroom masonry home with views from a "breezy mountaintop location" for $1.495 million.

Most houses for sale on St. John are in short-term rental programs, which at least brings homeowners some income and keeps the homes occupied. Indeed, the $895,000 listing by Islandia, comes fully furnished and has "excellent income potential with long- or short-term rental."

Islands

In many parts of the world, what second homebuyers want is either a view of the water or to be on the shore. The Virgin Islands is one of the few places where you can go one better. Remember, the territory consists of 68 islands and many are privately owned. Yes, in the Virgin Islands you can actually own an island and every now and then one comes up for sale.

"We have an island for sale," Sauter-Frett told me. "It's called Lonvango Cay [between St. Thomas and St. John] and the price is $6 million. There are two or three homes on it, fresh water, and electricity."

At the time I was in the Virgin Islands, Sauter-Frett listed a couple of other islands for sale including the better known Big Hans Lollick and Little Hans Lollick.

While it sounds idyllic, owning one's own island isn't without challenges. First of all, it's very isolated and you would definitely need to own a boat to commute. In addition, many of the islands do not have utilities or water. And finally, even though that island may be yours, you still have to submit development plans to the territory government.

"There was a gentleman who bought Big Hans Lollick for the sole purpose of putting up a hotel and condominium," Sauter-Frett said. "But there was an activist group on the north side of St. Thomas that opposed the plan because they thought buildings would spoil their view. The island owner did get approval for development but only for low-density homes, which didn't work economically, so the island is for sale again."

One fellow who did buy a piece of an island is Wally Leopold, who happens to be the uncle of a close friend of my wife. I gave him a call.

Leopold, who owned a small chain of casual furniture stores in St. Louis, first came to the Virgin Islands 25 years ago to semiretire. I say semiretire because Leopold, after moving to St. John ran a fishing charter business, and in 2001 one of his clients had a bead on some property on an island located 1.5 miles north of St. John. "He told me he wasn't going to do anything in the Virgin Islands, so I went and got myself a Realtor to see about this island," Leopold said. "The property totals three acres and runs 250 feet from the beach up a hill through the top of a ridge. It was a beautiful piece of ground with an old wooden dock, a 12-foot by 12-foot stone cottage and no infrastructure or utilities."

Leopold decided to buy it for $750,000. The problem was at that moment he wasn't liquid for that amount so he came up with a solution to raise the capital. He divided the acreage into six lots and sold five of them for $150,000 to $200,000 to friends and associates. "It was one of those situations where everything fell into place," he said.

Because this was an island with no infrastructure, Leopold and other landowners built a solar, wind, and backup electric generator and installed a reverse-osmosis desalinization system that could make 75 gallons of water an hour. Then, over the next 14 months he built his dream house.

To get to the point where Leopold was ready to buy part of an island took 25 years of residency on St. John. He and his wife arrived in the Virgin Islands because they wanted to buy in the Caribbean and, as he said, the Virgin Islands "have the American flag flying over them."

While they were on their first visit, Leopold stumbled across a quarter-acre lot on the east end of St. John and plunked down $12,500, but a few days later he ran across a half-acre lot on a mountaintop with gorgeous views and bought that too for $24,500. The story gets worse. While on the island, Leopold began subscribing to the local paper and came across a property on the north shore of St. John that was an acre and a quarter and on the market for $60,000. He purchased that as well. To help finance that deal, he put the other two properties on the market, selling them just a few months after he purchased them for $15,000 and $30,000, respectively.

About two years later, a Realtor called to say he had a beautiful property with a small house and a view to "knock your eyes out," Leopold said. The price was $395,000. "I made an offer for

$315,000 and they took it. Then I put the $60,000 lot on the market and sold it immediately for $225,000."

Over the years they lived there, the Leopolds pumped another $300,000 into the property only to divorce in 2000. The house had to be disposed of and it went for $2 million. With his part of the settlement, Leopold paid $650,000 for a house and an acre of cliff top land overlooking the sea below. "I put another $100,000 worth of renovation into the house," Leopold said. "I thought this is where I would spend the rest of my life."

It wasn't much later that a client of his told him about the island.

Condominiums

When I was in St. John, I asked Merry Nash about the condo market there, because I hadn't seen very many condominium projects while I was in the islands. St. John, she explained, was really a single-family-home market and of the condos that did exist, 95 percent were built during the late 1980s.

That changed around 2004, when six new condo projects (in the 40- to 50-unit range) either were planned or under construction. Taking those into consideration, the number of condos on St. John would triple. Prices varied from $700,000 for a small studio to units costing a couple of million dollars.

When I met with Marsha Maynes in St. Thomas, I also asked her about the condo market. While, as noted, Maynes scored big with an estate sale in St. Croix in 2006, she was working a number of condo developments when I met her the following year.

Maynes, who ran a well-known restaurant called Miss Ruby's in the Berkshire mountains of Massachusetts, came down to the Virgin Islands in 1981 and decided to stay. Around 1997, she began working at RE/MAX. At the time, Maynes was living in a condo on Mahogany Run for which she paid $115,000. Today, that same condo could fetch $400,000, she said. "Along with single-family homes, almost every condo in St. Thomas has doubled or tripled in value during the last five to six years," she told me.

While that kind of crazy appreciation has slowed, Maynes didn't expect the condo market on St. Thomas to collapse as it did, for example, in Florida. "We are a small boutique market," she said. "At any given time we don't have more than 100 condos on the market. Upmarket or down market, you will see the same kind of inventories."

Traditionally, St. Thomas condos were small studios or one-bedroom units. Now people are looking for more space, and builders, especially those creating luxury product, are meeting the demand for two- and three-bedroom units. At the upscale Preserve at Botany Bay on the west end of the island, the villas (attached homes) will all have three bedrooms.

Other new developments Maynes is representing include the Mahogany Run Golf Resort, which is offering two-bedroom condos from $295,000, and The Mandarin, located within the Mahogany Run Golf Course, which will be just 27 units almost all of which have two bedrooms and prices starting at $635,000.

"The condo market is still appreciating," Maynes said, "because it is a supply-and-demand issue. New construction costs are high, so the older, existing condos are a better deal. They are also in some of the best locations. For the most part, the older condos are in good shape, they just need some remodeling."

The Crime Issue

There is a rising tide of crime everywhere in the Caribbean, mostly stemming from the ongoing drug trade that crosses these waters. Boats of all sizes and descriptions ferry illicit drugs from places like Columbia to destinations in North America.

Violence has come to many of the peaceful Caribbean islands, and one place that has gotten a reputation for being dangerous is the Virgin Islands. I'm not saying this reputation is warranted for I certainly saw nothing to worry me while I was visiting there, but most tour books now bring up the subject.

As a blogger, allegedly quoting a guidebook, noted, "St. John is relatively safe, even at night, but St. Thomas, especially around its capital, Charlotte Amalie, has the highest crime rate in the Virgin Islands. You may want to avoid it at night. St. Croix has less crime than St. Thomas but caution is advised, especially if you plan night visits to the dives of Frederiksted or Christiansted where muggings might occur."[1]

Or, this comment, "Because of St. Thomas' thriving commercial activity—as well as its lingering drug and crime problems—the island is often referred to as the most 'unvirgin' of the Virgin Islands."[2]

I didn't visit St. Croix and most of my stay in the Virgin Islands was on St. Thomas, so the views I solicited were probably a little biased. When I asked about the crime problem, almost everyone said they felt perfectly safe living there. "I don't see crime as a major issue here," said Mis. "I feel completely safe here. Sometimes we still don't lock our doors at night."

Mis, like others I interviewed on St. Thomas, told me that if crime was a problem, it wasn't on that island but on St. Croix. "They have a higher incidence of crime there," Mis said. "I can tell you I know people who have gone there and have gotten mugged and assaulted."

The problem for St. Croix may simply be one of perception; the island has never lived down what is probably the most gruesome mass murder in the Caribbean in modern times. In September 1972, eight people were killed and another eight wounded on a St. Croix golf course by submachine gun fire. The incident, often referred to as the Fountain Valley Massacre, is still brought up every now and then as if it happened just yesterday.

"That crime is something that haunts St. Croix, and the island has never really come back since," Sauter-Frett said.

Rising crime in the Virgin Islands may not be a worry for most people, but it is definitely an issue. An October 2006 post on the Virgin Islands Law Blog reported, "Crime Tops Voters Concerns." The author noted that one of the top four issues cited by voters was public safety and went on to comment: "Crime has long been a concern to the Territory's voters with many pundits citing its impact on the Virgin Island's leading industry, tourism, as well as upon quality of life for residents."[3]

How to Buy Property in the Virgin Islands

When Maynes lived in Massachusetts, she got her original license to sell real estate. She has since sold some land there and bought a house. "I was surprised," she said, "Massachusetts law is very similar to the Virgin Islands."

Basically, buying a house in the Virgin Islands mirrors the experience in almost any U.S. state, with about the only difference being higher closing costs and probably higher mortgage rates.

Maynes recommends having an attorney. "On the mainland, the title companies close deals, but down here an attorney dictates the deal. If a lender is involved, the bank's attorneys are involved. They attend closings and do paperwork."

Sauter-Frett also recommends getting an attorney because unusual problems are not out of the ordinary. Sometimes property lines were drawn on incorrect government maps, or titles were not registered, or there are probate issues. Actually, there are a lot of probate problems because, in a typical situation, a retiree who was living on the island gets ill and goes back to the States for treatment. The retiree never recovers from the illness and passes away, say, in New Jersey. Probate gets done in that state but not in the Virgin Islands where there is property. "Probate here can take two to seven years to resolve," explained Sauter-Frett. "If you drive around and see properties that are old and empty, it is usually a probate issue. If the courts are not done with probate, you cannot get a clear title."

Closings typically take 30 days although it is not unusual to go 60 to 90 days. In regard to closing costs, the transfer tax is based on a graduated scale of 2 percent for sales up to $350,000 and 3.5 percent for anything over $5 million, Sauter-Frett said. "Typically, the seller pays the transfer tax, but it is negotiable at the time of sale. I've seen buyers pay half and I've seen buyers pay it all."

While property taxes are low in the Virgin Islands (value of property multiplied by a tax rate of 1.25 percent of 60 percent of the property value), the real killer is insurance, which can be 2 to 3 percent of the value of the home. That could mean $30,000 on a million-dollar property. I guess if you can afford a million-dollar home you should be able to afford an extra $30,000 in insurance premiums.

If you want to build your own home, don't expect to get a direct answer as to how much it will cost from a builder. He doesn't want to depress you. Building costs are at least $300 a square foot and could easily run to $500 a square foot.

10 Things to Know about Buying Property in the Virgin Islands

1. If you are looking for property, go with a Realtor. Driving about on your own won't accomplish much.
2. Real estate is expensive in St. Thomas, but even pricier in St. John, the two major second home markets in the Virgin Islands.
3. A decade-long run-up in home values finally began to moderate in 2006.
4. Appreciation on St. Thomas is now about 3 to 5 percent annually; St. John's middle market is flat to negative.
5. You can buy an island here.
6. Be careful what you wish for as most smaller islands, or cays, do not have utilities.
7. The condo market in St. John is getting a boost with new development.
8. New condos are bigger than the old product. Demand generally outpaces supply.
9. Crime, or at least the perception of crime, haunts St. Thomas and St. Croix.
10. Forget about property taxes, the big hit to the pocketbook comes from insurance.

GUAM

MILITARY BUILDUP ROLLS BACK REAL ESTATE DEPRESSION; TAKE A SECOND HOME HERE AND TRAVEL TO ASIA AND OTHER PACIFIC ISLANDS

hen I was in American Samoa, an experienced Pacific island traveler who heard I was heading next to Guam, told me the island wasn't nearly as pretty as Samoa. My first impression of Guam was that the traveler was correct, but I eventually changed my mind.

As my plane approached Guam I looked out the window to see below a plateau that seemed to have risen from the sea as one huge, flat plain. However, the island, which is only 30 miles long (its width varies between 4 and 12 miles), is actually two geological formations. The plateau resting on steep cliffs above the sea derived from coral reefs and makes up the northern part of the island, while the southern area is volcanic in origin.

I didn't visit the southern part of the island on my first visit to Guam because most of the population lived on the plateau, but I was told that it was mountainous and tropical with thick rainforests. I could see the mountains away in the distance from my hotel window, yet, because the native flora of the island's northern land mass was neither tropical nor attractive, I had a hard time envisioning rainforest until I was told this *Ripley's Believe It or Not* story by Phillip Schrage, general manager of the island's modern Micronesia Mall.

During World War II, Guam was taken over by the Japanese military. U.S. forces came back in 1944 and reclaimed the island from the invaders. About 20 years later, a sole Japanese soldier was found hiding in the jungle. When the U.S. forces took back Guam, the soldier had hightailed it to the jungle, lived in a cave, and when his uniform fell apart he made new clothing from the bark of a tree. He had no idea the war was long over until he was found.

I was impressed. For someone to hide in the rainforest for 20 years on a small island and never be seen, must mean there was some incredibly thick flora that I hadn't seen yet.

Schrage told me the story because the bark clothing the Japanese soldier was wearing when he was found could be seen in the American Samoa Museum, which was being temporarily housed in the mall while funds were raised for a permanent site.

In 1987, Schrage came to Guam on a three-year contract to manage a new mall being built by Philippine industrialist Lucio Tan (ranked by Forbes as the richest man in the Philippines). A native of upstate New York, Schrage had worked in management and other retail positions from South Carolina to Louisiana and decided the new mall looked like a good opportunity for him. The first three years went by quickly. When it was time to renew his contract, Schrage decided he liked living on Guam, signed up again, and has been here ever since, marrying a Filipino lady he met in Guam.

I bring up Schrage's story because, when Americans from the mainland visit Guam, they find something immensely appealing about the island and they will often stay. Unfortunately, unless mainland Americans are in the military, they will probably never visit Guam—even if they are among the few knowledgeable ones who know the island is an U.S. territory.

Island Economy

There are really two legs of the Guam economy. First, is the U.S. military, which traditionally, especially the Air Force and the Navy, has had a huge presence on the island. Deployment to Guam has waxed and waned over the years since World War II. Recently, with so much U.S. military action in Asia, the U.S. government announced it was beefing up its position in Guam with 8,000 marines to be stationed there. Guam's importance to the United States' defense can be inferred by recent visits to the island by former Secretary of Defense Donald Rumsfeld and Vice President Dick Cheney.

The U.S. government is committing some $15 billion to Guam over a 10-year period to build up infrastructure.

Guam citizens might laugh about "the marines are coming, the marines are coming," but it is heartfelt jocularity. Just the anticipation of the infusion of people and dollars has reignited the local economy. After an economic slump of more than a decade, the island is bustling with new building and the long-dormant housing market has been taken off the respirator. Home prices are accelerating and speculative fever is in the air.

That brings us to the second leg of the Guam economy: tourism. Once again, one needs to take out a map. The island is located in the Northern Marianas, a group of islands due west of Hawaii (about a seven- to eight-hour plane ride from Honolulu). This area is known as both the Western Pacific or the Philippine Sea. Obviously, Guam is much closer to Asia than either the American mainland or even Hawaii. So, while Americans would never think of vacationing in Guam, Asians, particularly the Japanese, just love the place.

An average of 1.3 million visitors come to Guam each year. In fact, "Guam receives more tourists annually than does the entire continent of Australia," Schrage wrote in a brochure about his mall. "Ideally situated, only a few hours flight time from major markets such as Tokyo, Hong Kong, Manila, Seoul, Sydney, and Honolulu, Guam is at the crossroads for Pacific, Asian, and American business and pleasure travelers."

Guam boasts direct airline service to 13 cities in Japan and serves as a regional hub for Continental Airlines.

Think of Guam as a smaller version of Oahu. The main tourist center is the Tumon Bay area and it has even come to be called the Waikiki of Guam.

On the west coast of Guam just north of the center of the island, two perfect semicircular bays were formed by reefs and waves, each with a narrow band of fine, sandy beaches. The northernmost of two, Tumon Bay, remains the most consistently developed with a line of high-rise hotels (Westin, Hilton, Marriott, and Nikko among many others) stretching to a line of cliffs—and the famous Two Lovers Point—that cap the bay at the north. The main street here is also known as Tumon and the center of the action, near the Outrigger Hotel, is called Pleasure Island.

Tumon Street is an odd mix of low- and highbrow. A new mall, called Tumon Sands Plaza, boasts nothing but high-end shops— Burberry, Cartier, Tiffany, and so on—while up and down the street one can find massage parlors, adult video shops, and strip clubs. Obviously, all those servicemen on the island have to go somewhere on the weekend.

The first thing a mainland American notices in Guam is that almost everything is written in two languages, English and Japanese. That's because tourism is really defined by the extent of Japanese visitations. As of 2005, 80 percent of visitors to Guam were Japanese. Indeed, Guam has been a getaway island for the Japanese for the last 40 years and that has not changed. As I walked the main street of Tumon it seemed to my eye the majority of the pedestrians were

Japanese honeymooners. Indeed, Japanese weddings on Guam are a major attraction.

"To a great extent, as goes Japan so goes Guam," noted Nicholas Captain, whose eponymous real estate consulting firm, The Captain Company, is a key source for Guam real estate data, as well as other economic information for most of Micronesia. Captain maintains that Guam's real estate values, for example, have tracked Japan's since 1985. That's not really a surprise, Captain wrote in an article published in *Real Estate Issues*, because the Japanese have been the biggest investors on the island, and "the subsequent contraction of Japan's economy in the early 1990s started the longest downward spiral in real estate values in Guam's modern history."[1]

Although a U.S. territory like Puerto Rico, Guam faces west toward Asia, not east. After Japan, the second biggest group of visitors comes from South Korea, with third place belonging to Taiwan. The current estimated population of Guam now stands north of 170,000 with the biggest ethnic group being the indigenous Chamorro people who account for 37 percent of the population. The next largest group is Filipinos at 26 percent. Caucasians are only 7 percent of the population, with the remainder made up of Koreans, Japanese, Chinese, and other Pacific Islanders.[2]

One morning while I was on the island of Guam, I sat and had coffee with the two principals of a small residential brokerage called Real Estate Guam. They were fairly representative of the island ethnically. Ramon Puangco was from the Philippines and his partner, Suki Nicole Sul, came from South Korea.

Puangco, originally an architect, came to Guam in 1998 to work on a hotel and decided to stay. After working with some architects on residential homes, he decided to become a real estate agent in 1992, just when the Japanese boom began to collapse. Nevertheless, he stayed with it and after working with numerous companies over the years finally decided to create his own firm, and in 2005 he and Sul formed Real Estate Guam.

"I fell in love with Guam," he said. "It's a nice place with fresh air and blue skies. The people are friendly."

Sul didn't arrive in Guam until 1998, when she came with her husband, who had a business in Japan and Guam. The marriage folded, but Sul, too, decided to stay on the island. She had been working in a bank and dabbling in real estate. Eventually, she had to choose.

"The bank told me I could be a banker or a Realtor, but not both," said Sul. "The market was going up so I decided to give it a shot."

Since she was Korean, Sul felt her language skills would be very useful as the South Koreans represent the next big wave of investors on the island. "I'm bilingual," she said, "so this was a good opportunity to get into the real estate business where buyers are Asians. Now it's mostly Koreans who are buying."

As noted, the Koreans have become the second largest visitor group to the island, and why not? Winters are brutal on the Korean peninsula and perpetually warm and sunny Guam is a relatively short three-hour plane ride away.

Like the Japanese pattern, Korean investments followed Korean tourism, this was especially so since a recent change in Korean currency laws, explained Captain. "Korea now allows individuals to take an equivalent of $3 million out of the country if they want to invest in overseas real estate; so what we are seeing now is a lot of speculative money coming to Guam from Korea."

In the past few years, Koreans have closed on about $40 million in real estate deals. A couple of transactions involved Koreans buying land with the intention of developing luxury, condotel communities where individual units will be sold as second homes mostly to Koreans.

In addition, Sul says property is very costly in South Korea. "The price for real estate is very high. Initially many Koreans looked to invest in California or New York, which is also high. Then they discovered Guam. Real estate here is reasonably priced and with the U.S. military bringing in the Marines, Korean investors expect high returns in the future."

Koreans like to buy properties with ocean views, Ramon added. "Some Koreans are buying land, expecting to build condos that would be sold to Korean senior citizens who are planning to retire. It's not cold here and they say if you retire in South Korea, even with $2 million you cannot live comfortably. A $2 million condo in Korea is very small. Here you can buy a condo, still have a million in the bank, and live comfortably on the beach with fresh air, blue skies, and less traffic."

Sul also mentioned that she was seeing an influx of mainland U.S. and Hawaii-based investors interested in 1031 exchanges.

The phenomenon of the mainland investor also caught the eye of economists at the First Hawaiian Bank, which reported in its Guam 2006–2007 Economic Forecast: "Traditionally, Guam offshore demand has mostly come out of Asia, but now more of the players are from the U.S. mainland and Hawaii. Realtors observe that inquiries from the U.S. really are not so unusual, but more of that interest is now culminating in actual sales. Asian demand is still important, driven by improving economies there. But the advantage for U.S. investors in Guam real estate is that it is a dollar-denominated investment in what is essentially an Asian economy. Guam's 'America in Asia' image seems to be paying off."

Taxes

"My father is a genius," 10-year-old Matthew Schrage told me. We were discussing the famous digitally dancing Christmas tree light show his father had created at the mall. Indeed, the elder Schrage had a knack for promotions and marketing, and knowing that some visitors to the island, such as journalists, are curious about what makes Guam tick, he had put together a combination promotional package about his mall and fact sheet on the island.

What I found interesting in Schrage's packet was a one-page backgrounder entitled, "Guam Is a Business Friendly Market." Instead of explaining why, Schrage hit on a number of bullet points, such as: no consumer sales tax, no state income taxes, no unemployment insurance tax, and no export duty taxes.

It is important to understand that Guam is an unincorporated U.S. territory. As a result, its laws and processes, such as buying real estate, are the same as on the mainland. However, just as the tax structure for New York City might differ from that of Houston, taxes to some extent are different on Guam as well.

Key points on taxes:

- There is one legal tax authority for the island, no separate municipal or district taxes.
- The tax structure includes an income tax levied on U.S. citizens, which is paid to the U.S. government or the government of Guam, depending on where the citizen resides on the last day of the calendar year.
- Businesses incorporated in Guam also pay a corporate income tax on all worldwide income.
- A 4 percent gross receipts tax applies to local transactions; and a 4 percent use tax applies to all personal property imported into Guam for local use or consumption.

- Real property taxes on land or improvements are lower than on the mainland, generally 1 percent of assessed value for land and one-fourth of 1 percent of assessed value for improvements (the assessed value is 35 percent of the appraised value.)[3]

The Last Real Estate Boom

In 1967, Pan American World Airways started flying to Guam, bringing tourists from Tokyo, and the strange, post-WWII relationship between Guam and Japan began to develop. This occurred at a divergence in the economies of the United States and Asia. After the Vietnam War years, the U.S. plunged into a rolling recession that lasted into the 1980s. However, on the other side of the Pacific Ocean, the economies of the Asian Tigers such as Korea, Thailand, and Malaysia were getting stronger. Probably no Asian economy was booming more than Japan's.

While only 20 years ago, it's already getting hard to remember that Japanese investors and businesses were so flush with cash they departed their native shores for the United States and started buying everything in sight. Office buildings, golf courses, hotels, even Rockefeller Center was swept up in a wave of Japanese real estate investing.

Since the Japanese were already familiar with Guam, which was turning into a major vacation market, they dived into the island's real estate market with huge development schemes. Many of the mid-rise and high-rise hotels along Tumon Bay and elsewhere on the island were financed by major Japanese investors. Smaller investors were buying up almost anything else that wasn't nailed down.

"During my years here at the end of 1980s when I was still an architect, the Japanese were literally carrying suitcases filled with cash, knocking on doors and buying properties," recalled Puangco.

Although a little more speculative, Guam was experiencing a real estate market not much different from that of the mainland and Hawaii during the 1980s. It was a boom time for both the commercial and residential markets, and properties everywhere were appreciating at an extremely fast clip. By the early 1990s, two things happened: the real estate market in the United States started to fall apart, while in Asia, go-go Japan turned out to be ephemeral Japan; and the speculative bubble deflated so badly in

Japan, that it is only now that the Japanese market is beginning to recover.

Oddly, tourism from Japan held up through most of the 1990s, peaking in 1996, but the economic relationship between Guam and Asia was so tight, the island's economy and real estate boom began sinking like an anchor tossed off a fishing boat.

I've often noted Hawaii real estate markets exhibit marked radical boom-and-bust cycles. Guam, as a small version of Hawaii with an even more limited economy, has struggled through more dramatic boom-and-bust cycles.

Going back about 40 years, Guam first rode the military buildup in the Vietnam War years to its first real estate boom, including its initial $1 million land deal. Then came the oil price hikes of the 1970s, and the island's economy collapsed leading to Guam's first major real estate bust. A decade later, as the value of the Japanese yen versus the U.S. dollar doubled, Japanese tourists to the island realized the currency difference made Guam land prices dirt cheap and the island's second real estate boom was launched. Then it all got nasty again.

Unimproved land in the Tumon area once went as high as $1,500 a square meter, now that same land could be bought for $250 to $300 a square meter, Sul said. "There was a plot of land used for a parking lot. The Japanese offered $5 million and the owners didn't bite. Now they cannot sell the land for $500,000."

During the peak of Guam's second real estate boom in 1990, the prices for the highest-demand land had increased nearly 10 times within a three-year period. "By 2002, numerous properties that sold during the 1989–1990 market peak subsequently resold at small fractions of their original purchase prices," Captain said.

How bad was the 1990s real estate bust on Guam? Captain claims that it was the worst speculative financial disaster since the Tulip Bulb bubble in Holland back in the mid-1600s when the speculative price of tulip bulbs rose an astounding 5,900 percent from 1634 to 1637, then collapsed 93 percent. From 1985 to 1990, during the Tumon land rush, prices rose 1,100 percent, but the ensuing decline in prices was 95 percent.

What did that magnificent bust mean in regard to individual deals? Captain has a number of examples: 24.7 acres of oceanfront land sold for $63 million in 1989–1990, then during the downturn was resold for $7.5 million; 20.2 acres of oceanfront land sold for

$40.5 million during the same period, then during the bust was resold at $2 million; in the interior of the island, 1.2 acres of land sold for $2.3 million at the height of the boom only to be let go during the bust for $130,000.

Captain's most notorious example of real estate bought and sold at exactly the wrong moments in a cycle concerns 5,524 square meters of nonoceanfront land near the Hyatt resort that was acquired for $18.2 million, or a then-record $3,295 per square meter. The land was then consolidated with two other purchases increasing the whole plot to 9,843 square meters. Between 2003 and 2005, Captain said, the entire property was finally sold at a bottom-feeder price of $520,000, or $55 per square meter, reflecting what he called a total "meltdown decline ratio of 97 percent."

Captain's database reports for the fourth quarter of 1999, indicate that there were 114 single-family dwelling transactions with a median price of $154,800. By the second quarter of 2003, transactions increased to 168, but median sale prices collapsed to $106,500. For condominiums, the median sale price peaked at $133,580 in the third quarter of 1999 before falling off the edge of Two Lovers Point, bottoming out at $65,000 during the second quarter of 2003.

The Comeback

Guam is now four years off the worst of its most recent real estate bust and prices that were crawling back slowly have now began to accelerate. In 2006, according to Captain, condominium sales were strong all year, and by the fourth quarter, median sale prices hit $115,125.

Single-family dwelling sales also were robust in 2006 with prices jumping to a median sale price of $170,000.

Captain, himself, could be affecting the market numbers for 2007 as he bought oceanfront land on the more rural southern end of Guam for $450,000. Not bad for the one-quarter-acre property with 3,000 square feet of living space. That would include a one-bedroom apartment currently leased to a serviceman. As he told me about his latest purchase, I could tell he was very enthused, rambling on about the beauty of that part of the island.

Captain was born in California and raised in Connecticut. His father had been to Guam because the woman he married was in the military, and by odd chance was a captain. Thus, she was known as Captain Captain. Eventually, the younger Captain made his way to

Hawaii, where he met someone whose job involved flying back and forth between Honolulu and Guam. Captain began working for his friend and opted to move to Guam, getting into the real estate business in 1991. The Captain Company opened in 1997.

"This place is paradise," Captain said. "It is one of the most wonderful places in the entire world. It's part of America and there are business opportunities everywhere you look."

Captain doesn't just advise on real estate, he also invests. One of his most recent deals was a condominium he and partners acquired. The oceanfront units in the investment originally sold for $700,000 (1,750 square feet of space). Captain and the other investors made their deal in the bottom of the market (2003–2004) paying just $400,000 per unit.

"From 1988 through 1990, lots of projects were developed for the Japanese second home market," Captain explained. "Unfortunately, when the Japanese economy collapsed, those second home properties were sold off at a discount or left vacant."

Asked what he thought the condos in his buildings could be sold for today, Captain said $600,000. Not a bad return on his investment after three years.

"The investors who are buying now are people who know the Marines are coming to Guam. There is a run in the market," Liz Duenas explained to me as she whipped in and out of traffic along the main roads of Tumon, Tamuning, and other locations in this metro area. "Prices have spiked over the last couple of years. Now they are stabilizing. We are waiting for prices to spike again. Then they will stabilize and spike again. Prices are still rising but not at that drastic jump we just experienced."

With one hand on the steering wheel of her car and the other pointing out properties, Duenas is a maestro of the drive-by. "Prices have hit bottom and now we are coming back up. The only reason prices have come back is because of the Marines. You see this [condo] complex [near Tumon]. A couple of years ago, I sold a unit for $150,000, then it sold for $199,000 in 2005. The most recent comp came back at $235,000. It was owned by a retired teacher who later moved to Florida and asked me to sell it. In 2000, the price went as low as $110,000. I had a buyer, but he couldn't come to terms, quibbling over a few thousand dollars. He was the one who eventually bought it for $150,000 cash."

One has to pay attention because Duenas talks fast.

"In Tumon, land values are higher than anywhere," she contin-ued driving and pointing. "This is Tumon Holiday Manor. I have a unit here for sale at $571,000; it is 2,100 square feet of living space with four bedrooms and two baths. That unit there sold for $460,000 or $480,000, but they pretty much had to gut it."

Like Puangco and Sul, Duena has been dealing with an increas-ing number of Korean investors. However, what she finds interesting is a spillover of Hawaiian investors. Apparently, there is enough capital moving to Guam that a number of Realtors from Hawaii have gotten licenses in Guam to manage deals and properties for their Hawaiian and California clients now investing in the small island. "They are doing 1031 exchanges out of California, where they are selling high on existing real estate investments and mov-ing the dollars to where they can stretch their money a bit more," Duenas explained. "Prices are on the high side in Hawaii, so when they come here real estate looks like a deal."

One Hawaiian broker has put together a pool of investors from his own investor list and has been bringing them all to Guam.

Duenas told me this story. One individual she was working with sold his home on Guam and relocated to Hawaii to invest there. When he got to Hawaii, he discovered all his friends were pooling their monies to come to Guam.

Duenas, who stands about five feet tall, is a powerhouse selling machine. She was born in Guam as her mother was a local girl who married a man from the Philippines. She entered the real estate business with her husband John in the 1990s, creating Diamond Realty. They took on a partner in 1999 before becoming a RE/MAX franchise in 2001.

"We sell a lot of homes; we have about 20 percent of the mar-ket," she said, which in any market is a considerable achievement because residential real estate is typically fragmented among hun-dreds of individual agents.

To unwind, Duenas and friends will fly to the Philippines, stay at a resort-spa for a long weekend, get massages and manicures, then fly home. Of course, this is the lure of Guam, it is a relatively short plane ride to most of Asia. One can own a home on Guam, which has excellent airlift to Asia, and use it as a hub to travel to the Philippines, Hong Kong, Bali, Tokyo—whatever one's poison.

Or you can go the other way and visit the islands of the western Pacific.

Anthony Godwin, a resident of Tamuning and principal broker with Today's Realty in his hometown, waxes rhapsodically about traveling to neighboring islands like Palau or Truk in the Caroline Island Group.

"Palau is about two hours by air," according to Godwin. "That's a Continental flight. Continental has taken the responsibility to service these other islands. They are all accessible from Guam by air."

Godwin's family moved to Guam in 1968 when his father's job transferred him. Godwin, himself, was born in North Carolina, but for all practical purposes grew up in Guam, then went to the University of Guam before entering the real estate profession in the early 1990s—just in time to experience the last of the Japanese boom before the bust.

"Real estate in Guam goes up and down," he said. "This is the second or third cycle I've been through." That experience allows Godwin to take a long view of the local market. In his first year as an agent, for example, he sold a condo in Tumon for $550,000, then saw it go back on the market five years ago for $250,000. Now, the value has climbed back to $400,000. There were other condos built as second homes for the Japanese in the Tumon area that sold in the $400,000 to $500,000 range. At the bottom of the bust they were on the market for half that original price. Today, they are back on the market selling between the bottom and the old top.

Godwin, himself, has dived into the market. He bought a 1,400-square-foot condo in the heart of Tumon for $125,000 15 years ago. At the end of 2006, it was put on the market at $190,000. Godwin bought it to be a rental property; it leases for $1,700 a month. He also bought a number of single-family dwellings through foreclosure. "I bought those at good prices, renovated them, and then resold," he said.

"This is a good time to invest," Godwin added. "This year and last year were market recovery years. We are seeing numbers come back up."

When Duenas was driving me around the Tumon/Tamuning metro area, I had to admit I was a little underwhelmed by the quality of the housing. It wasn't that there weren't some very nice homes, but everything was too haphazard. A large manse could be sitting next to what looked like a clapboard shack. That's not an exaggeration, and I saw numerous examples of just that kind of situation.

Duenas showed me a handful of planned communities where there was at least minimum consistency among the individual homes, but there were not a lot of those types of developments close to Tumon/Tamuning.

Prices are all over the map as well. The local newspaper, the *Pacific Daily News,* listed an ad with three different homes in Tamuning: a new house (five bedrooms, three baths, 3,200 square feet) for $460,000; another house (three bedrooms, three baths) in the same area of town was going for $250,000; and a third that was three bedrooms, three baths and two stories was advertised for $368,000. Meanwhile, a Tamuning condo (two bedrooms, one bath) was offered for just $70,000.

Since most waterfront areas in Tumon/Tamuning were built out with hotels and commercial buildings, good residential locations are scattered through the higher elevations surrounding the city, especially where there is a good view to the ocean. Occasionally one finds a condo project. Indeed, there were a couple of mothballed high-rise hotels that I was told were recently acquired and would be converted into either condos or apartments, the latter would be marketed to the military.

It's not that rents are cheap on Guam. A good rental, either condo or single-family dwelling, generally averages about $1,200 a month. The highest rent Duenas quoted to me was $1,700 a month. Not New York City prices, but higher than what my sister was paying for a two-bedroom, two-bath condo in the Orlando, Florida, area.

Scanning the local newspaper, I saw one property for rent in Barrigada Heights, a hillside development that overlooks Tumon Bay. The location is great, but again, the quality of homes extremely erratic. This "very unique and comfortable home in central location" was going for $1,800 a month.

Even so, Duenas warned, while this is still a good time to buy a condo as an investment, cash flow remains difficult because rental values have not caught up with the recent spike in pricing.

How to Buy Property in Guam

A tutorial is not needed for Guam, because the transaction process is the same here as in the mainland United States.

There are a couple of things to note. When I was visiting the island in spring 2007, the always cash-strapped government was looking to tap into the resurging real estate market as a way to generate more income. The governor of Guam proposed to increase two sets of fees in regard to real estate transactions: deed recording and conveyance tax. To record the deed for the sale of a $200,000 property cost $200, but under the new proposal that would climb to $1,000; the realty conveyance tax was $1 per $1,000 of property value, but the new proposal would lift that to $5 per $1,000 of property value.[4]

While researching Guam before my visit, I came across a blog written by a Guam resident. She had her own list of things to consider before buying or renting on the island, including:

- **Typhoons:** Just as Florida is in the hurricane zone, Guam sits in the western Pacific typhoon zone, and in the past decade has been hit by two supertyphoons. Considerations: Tin-roofed houses, which are fairly common, may not be eligible for typhoon insurance (you need to inquire); everyone wants a beach house, but when the typhoon hits, you probably would prefer to be living inland; and if renting, a landlord should supply typhoon shutters.[5]
- **Water:** On a small island surrounded by the great Pacific Ocean, there are some areas that have notoriously low water pressure. Again, this is something your real estate agent needs to inform you about.[6]
- **Bugs:** Guam has a lot of termites, which is why most people do not build with wood. This doesn't mean that termites can't still be a problem as even concrete block homes use wooden doors and molding. Termites can even get into your books and furniture.[7] I don't know if ants are a huge problem in Guam, but I was staying on the 10th floor of a high-rise hotel in Tumon Bay and my first room had a huge ant infestation. In fact, I had to move to another room. As for my Guam blogger, she notes, "Guam has too many ants. Not only are there too many of them, but they all want to move in."
- **Snakes:** Probably the one thing everyone knows about Guam is that the island is plagued by the nasty looking brown tree snake. If the reality lived up to the hype, I should have been tripping over snakes with every step I took. I never saw one except at an exhibit in the local aquarium. People I spoke to on the island said they rarely see them.

10 Things to Know about Buying Property on Guam

1. Guam is an important beach resort location for Japanese sunseekers, tourists, and honeymooners. Almost all signs and public announcements are in English and Japanese.
2. The island also boasts a large U.S. military presence, which will only get bigger in the years to come.
3. Think of Guam as a smaller version of Oahu, but with much, much cheaper real estate.
4. After a decade-long economic slump, the island's real estate market fell into a virtual depression. This only recently lifted as the U.S. government has decided to create a new base for about 8,000 Marines.
5. Guam, like Hawaii, has a bit of a boom-and-bust real estate market, but more severe. Beginning around 1998, the island's economic bubble burst and property prices plummeted.
6. Real estate has remained extraordinarily cheap compared with Hawaii and the mainland United States, but prices have been climbing since 2005.
7. Asian real estate investors are slowly being replaced by Americans, who are finally beginning to realize that the United States governs another major resort island in the Pacific.
8. The process of acquiring real estate in Guam is no different from buying property in California.
9. Plenty of oceanfront and ocean view properties are available.
10. Guam boasts great airlift to Asia and the Pacific Rim, which makes it a perfect hub for someone interested in holiday jaunts to places such as Japan, Korea, Bali, Thailand, or Palau.

CHAPTER

SAIPAN

THE LAST REAL ESTATE BARGAIN UNDER THE STARS & STRIPES; FEDERALIZATION, LEASEHOLD LAW LIBERALIZATION MAY BE NEEDED TO SAVE THIS ECONOMY

Y ou know things are really bad in a country when the taxi driver taking you from the airport to your hotel, while trying to entertain you with small talk, ends up regaling you with a litany of local problems, from a wrecked economy and lack of jobs to inept government.

I arrived in Saipan about nine o'clock one evening after a short flight from Guam and one of the first things I noticed as we slid into the village of Susupe, where my hotel was located, was a number of small establishments with bright neon signs advertising poker. "What's up with that?" I asked my taxi driver, and he explained that these were places that had poker machines, which I supposed were slot machines, and that recently these places had suffered a string of robberies.

Never discount the words of a taxi driver, because the next day, a headline in the local newspaper screamed, "Four Suspected Poker Robbers Fall." The less-than-tabloid prose exclaimed: "Detectives arrested on Tuesday four men who were allegedly responsible for the recent armed robbery of a poker arcade in San Antonio."

"Armed robbery?" Where were the perpetrators going to hide? Saipan, the capital of the Commonwealth of Northern Mariana Islands, is a small island of just 71.4 square miles and a population of 58,000 people. Did they think no one would figure out who they were?

I got word of Saipan's problems prior to my visit, especially when I was in Guam. Whenever I told anyone I was headed next to Saipan, stories began to unwind: no money to pay teachers, slave labor problems, one of the lynchpins of the local economy—the garment industry—was going bust, and major airlines were dropping Saipan.

One woman even managed to scare me, telling me stories about the Russian mafia and the Japanese Yakuza moving onto the island to launder their money into dollars and Russian prostitutes working the island because prostitution was legal on Saipan. She told me to look closely at the men because some of them are missing part of their index fingers—cut off as part of a traditional penalty in mob society.

The woman was no hysteric. Her name was Donna Ysrael, scion of one of the largest development (Tanota Partners) families in Guam and a successful businessperson in her own right as founder of Dizzy Inc., a Guam beachwear chain with stores such as DNA, Splash Guam, and DNA Evolution.

After her rant, I told Ysrael I would like to record her comments for a book. She nodded, then launched into a more moderately toned ramble: "Saipan has so much potential—beautiful weather, wonderful beaches, and the people are nice. But it is like a cowboy town. It is the Wild West. The government is deep in debt and the economy is dying a rapid death—it used to be a slow death, but not anymore. They are just surviving by strings. You almost feel as if you are in a third-world country even though you have the luxury of being in the United States, speaking English, using the U.S. dollar, and being protected by U.S. laws—but not all laws. In Guam, we have taken the California code and copied it to form the Guam code, not in Saipan."

The Commonwealth of Northern Mariana Islands, often locally referred to as CNMI, is a dominion of the United States. How could all that possibly be going on? This was going through my mind as my taxi pulled up to my hotel, a large, sprawling complex. Milling about were other guests most of whom seemed to be single women from Japan and Korea. They seemed complacent. "Hey, did I just get a look? Wow, maybe this won't be such a bad place to visit after all."

The next morning I awoke to a dawn so beautiful my heart skipped a beat. From my window on the fifth floor of a 10-story tower, I looked out to see the bright sky of a Pacific morning, with the coastal waters moving gently in hues of dark blue and aquamarine. Palm trees lined the beach and they slowly waved in the morning breeze. I stepped out onto my patio to a warm day without the thick humidity that makes you tired just being alive. The two previous islands I visited, American Samoa and Guam, were extremely humid and the air always felt encasing. The world was a little crisper here on Saipan.

If Guam was a small version of Oahu with its own little Waikiki, then as a Guam resident explained to me, Saipan should be considered "our Maui." And the good news about Saipan, that person added, is that the weather is better and so are the beaches.

In the Northern Marianas, Guam was the big city, and Saipan the small town. And I'm going to say this now, before I go any further, Saipan is a lovely place to visit with, I might add, all the amenities of a resort island.

As Ron Hodges, a mainlander from Cincinnati who now lives on the island told me more than once, "I love it here."

In 1995, Hodges moved to Saipan from Kentucky to teach. Around 2004, he segued into the real estate business. "I started out teaching in the Saipan schools and when I arrived I immediately fell in love with the island," he said. "I probably decided in the first month I was here I would never leave. It had tranquility, peace and quiet, water, and no traffic. I would not trade Saipan for anywhere."

Part of the attraction of Saipan was that it was a good base for traveling in Asia, and Hodges made the most of it visiting the Philippines, Bali, China, Thailand, and places in between. That lasted until about 2003 when he meet a young Filipino woman and got married. When I visited Hodges, his first child was already 18 months old.

Since Hodges was one of the three licensed real estate brokers on the island, he understood the local property dilemmas and early on realized he was living in a true market collapse. Smartly, he began to invest heavily in island real estate.

I should add, and read closely: Saipan's economic structure has the dilapidated, hopeless feel of a Pacific island after a tsunami, but if there are any bargains left anywhere in property markets under the American flag, this is indeed the place. I visited Hodges' home, a freestanding condominium in a gated community with a pool on the highest mountain in Saipan. The views were stunning. The homes were originally built for the Japanese, who had dominated the island's tourist trade and then the real estate market before everything went to crap. The original price on the condo had been set at $375,000. Hodges picked it up for $50,000. Not far away on a plot of land that Hodges said had "the most beautiful views I have ever seen," he nabbed almost two acres of raw land for $45,000. It had originally sold for $1.5 million.

Here's one more crazy example. The Hotel Nikko Saipan, one of the island's major luxury accommodations built in the 1980s for about $65 million (if built today would cost hundreds of millions) recently sold for $10 million. You can't even buy a good penthouse in Manhattan for that price.

Hodges was just one of approximately 5,000 mainland North Americans on the island (including Canadians), who visited, said "wow," and stayed.

"There used to be a large expatriate community on Saipan," confirmed Ysrael. "A lot of people from Canada used to go there because it is a good tax haven. I knew someone who visited Saipan and started a company. The government wanted the new business so badly he doesn't have to pay taxes to the government of the Commonwealth of the Northern Mariana Islands for 10 years. He moved all his companies there and does not have to pay taxes."

Frankly, as I toured the island, I couldn't believe how beautiful it really was; needless to say, I also couldn't believe how upside down many investments were and how desperate those owners were to get out from under them.

"This is the coldest real estate market on the planet," Hodges exclaimed. "You can't even give properties away. I auction houses that have gone into foreclosure. Sometimes I can't even get a $500 bid."

He added, "I get calls every day from people trying to unload property," and then he launched into a tale about a young woman who owns a beach apartment complex with 24 units. The woman owes $1.6 million on the property. Of the 24 units, 20 are occupied but only doing $400 a month in rentals. Not even figuring expenses, the woman's five-year earnings stream stands at about $500,000. "For $500,000, I would not buy that place," Hodges noted. "I would value it between $200,000 and $300,000."

That is the point. The real estate market has collapsed so deeply that for bargain hunters Saipan may be the last great American frontier.

Saipan is a market with extreme risk, and everyone I spoke to guessed that the floundering economy of this Commonwealth has another two years of recurring bad news, but already signs of investment life are sprouting and the seeds of some recovery are being established.

A Little Background

After World War I, Japan occupied a number of island groups in the western Pacific including the Mariana Islands, a string of 15 islands, the biggest being Saipan, Tinian, and Rota. (Guam belongs to the Mariana group, but it had been under U.S. control since 1898.)

As Japan's martial aims expanded in Asia, it began to fortify some of these islands. Saipan, in particular, had a large contingent of Japanese military and civilians.

That state of affairs remained in place until World War II when the United States military slowly retook Asian territory and Pacific islands that had been conquered (including Guam) by Japan. In the Pacific, one of the United States' toughest and costliest confrontations with the Japanese was the battle for Saipan.

The objective of the Mariana Islands was strongly influenced by the introduction of a new airplane into the war, the B-29 Superfortress long-range bomber. If the U.S. could take the Marianas, then Japan's major cities, including Tokyo, would be well within its range of 1,500 miles. (The Enola Gay, the plane that infamously dropped the first atomic bomb, took off from Saipan's neighboring island of Tinian.)

The Battle of Saipan began on June 15, 1944, and concluded after almost a month of solid fighting on July 9, 1944. As on other islands such as Iwo Jima, the Japanese would not surrender and fought to the last man. Before the battle, there was a large Japanese civilian population on the island and it tragically followed the military into death. Hundreds of Japanese civilians committed suicide jumping from two sets of cliffs on the north end of the island. Today, memorials have been erected at these sites, and they are known as Suicide Cliff and Banzai Cliff.

When the smoke finally settled over Saipan, 14,111 American soldiers were killed, wounded, or missing in action, while 30,000 Japanese soldiers and 22,000 Japanese civilians died.[1]

After World War II, the Mariana Islands were administered by the United States as part of the United Nations Trust Territory of the Pacific Islands. That administration lasted until the 1970s, when instead of seeking independence, the island group opted to accept U.S. territorial status. In 1978, the Commonwealth of Northern Mariana Islands arrived with a new government and constitution. Legally entitled Northern Mariana residents qualify for U.S. citizenship.[2]

Sweatshops

It would be nice to report CNMI has done well as a U.S. territory, but the fact is, in the spring of 2007, when I visited the island, its economy was catatonic. The government had managed itself into a disaster.

The country's biggest economic sector has traditionally been tourism, but in the 1990s, a garment industry blossomed. Unfortunately, those blooms were poisonous.

The Northern Mariana Islands successfully used their position as a free trade area within the U.S., which, at the same time, is not subject to the same labor laws. For example, the $3.05 per hour minimum wage in the Commonwealth is lower than that in the mainland U.S. and some other worker protections are weaker leading to lower production costs. This allows garments to be labeled "Made in USA" without having to comply with all U.S. labor laws.[3]

Unfortunately, a number of garment manufacturers took advantage of Northern Mariana being outside U.S. labor laws, and very ugly allegations of sweatshops, slavery, and child labor began to surface. A large number of female Chinese migrant workers were brought to the island to work in the garment industry, and since the collapse, many I'm told now work as prostitutes.

Remember Donna Ysreal's rant about Saipan including the Russians and legal prostitution. She was partly right and partly wrong.

Roy Alexander, president of Alexander Realty & Development on the island of Saipan, enlightened me further: "Prostitution used to be legal and now it is illegal, which is worse, since it now has become a real eyesore to the community. A lot of it had to do with the garment industry employees who were working nights, but to make extra income they worked as prostitutes. When it was legal, it was regulated, and now that it is illegal the prostitutes are on the street and aggressive. It has driven a lot of the tourists away."

Alexander's explanation probably was closer to the truth because while researching Saipan, I came across a reprint of an article from a local publication with a headline that declared, "Japanese Call Saipan 'Prostitution Island.'" I can truthfully say I didn't see one prostitute during my three days on the island, but my hotel wasn't near the downtown area, which was a couple of miles up the coast.

The rapid decline of the garment trade, particularly on Saipan, was the direct result of the World Trade Organization lifting restrictions on imports from other countries, such as China, where the cost of production is far below that of Saipan.

"Since 2005, the garment factories have started pulling out. We had a garment factory here, but closed it because there are no more quotas required for countries such as China, Cambodia, and

Vietnam," said Mustafa Shakir, president of his own entrepreneurial enterprise called Shakir's CNMI Inc., a company that does a lot of things, but mostly dabbles in real estate. He was born in India and came to CNMI in 1989 because his father, who was born in Indonesia, was having problems exporting garments to the United States and had to reestablish in Saipan. Shakir came to help out but in 1993 decided to go into real estate.

A First Hawaiian Bank economic forecast for 2006–2007 reported: "The contraction of Saipan's garment industry is staggering. For example, from October 2006 through June 2007, garment certification user fees have fallen 25.2 percent as compared to the same period the year before and 44.3 percent from the same period in fiscal 2001."

The U.S. Government Intervention

The problems with the garment industry in Saipan encompassed two important issues, self-regulation of the territory's labor and immigration. From a mainland U.S. investor's perspective, the outcome of all these problems looks to be increasing "federalization," which means the territory will have to conform fully with U.S. labor and immigration laws and procedures. That would mean, among other things, the same minimum wage as on the mainland and the same immigration controls.

When I was on Saipan, U.S. Deputy Assistant Secretary of the Interior David Cohen told CNMI that the federal government was working toward controlling CNMI immigration without harming the local economy. He was calling the process, "flexible federalization."[4]

This was a big change from the early Bush administration years. Somehow, even Saipan got caught up in the Jack Abramoff-Tom DeLay scandals. According to online reports, Abramoff and his law firm were paid $6.7 million by the Commonwealth from 1995 to 2001; part of that money was used to finance trips by Tom DeLay and his staff to Saipan. Delay then crafted a policy report that extended exemptions from federal immigration and labor laws to the island's industries. Magazine and Internet blogger reports looking into the sex slavery and the garment workers industry on Saipan were attacked in Congress using statements prepared by Abramoff's lobbying team.[5]

The immigration issue was particularly important because of the relocation of 8,000 Marines to Guam and buildup on that island. The U.S. government also controls a major portion of Tinian Island and an increased military presence was expected there as well. Security (immigration) was going to become an issue.

The problem is, the Saipan government and garment industry has worked hard, for obvious reasons, to convince Saipan citizens that it was important that labor and immigration should be independent of federal oversight (just as Abramoff was paid to do the same for Congress). "For the last 15 years, the locals have been hammered with the message that it is important for us to keep control of labor and immigration, so most people believe that it's true. The newspaper, which behaved like a mouthpiece of the garment industry, has been telling them that for 15 years," said Ron Hodges, owner of A1 Real Estate Hotline on Saipan.

Hodges is one of those who would like to see the federal government taking on the immigration and labor oversight responsibilities. "We should federalize labor and immigration because it means a large department that would be paid by the federal government and that would relieve the Commonwealth, which has no money," he said. Most issues, even immigration and labor are not so cut and dry. Alexander, who runs numerous businesses on Saipan said, "To get foreign laborers here, they have to bonded, airfare paid for, and employers are responsible for housing, electric bills, and transportation as well as food and medical expenses. Our minimum wage is $3.05 but net to the employee with all those other expenses, they are actually averaging $8 to $10 an hour. If we go to a minimum wage and drop the mandatory expenses foreign laborers would have a more difficult time here than they presently have."

Tourism

If I dwell on history and economic development more with Saipan than with other locations, it's for good reason. First, it's probably least known of all U.S. territories and solving economic problems should result in stabilization, which will only benefit the qualms of mainland investors. For that reason, I need to also spend a bit of time on tourism to the island, because the real estate market, for better and definitely worse, has followed the tourism trade.

The Marianas, Guam included, are the closest tropical islands to much of eastern Asia, as such, they evolved into a vacation destination similar to the Caribbean for mainland Americans on the East Coast or Hawaii to those on the West Coast. Guam, with its better infrastructure, captured the bulk of the sun lovers, but CNMI didn't do badly either. For every million visitors to Guam some 300,000 came to the Marianas.

The most important point of origin for visitors has traditionally been Japan. As Japanese continued to visit Saipan from the 1960s to the 1980s, investment followed. Not only did they build the major hotels, shopping centers, and a few commercial properties in Saipan, but individual investors began buying up properties. To some extent these were the glory days of Saipan's economy and real estate market.

Tourism and investment held up somewhat after the bursting of the Japanese speculative bubble, which grew from the late 1980s through the early 1990s, but after the Asian economic crisis at the end of the 1990s, tourism began to collapse and so did the real estate market—mostly because it was created and supported by Japanese investors who were no longer coming to the island. By 2003, Japan Airlines on its Tokyo to Guam route cut flights from 14 a week to 7 a week. The airline eventually pulled out altogether.

As to why Japan Airlines pulled the plug, that is open to some debate. Subsidiaries of the airline built hotels and the major shopping center in Saipan. The latter has since been shuttered, and the hotels sold off with massive losses. Partly, it was a matter of economics for Japan Airlines, but Ysrael told me the island native lands provision, or Article 12 of the CNMI Constitution, was also a problem.

Things only got worse for Saipan's tourism industry. In 2006, Northwest Airlines cancelled its evening direct flight from Narita (Tokyo); that was after dropping its direct flights between Saipan and Osaka and moving to smaller planes for its remaining flights.

While I was on the island in the spring of 2007, I picked up the local newspapers to read two stories that summed up the tourism situation in Saipan: the decline of Japan and the ascendancy of Korea. The first story said that Japanese arrivals had fallen 15 percent during the first six months of fiscal 2007. The second story reported Asiana Airlines was adding four daytime flights a week from South Korea to Saipan. As happened with the Japanese, Korean investors are following the tourists, not only investing in commercial properties but vacation homes and condos as well.

How to Buy Property in Saipan

I briefly mentioned Article 12 of the CNMI Constitution, but it is the most important impediment to a thriving real estate industry in Saipan. Even as an American citizen, you cannot own CNMI property unless you are descendent of Mariana Islands native peoples.

When the Commonwealth was formed, the United States felt it was necessary to protect the property rights of the island's indigenous peoples, mostly Chamorros, from rapacious foreign and domestic real estate investors and developers. As a result, Article 12 of the Commonwealth's Constitution restricts the acquisition of permanent and long-term interests in real property within the CNMI to persons of "Northern Marianas descent."

However, there is some leeway in that the island currently allows investors to get a 55-year lease on private property. In addition, leaseholders can buy, sell, trade, mortgage, and renew the leasehold, which, in effect, makes it as close to ownership as possible. (When I mention properties bought and sold in this chapter, I'm referring to leaseholds bought and sold.)

"The one thing we have here is Article 12," explained Alexander, "that has been a deterrent to property investment to many mainlanders and institutional investors because you cannot own property here even as an American citizen. You are only entitled to a leasehold for a maximum 55 years. The trouble is Americans are just not used to working with leases."

Big investors often found ways to circumvent this law. For example, one of the early investors in Saipan (and discoverer of the island's beneficial tax laws) was Larry Lee Hillblom, a founder of DHL Worldwide Express, who discovered corporations with majority CNMI ownership could own land, so he formed business entities where he would have 49 percent of the ownership, but he would find at least three local partners to make up the 51 percent ownership. He fulfilled the law's requirements but still held the most important ownership position as compared to other partners. The courts determined that was legal until the CNMI legislature changed the loophole—by that time Hillblom's investments were grandfathered into legality.

Partnerships with locals have been a sticky business ever since then. When Japan Airlines entered the Saipan market, the parent company invested heavily in the island, with a Nikko hotel and nearby, a shopping mall. Apparently, the same issue of corporate ownership was involved in the purchase of the land for the hotel and mall, and when local parties took issue with the ownership they dragged the Hotel Nikko Saipan and Japan Airlines into court. The case was finally settled in 1997 by the CNMI Supreme Court and not in favor of the Japanese.

Whether the case should have come to court or whether the decision was fair, the result has been a disaster for Saipan.

"There was an aggressive attorney on the island back then and he took the Japanese to court," explained Alexander. "He tried to say all the leaseholds were null and void and as a result the hotel belonged to the indigenous people. This court case went on for five years and really put a halt to new development on the island. The Japanese government and Japan Airlines felt it was a slap in the face to them. That might have something to do with them pulling out of this market."

Japan Airlines was the island's major carrier. But no more. Fourteen flights between Japan and Saipan ended in 2005.[6] In addition, the mall was shuttered (recently acquired) and the Nikko Hotel sold.

As noted, the decline of Japanese tourists coincided with a rise in Korean tourists—and investors. Unfortunately, Korean investors are not comfortable with leaseholds so while the expected flow of investment capital from Seoul has been good, it has not been as good as it could be.

With the economy in the doldrums, the CNMI government needs to attract more investment capital and one thought is to make land ownership less restrictive to non-Mariana islanders.

In 2012, CNMI has an opportunity to amend its constitution and there is a debate going on right now as to what do with Article 12, noted Shakir. "One suggestion is to try to fix the leasehold, extending it from 55 to 75 years, and the other solution is to totally abolish it."

Business people are now lining up behind change. At the end of 2006, Saipan's incoming Chamber of Commerce president spoke out: "CNMI practically has no market for real estate. A two-bedroom, one-bathroom house in the CNMI costs $51,000 on average. In Guam, the same package would cost $160,000, while in Hawaii, it would be worth $480,000. What is that telling you? It is telling you there is no market for real estate on Saipan because of this land ownership issue. If you're an investor would you put more capital here or in an area where the value of land goes up?"[7]

Or as Hodges wrote me, "The original intent of Article 12 was to save the island for future generations but it was economic ignorance. Prices are based on supply and demand and when you take the Chinese, Japanese, Koreans, and mainland Americans out of this market, the only buyers are local. We have denied ownership to an affluent tourist market and that is the primary cause for our low real estate prices."

Bargains Galore

Is Hodges a pessimist? Actually, no. His blog notes: "There are bargains in a cold market. A new Tokyo airport will open routes for tourism, and while that is a couple of years away, Saipan is still a favorite destination for Japan. China granting CNMI favored destination status will open the door [to tourism from] the world's fastest growing economy. Affluent Chinese tourists could spark enormous economic development. Real estate prices will continue the seven-year downward spiral, but the more properties you can acquire in the next two years, the richer you will be. The completion of the Tokyo airport and the Chinese invasion alone will drive real estate up."

Alexander came to Saipan in 1988, getting hired by a Larry Hillblom partnership. He stayed. "I do love the lifestyle, the weather, and the sports—scuba diving, fishing, and golf. What more can you ask for?" In 1989, Alexander sold a plot of Saipan land to investors for $8.8 million, and recently bought it back for 10 percent of that cost. Judging from Alexander's and Shakir's comments, real estate does seem to be going for about 10 cents on the dollar.

Beachfront land used to sell for $1,000 to $1,500 a square meter, now it goes for $150 a square meter, Shakir said.

In the spring of 2007, Alexander took 24 acres of mountain land that had originally been acquired by a Japanese investor for $3.3 million, and sold it for $300,000 to a Russian. (Remember, Saipan is just 3.5 hours from Asia and that includes eastern Russia. Saipan is negotiating to bring charter flights in from Khabarovsk, Russia, twice a week.)

Alexander has been conducting a number of single-family dwelling auctions of late. He gave me two examples. The first is a 4,000-square-foot home that was appraised at $750,000 in 1995. A doctor's wife picked it up at auction for $55,000. Even better was a 5,000-square-foot home with ocean views on a quarter acre of land. It was appraised seven years ago for $235,000, has a mortgage of $180,000, and was abandoned two years ago. Alexander intends to buy it for $55,000 and then divide it into two rental units.

For some reason, $55,000 seems to be a popular number. Shakir told me about a 900-square-foot condo unit that originally sold for $165,000, but he brokered for $55,000.

Next to my hotel in Susupe stood the immense, 317-room World Resort. Alexander told me that it had recently changed hands for the ridiculous sum of $7 million and the buyer pumped another $14 million into renovations. (Part of the reason for the cheap price is that the term of the leasehold wasn't far into the future.)

One more startling deal. Kumho Asiana Group, the Korean parent company of Asiana Airlines, bought the LaoLao Bay Golf Resort (Greg Norman-designed 36 holes on government leasehold land) for the almost giveaway price of $17 million.

One afternoon, Shakir picked me up at my hotel. Driving and acting like a tourist guide, Shakir circumnavigated the island. Along the way, he would point out buildings for sale, homes on the market, and properties that had recently changed hands. He confided to me that he was going to alter his investment strategies, which heretofore had been very conservative, to take advantage of some great buying opportunities.

At the end of the day, Shakir took me to his favorite watering hole, an outdoor table on the beach at one of the island's resorts. We ordered a couple of beers, some bar food, and got set to watch the sun fall into the western ocean. In a heartfelt statement, Shakir said he couldn't believe how lucky he was to have ended up on Saipan. With the sinking sunlight reflecting in his misty eyes, he said once again to me, "I feel blessed."

10 Things to Know about Buying Property in Saipan

1. The economy is in turmoil.
2. Real estate is selling for 10 cents on the dollar. Could this be the last bargain location left in U.S. property markets?
3. The island is a resort location marketed mostly to Japanese and Korean sunseekers. The Japanese were the first big investment group, creating the island's second home market.
4. Saipan is a good tax haven.
5. The federal government may need to step up its oversight of the Commonwealth of Northern Mariana Islands, which probably would be a good thing for investors.
6. Much of the island's land cannot be directly sold to persons who are not of Northern Mariana descent. It's possible this restriction will be eased in the near future.
7. Most real estate investment is done through long-term leaseholds.
8. North Americans are slowly discovering Saipan and the rest of the Marianas. The current wave of investors originates in Seoul, Korea.
9. Saipan boasts absolutely fabulous beaches. Oceanfront and ocean view properties are available.
10. There is a lot of World War II history here. Remains of past battles still can be seen in the countryside and along the coast.

CHAPTER 8

AMERICAN SAMOA

STORIED TROPICAL PARADISE IN THE HEART OF THE SOUTH PACIFIC; COMMUNAL PROPERTY OWNERSHIP A REAL IMPEDIMENT TO DEVELOPMENT

arrived in American Samoa at night after a five-and-a-half-hour flight from Honolulu. Much to my surprise the flight was absolutely full, most of the passengers being Samoans returning home.

For those of you who don't know your geography, there are actually two Samoas: an independent country, Western Samoa, and the U.S. territory, American Samoa. One might say they are neighboring islands, although the word "neighboring" is a relative expression in regard to the South Pacific. In fact, they are about 60 miles apart. If you were willing to pull out a map and take the time to locate American Samoa, you would see the Cook Islands are to the east, Tonga is to the south, and the more well-known Fiji Islands lie off the horizon to the southwest.

Although all these places sit in the same region of the South Pacific, interisland travel is not always very easy or convenient. So, each island has certain airlift tied to major population centers that are important lifelines. The Cook Islands, for example, is a popular beach location for folks from Australia and New Zealand so the lift is in that direction. Fiji does very well with Europeans and North Americans, so it has excellent connections from the West Coast of the United States and through to Asia and Australia. Tonga has close ties to New Zealand.

As far as being a vacationland, of that set, I had been to Fiji, which has massive tourism infrastructure and a small second home market. I have also journeyed to Cook Islands, and although it, too, has a decent tourism infrastructure, it does not have a large land mass and the ex-pat population seemed small but intense.

This was my first trip to American Samoa, a U.S. territory since 1899, and I was surprised that the flight attendants made all the announcements in two languages, English and Samoan. Indeed, all around me on the plane I could hear the babel, some of it in words that I understood, and some a rolling dialect that I had never heard before.

In 1916, the writer Somerset Maugham arrived in Pago Pago, the port of American Samoa, on board a boat from Hawaii.

He turned the experience into his well-known short story "Rain," which introduced the character Sadie Thompson to the world. Maugham wrote at the beginning of his story: "The ship turned sharply and steamed slowly in. It was a great landlocked harbour big enough to hold a fleet of battleships; and all around it rose, high and steep green hills. Near the entrance, getting such breeze as blew from the sea, stood the governor's house in a garden. The Stars & Stripes dangled languidly from a flagstaff."

Considering the United States had such a long history in Samoa, I was surprised when I arrived at the airport that I had to go through customs and have my passport stamped, and then, when I retrieved my bags and flagged a cab to take me to my hotel, the driver could barely speak English. He seemed to think he was speaking English, but I didn't have a clue as to what he was saying. When I asked how much the cab ride was going to cost, his response was gibberish to my ears. As it turned out, this was a bit of disingenuousness on his part.

After about a 20-minute drive along the seashore, we arrived at the hotel. My bags were taken out of the trunk and I asked the cabbie once again, "How much?" He responded, "Forty dollars." I looked at him with disbelief. "How much?" He repeated, "Forty dollars." I said, "No, I'm not paying that much." A quick, absurd argument ensued that to my ears contained few words of English. Finally, I yelled in exasperation, "Can't you speak English?" To which he responded quite clearly, "Yes." "Then how much is the taxi ride?" "Twenty-five dollars," he whispered to me. That didn't please me either, but I paid it.

A few minutes later as I was checking into my hotel, I asked the receptionist how much a cab ride should cost. She told me the cabbies who pick people up at the hotel to take them to the airport charge $10 to $15. Welcome to American Samoa, my friend.

Beauty in the South Pacific

I had arrived on the island at night. Tired, I fell asleep quickly in the quiet. But I awoke early and waited for morning to arrive. Since the dark curtains were shut, I was still thinking night. Then I heard the birds chirping in the earliness and I opened the curtains. My sleepy eyes beheld a truly magnificent sight: a red dawn breaking over Samoa harbor. My view to the beach was uniquely framed by a palm tree to the right and thick, tropical vegetation on my left.

Further out along the water's edge, a series of clumpy hills, still dark, defined the harbor, and the horizon beyond shown splendidly a variegated sky dappled with crimson and gold.

All the trespasses of the night before were forgiven. I was in a Gauguin paradise. In regard to tourism, and by extension, a second home market, this was virgin territory.

Except for the cruise ships that made a port of call in Pago Pago, the island's capital city and commercial center, the tourism infrastructure of the island was almost nonexistent. Having traveled to more than 120 countries, islands, and territories around the world, I could barely recall a place—so inspiringly beautiful—that had so little regard for visitors. There was only one major accommodation on the island, a Clarion hotel; a couple of sharp, smaller hotels; and a handful of prospering and interesting bed-and-breakfasts. There were no curio shops and when I sought a guide to organize a tour of the island for myself, none were to be found, although somewhere I had come across a list of such companies.

In my hotel, a charming, small property on the edge of the harbor, called Sadie's By the Sea, I picked up a local tabloid, *411*, which ran a *New York Times*-ish boast, "The More You Know the More We Grow." With interest I scanned a page of economic data culled from the 2002 Economic Census that reported revenues from the island's 13 main industries. Tourism was nowhere to be found.

Curious, on my first day in town, I strolled over to the island's Department of Commerce and picked up a copy of the *American Samoa Statistical Yearbook 2005* (the most recent edition). A small section on tourism read: "Although it has always been a challenge to ascertain the true value of tourism in the American Samoa economy due to the lack of consistent and accurate visitor data, experts expected the tourism industry to generate revenues of over $10 million a year." That, indeed, was why it was not listed as a major economic sector; the last of the big 12 revenue-makers was "Professional, Scientific, and Technical Services," which generated revenues in excess of $16 million.

The wonder of it all was that American Samoa was an amazing tropical land consisting of seven volcanic (extinct) islands and islets, the largest being the island of Tutuila, home to Pago Pago, the international airport, and most of the territory's approximately 65,000 people.

Much of Tutuila was dominated by an impressively steep mountain range dressed in the deepest tropical flora. Pago Pago itself was a thin strip of a village bordered by its harbor and a wall of mountains most of which was a national park—the only paleotropical rainforest in the United States and habitat of the rare flying foxes, actually a species of fruit bat.

The islands came into the possession of the United States at the turn of the twentieth century, when Western nations were still carving up the world. In 1900, Germany and the United States both claimed the Samoan islands and after Germany annexed several islands (now the independent Western Samoa), the United States took Tutuila to use Pago Pago and its deepwater harbor as a coaling station for naval ships.

Technically, American Samoa is a territory of the United States, and its people are not U.S. citizens, although they are classified as U.S. nationals, carry U.S. passports, and have freedom of entry into the continental United States. To this day, many Samoans join the various U.S. armed services.[1] I was told during my visit that Samoa, for its size, has suffered a very high percentage of military deaths during the Iraq War.

The people of Samoa are Polynesian and the extended family is the traditional social structure. They are very communal and this has been a blessing of stability on the island and a curse in regard to almost anything else, in particular development. There are two reasons for this: first, because most of the land on the island is communally owned it cannot be sold, and second, the communal mindset is very socialistic and that strain runs through the local government, which often acts paternally and, more important, finds it difficult to privatize what it already controls.

Restraints

As noted, there are few hotels on the island, no condominiums and few, if any, traditional vacation homes.

When I was on the island I was invited to speak at a local Rotary Club and afterward a number of people spoke to me about what I perceived as opportunities for tourism and real estate development on American Samoa. There seemed to be a small group of active businessmen who were chomping at the bit to bring this kind of investment to the island.

One of the most enterprising local entrepreneurs I met was Tom Drabble, who owned two of the best-run small hotels on the island. He was a longtime American Samoan businessman, who had successfully worked within the confines of the island's land ownership situation—although not without a struggle.

Drabble was a native of New Zealand and had come first to Western Samoa as a young man back in the mid-1960s. He got a job with a construction company and after that contract ran out, still seeking travel and adventure, he continued further east, ending up in American Samoa in 1966. He liked the island so much he never left. "Living was easy here," he said. He married on the island, had two children, and after that marriage petered out after 20 years, he married again and had another child. His current wife of 18 years, who helps him with his enterprises, is a very lovely Western Samoan woman with the exquisite name of Ta'aloga. He joked with me, "I tell her she has just two years left in this marriage."

Perhaps because he was an accountant by training, he was able to figure out how to develop land within the boundaries of communal ownership and take advantage of opportunities when they arose.

Drabble is best known on the island as the proprietor of two small hotel properties named for the Somerset Maugham character, Sadie Thompson. The first is the Sadie Thompson Inn, which is the original building both Maugham and the real-life Thompson stayed in when they arrived in Pago Pago in 1916.

In the early 1980s, Drabble leased the property for 30 years, but about halfway through the lease it was obvious the building needed a lot of repair and renovation. It required a huge investment, so Drabble went to the landowner and said he was willing to make the large financial commitment if he could get a new lease (the law had changed allowing for 50-year leases) or, because the building stood on freehold land, he offered to purchase it if the owner wanted to sell. The landowner preferred to sell and Drabble became an American Samoa landowner and successful hotelier.

It was because of Drabble's success with the Sadie Thompson Inn that the governor of the island offered him an opportunity to do something with one of the island's great investment disasters, the old Intercontinental Hotel, which sat in ruins like some lonely archaeological site before discovery.

Back in 1961, Pan American World Airways had a Los Angeles to American Samoa to New Zealand run. The governor of the island had decided that American Samoa would raise the money to build a hotel, the Intercontinental, because it would create jobs and become an investment for the island's retirement fund. In a sign of things to come, the government could only sell 20 percent of the ownership shares for the hotel, so it ended up owning 80 percent through the governmental body, the American Samoa Development Corp.

Pan Am stopped flying to the island, American Airlines took its place, and the hotel took on a new brand. American Airlines then pulled out, and the government brought in a professional management team to run the hotel. The hotel at that point wasn't making any—or at least not enough—money, so the government figured it could do a better job itself. Wrong!

For years, the government tried to get rid of the abandoned property and was thinking of demolishing it when the governor approached Drabble, who recognized two things: the market could use some but not all of the rooms, and this property had a fantastic small beach. He leased half the property from the government and the result is Sadie's By the Sea, where I stayed on the island.

While I was on the island, rumors were floating about that some Texas investors were interested in the other part of the old hotel.

How to Buy Property in American Samoa

How to buy property in American Samoa? The simple answer is, in most cases, you can't. There is some freehold land but not a great deal. By one estimate more than 90 percent of the total acreage in American Samoa is communal family land. Even the national park is leased from communal lands. What freehold land there is can be found in the Pago Pago area, Tafuna Plain, and the Village of Leione.[2]

Should you avoid considering American Samoa? The answer is no, because it is truly a beautiful island. And think of it, how many places can you go in the South Pacific and still be on American territory? The answer is just one, American Samoa.

A little background first.

American Samoans retain what is called the *aiga*, or extended family, as the basis of their social structure. In this uniquely communal system, the *matai* (chief) holds control over the extended family's land and property. While the land is passed on from generation to generation, for the current generation, the *matais* can assign holdings to family members on a lifetime basis. Most important, American Samoa's existing law on land tenure prohibits the transfer of land ownership, except freehold land, to any person whose blood is less than one-half Samoan.[3]

So how does one get land for development? To figure that out, I turned to Henry Kappel, an attorney with the local law firm of Rose Joneson Vargas.

Back in 1993, Kappel, who was living in Norman, Oklahoma, faced a change of life. His marriage had broken up and his ex-wife was going to take the children and move to Cincinnati. His oldest child would be heading off to college. "Everyone was leaving town," Kappel joked. "I had a buddy who was in American Samoa and said he could get me a job with the attorney general's office there. I had been in the Pacific—Okinawa and Hawaii—when I was in the Marines and always wanted to get back."

After serving in American Samoa's attorney general's office for three years, he moved on to the governor's office and then back into private practice. Along the way, Kappel married a local woman. "American Samoa is small and friendly," he said. "In a lot of ways it reminds me of back home."

Somewhere along the way, Kappel became an expert in American Samoa land issues, which is complicated because there are basically four classes of real estate in these small islands. This is how Kappel explained the land categories:

1. **Freehold land:** Property conveyed by what was then the independent state of Samoa before 1900. The good news is that there are no restrictions on the sale of freehold land; the bad news is that only 4 percent of the island falls into this category.

2. **Communal land:** Comprises the vast majority of land on the island. This land can be bought and sold but only to natives of the island or to someone who is at least one-half native blood. Land can be sold to someone who is less than 50 percent native but only if that person meets certain criteria such as if the person was born in American Samoa or lived in American Samoa for five years and has declared the islands to be the place of residence. Land may be conveyed to such people under a long-term lease.

3. **Individually owned land:** This is a concept that has developed over time on the island. It refers to property sold or owned by

a person who has at least 50 person native blood. The problem with individually owned land is that there is not a general statute in the island's laws that addresses this concept. This land can be long-term leased. Leasing, however, is really uncharted territory.
4. **Government land:** This land can be long-term leased, but not sold.

"Communal land comprises the significant portion of land, but throughout the years, the percentage has been reduced as more and more land gets parceled into individually owned property," Kappel explained.

Most major businesses on the island lease communal land as a lease can extend for 55 years (with an option to renew), although leases do require the governor's approval. "Any conveyance of real estate in American Samoa requires the governor's approval," Kappel said. "Any deed or lease is first filed with the territorial registrar and a notice is published for a period of 60 days. If there are any objections, they are considered by the land commission, which then makes recommendations to the governor."

Despite solid laws, conveyance of property can be bogged down in interpretation. For example, American Samoa has a statute that allows for corporate ownership of land, subject to the governor's approval. However, the actual statute uses phrasing that says the corporation is "without race." In American Samoa, there are those "native blood" requirements, but something without race cannot meet those specifications. "The current governor, who is an attorney, has taken the position that a corporation is without race and therefore cannot meet these restrictions," Kappel said. "He is not approving conveyance to any corporations."

Then there is the Drabble situation.

Back in 1970, Drabble developed a small shopping center, about 10,000 square feet, near the airport. Back then leases on communal land only extended 30 years, so around 2000 he signed a new lease. That's when things got ugly.

"In those days you could not get an option to renew the lease," Drabble recalled. "However, the lease stipulated the building, which sat on the land, was mine. The land was family-owned, and when the lease ran out I negotiated with the family and signed a new lease. But, family members living in the United States objected to the new lease. This is fairly common as most people on the island have no idea what land is worth and certainly family members living in the United States have no idea what the land is worth."

In 2002, the family members who lived in the United States hired a lawyer to stop the new lease. That case has been winding its way through the courts for the last five years. There were also a few intangible problems as well. The chief who signed the leases for the communal, or family, land was not registered as a chief although he had been signing leases on behalf of the family for 20 years. That problem has since been corrected.

The key issue the courts eventually have to decide is whether off-island Samoans have the right to dictate what happens to land that is held for people actually living on that land. Drabble expects the courts will eventually decide his lease will be upheld.

Legal System

American Samoa's government and legal system are quite unusual and need to be mentioned. For this I'll lean on Kappel and his law firm, Rose Joneson Vargas.

Since the Deeds of Cession, which created American Samoa, have not been altered from their original form as written in 1904, the island group has no formal legal structure as a state, commonwealth, or other form of government organization. Thus, legal scholars refer to American Samoa as an "unincorporated" and "unorganized" territory of the United States.[4]

Nevertheless, the U.S. Constitution applies in American Samoa and over the years, Congress has extended many federal statutes to the island. In regard to the judicial process, American Samoa has a District Court, which hears small claims and misdemeanor crimes, and a High Court, where land and *matai* title disputes are heard. There is no federal court on the island, so issues regarding federal law end up in federal courts in Hawaii or Washington, D.C.

Due to the strength of Samoan traditions (*fa'a Samoa*), even Rose Joneson Vargas feels obliged to warn: "The *fa'a Samoa* continues to coexist with American Samoa's formal legal system of governance because most of the people in American Samoa have continued to follow *fa'a Samoa* traditions by consensus. The tradition makes governing and administering justice in American Samoa unique."

A Residential Market?

The island's population center has moved to an area of less mountainous land south and west of the international airport. Except for
traditional industries such tuna canning, most industry has moved
here from Pago Pago; also located near the international airport is
the island's major hotel, the Clarion Tradewinds and a number of
small lodging properties and bed-and-breakfasts, as well as the only
golf course in American Samoa. (The latter is owned and badly run
by the government, but it's cheap. Local residents pay $7 a round
and seniors pay $4 a round.)

Much of the island's freehold land can be found here because
in ancient times there was little water so communities settled elsewhere such as around Pago Pago harbor. Decades ago, farmers
acquired the land, and now it can be bought and sold. I visited a
New Zealand entrepreneur, who married a local woman, and was
able to acquire coastline property where they were building a new
bed-and-breakfast. The property didn't have a beach, but there was
something better, a rugged, wave-pounded coastline, extraordinarily
dramatic and beautiful.

The communities on this end of the island are called Tafuna,
Vaitogi, Futiga, and Pava'lia'i and folks with money also have built
here, including the ex-governor who owns probably the biggest residence on the island (don't ask how he ended up in control of the
land). No one I talked to knew the size of his property, but Steven
Watson, the manager of consumer lending and credit administration at Amerika Samoa Bank, estimated its value at $750,000.
Standing outside the front gates of the huge manse, my own consideration of the property was that it was a bargain compared to anything else that size on the mainland U.S.

Watson, a native of San Diego, was practicing law in his hometown, when the travel bug bit him hard. A friend who had worked
for the High Court and the attorney general's office in American
Samoa suggested to Watson he come to the island and fill a vacant
slot as assistant to the attorney general. He liked the island so
much he stayed, married a local woman, and after that marriage
collapsed, met a second Samoan lady whom he fell in love with
and married. Deborah, a friendly woman who is a great cook, and
Watson, have one daughter. They also live in a spacious home with
a large garden of tropical plants. With the heat, sunshine, and more

than 200 days of rain, anything will grow on this island; the problem for gardeners is keeping it all under control.

Watson told me he owns the property where he has lived for 30 years, but that was a special case because he has worked with the Samoan family that owned the land for many years. In any case, his wife is Samoan, so property could be held in her name.

"I can sell my house, but I would not want to live anywhere else on the island," he said. "I'm not planning on moving." Watson, in a sense, has gone native Samoan, because that is the same mindset as the rest of the population. They will build houses on community land and live there the rest of their lives.

Kappel, on the other hand, just acquired a piece of individually owned land (his wife is Samoan and the property can be in her name). "We got wind of it and made the deal," Kappel said. "It was a little over a half acre and we paid over-market, but I justify it because it is very centrally located, the land has a rock wall around three sides, and it has a variety of fruit trees—grapefruit, avocado, papaya, guava, and banana. We paid $80,000."

The going rate for a quarter acre, Kappel added, used to be $30,000, but that has since climbed to $35,000. Building costs average $60 a square foot. The problem, of course, is that everything has to be shipped in so you as a developer have to be aware of shipping schedules, either from mainland U.S. or from Australia or New Zealand.

Homes on the island are not expensive, but they are not cheap either. A residence of 3,000 square feet can cost as much as $350,000.

"We [Amerika Samoa Bank] recently did the mortgage for a family that moved back from the mainland," Watson said. "They paid $400,000."

Amerika Samoa Bank (owned by an Australian company) does most of the lending on the island, with Bank of Hawaii holding down second position. "We've got 500 to 600 mortgage loans on the books, mostly with houses built in the last 25 years," Watson said.

There have been a few homes on American Samoa bought by people living off-island, but for a second home market to develop, it would have to be mostly condominiums as the extreme tropical climate is very harsh on buildings. Indeed, a home can't just sit locked up for say nine months of the year because, as Watson observed, "when you close buildings up here, things grow."

The problem is there are no condominiums on American Samoa and no large-scale development could happen without some legal infrastructure work. That probably won't happen anytime soon as the Samoan government suffers from inertia.

Oddly, a condominium demand probably already exists. More people of Samoan ancestry live on the U.S. mainland than live in American Samoa. Many would come back if there were such things as retirement homes.

"It could work here, but it would take a forward-thinking person who has the location," Drabble said. "There are several gorgeous bays on the island where no one is living. If someone had 200 to 400 acres and worked with a developer it could happen, but how you get someone here to understand that is the tough one."

Drabble says he had the idea for a small condominium project a number of years back when he developed the Sadie Thompson Inn. "When I started the restaurant 15 years ago, the owners were asking for offers on hillside property approximate to Sadie's," Drabble said. "I was thinking condos, maybe for retirees. They would use my restaurant; it would have been a natural fit for me. I was the only person to put in that kind of offer on the property and it was ignored. Meanwhile, the land still sits undeveloped and the owners are not getting a penny from it."

Watson's a little more optimistic. "Some very sharp, younger generation men are now leading the traditional family groups. They hold chief titles. Many were educated in the United States and have a vision for the future. They could work with their families to develop on communal land."

10 Things to Know about Buying Property in American Samoa

1. The island is extraordinarily beautiful, but remote. The easiest airlift from mainland United States is through Honolulu.
2. There is very little tourist infrastructure, although some cruise ships visit Pago Pago.
3. Most of American Samoa real estate is communally owned. This land can only be bought and sold to someone who is at least one half native Samoan.
4. There is some freehold land around Pago Pago and in the newer townships near the international airport.
5. Investors and developers would need to lease property, which can be done on a long-term basis of 55 years.
6. Any conveyance of property on American Samoa requires the approval of the governor.
7. The pricing for land and residences is much less expensive than on the mainland United States but not inexpensive.
8. Development of second homes would require a pioneering effort, but could be well worth it as American Samoa is the United States' only outpost in the South Pacific.
9. There are no condominiums on the island, but some smart developer will figure out how to get it done—and will probably be very successful given the number of Samoans who would move back to the island from the mainland.
10. For those who wish to travel through the South Pacific, American Samoa makes a perfect hub.

MEXICO

REVERSE MIGRATION AS AMERICANS HEAD SOUTH ACROSS THE BORDER; OWNERSHIP REGULATIONS COMPLICATED BUT TRUSTWORTHY

H ere's what happens when you land at Puerto Vallarta International Airport. After quickly going through customs and finding your luggage on the carousel, you walk from the secured section of the airport into the anteroom from hell. It all looks orderly as a phalanx of gentlemen carefully guide you to a counter full of smiling faces. They look like they are there to help you, but in actuality they want to sell you a timeshare.

Puerto Vallarta is crazy about real estate, but first you have to deal with the timeshare problem, which I have to remind people is not about real estate. Timeshares are a vacation scheme not an investment.

In 2005, over a half-billion dollars worth of residential real estate was sold in the Puerto Vallarta area, yet Brian Porter, an investor in local real estate and now an agent with Coldwell Banker in the city, told me that timeshares are the biggest business in the city. "There are 60 new projects under development in the area right now and a lot of those are dedicated to timeshare," he explained while sitting at my temporary office, which is the restaurant table closest to the beach at my hotel. For three mornings in December 2006, I sat here discussing Puerto Vallarta real estate with local agents and investors. Porter was my second visitor.

Porter, a successful, but itinerant, businessman has lived in Mexico on at least three different occasions and is married to a Mexican woman. He now owns a home in Bucerias just north of Puerto Vallarta, a condominium in the city (in his wife's name), and a timeshare. He's also looking to buy a small plot of land to develop a six- to eight-unit apartment building. Two months before I met him he joined Coldwell Banker.

Obviously Porter feels very secure about investing in local real estate, but nothing bothers him more than timeshares. That's probably because he was once an easy mark. Sixteen years before, while honeymooning in Puerto Vallarta, a timeshare salesperson stopped him on the street (this still happens today) and talked him into attending the orientation lecture. He and his wife bought in.

"They are a racket," he snarled. "Any investment you buy that is worth half of what you pay for it, is not a good investment. My timeshare has not appreciated at all in the last 16 years, and maintenance fees have gone from $150 a year to $400 a year. I'm giving the timeshare to my father-in-law as a Christmas present this year."

It's not that Porter didn't make use of the timeshare. He admits to coming to Puerto Vallarta at least a dozen times since his honeymoon, and, in fact, he and his wife are living in Puerto Vallarta because of the pleasant experience they've enjoyed in the small city. Of all the places in Mexico, "this is the place we like the best," he declared unabashedly.

And that's the thing about Puerto Vallarta, people just fall in love with the place. More Americans may buy second homes in Cabo San Lucas or even Cancun, but no one gushes about living there. Mexicans and North Americans who come to Puerto Vallarta really do adore the city.

This love-at-first-sight phenomenon associated with Puerto Vallarta is actually the reason why Americans have been coming here since the 1960s. It all happened because of a movie. Back in 1963, director John Huston decided to film his next project, *The Night of the Iguana*, down in Mismaloya, just south of Puerto Vallarta. He gathered a terrific cast including Ava Gardner, Deborah Kerr, Sue Lyon, and Richard Burton. Now Burton, just about the top actor of his day, was seeing Elizabeth Taylor, although they both were married to other people. Taylor flew down to the set, apparently to babysit Burton. She was closely followed by hordes of media as the Taylor-Burton romance was the Brad Pitt-Angela Jolie affair of its day.

This was the world's first real peek at Puerto Vallarta and the world liked what it saw. So did the principal players, Huston and Taylor, who owned property there. Although Elizabeth Taylor's house has had a couple of owners over the years, I'm told all of her things are still intact, including the original décor. In 2006, a source whispered to me that the home had been sold once again. According to my source, the new owner took over a lien on the house, but whether that person paid the $2,650,000 asking price was unknown.

In one of the older commercial areas, you can find a statue of John Huston. He's depicted sitting like a Roman Caesar. The good news is that the statue actually looks like him, which is not the case with the Elizabeth Taylor-Richard Burton statue at a restaurant nearby. Just who are those people anyway?

Puerto Vallarta was founded on the deep curve of a large, lovely body of water called the Bay of Banderas. The bay was supposedly named by the first Spaniards to visit the area in 1525 who were attacked by a multitude of natives carrying flags (*banderas*). The area remained isolated until the first permanent settlers started constructing homesteads around the middle of the nineteenth century.

The choice of location for Puerto Vallarta is somewhat strange as the old core of the city rests on a very narrow stretch of land between the water and a steep mountain range, while just to the north the land is flatter. The oddity of population movement continued well into the 1980s, as the first growth occurred to the south, where flat land was almost nonexistent. These neighborhoods were built on steep mountainsides that to this day rise tenuously further up the pinnacles.

Starting at the end of the 1980s, the first major developments began migrating north and here is where the growth will occur in the decades ahead. If one stares out into the bay and the Pacific Ocean beyond, to the left or to the north of the old city sits the hotel zone and the first real planned development, Marina Vallarta, which has been built out and now bumps up against the international airport. At this point, the state of Jalisco ends and you cross into Nayarit. Going around the bay, the next major planned development is Nuevo Vallarta, which is still being built out; the older town of Bucerias (undergoing a population boom); and then at the very end of the bay, the very exclusive planned development of Punta Mita. Punta Mita is already home to a Four Seasons Resort and many large residences owned by a heady mix of North American and European corporate mavens and entertainment personalities.

I made the whole journey around the Bay of Banderas courtesy of Giovanna Mosqueda Aldana, the owner of a Century 21 franchise in Puerto Vallarta. My wife and I jumped into Aldana's SUV and for a full day she drove us from neighborhoods south of the city, where Amapas and Conchas Chinas were flowering with condo developments, to every development all the way to Punta Mita.

Birth of a Boom

I've lived in the Valley of the Sun (Phoenix metro area) for 30 years and know firsthand something of real estate booms, but I have to admit I was astounded to see what was going on in Puerto Vallarta, where miles and miles and more miles of wild landscape have already been marked for development. By my estimate, just between Puerto Vallarta and the 45-minute ride north to Punta Mita, there was at least a decade's worth of building to consider. Already, I was told Punta Mita is considered established, and beyond the bay to the north, whole new planned communities were being mapped.

Frankly, at Punta Mita I didn't see much because access is very limited. One can't even visit the hotel without being a guest or having a documented appointment with a guest. Bucerias looked like just another scruffy Mexican town with the highway running through the middle until you looked toward the bay where modern, mid-rise condo projects pop up with regularity, palm trees blow in the wind, and the heady transformation of the local economy is already in bloom.

The entrance to Nueva Vallarta was a little weird. First, you have to maneuver your car past the aggressive timeshare salespeople and then the entrance to the golf course appears—it's hard to miss because the developers created a huge, two-story, arched Disneyland-like structure to impress visitors. Aldana told me golf course homes start at $800,000, but that doesn't compare to the big developments on the shore. I spotted numerous mid-rise condominium structures. Nueva Vallarta is so big that it makes room for a considerable number of nongolf, nonoceanview residences that drop in price to $140,000. I noticed a sign that read: Exclusive Marina Front Condos. No prices were listed.

From my hotel, a large Sheraton that also had a timeshare unit as part of the complex, I could look shoreside along the mountains to south. The buildings climbed progressively higher on the mountain, and included a very large condo complex in the early stages of construction.

Going south along the coast from downtown one crosses the Cuale River into a section of the city called Los Muertos or Los Muertos Beach—literally, the beach of death. Higher on the mountain above Los Muertos sits the Amapas neighborhood and then next to it to the south is Conchas Chinas. Consider these inner-city neighborhoods as opposed to everything from Marina Vallarta north. They are also in some regards the most chic sections of town, and, as you can imagine, the priciest for a number of reasons. Since the homes are on hillsides, there are a lot of oceanview properties; these neighborhoods are established; and finally for hearty souls (or soles), it's walking distance to the center of town. However, you probably need a four-wheel drive vehicle or at least a burro to get back up the mountain to your home.

I looked at a condominium called Playa del Sol, where I'm told a two-bedroom unit costs $400,000 to $500,000. It was high in the hills with a good view of the bay. A little further to the south and actually on the coast, a condominium project had two-bedroom units for $800,000 to $900,000.

Aldana took us up a steep hill through Conchas Chinas, locally known as the Beverly Hills of Puerto Vallarta. The only places to build here were higher up the mountain and, indeed, there was plenty of activity. Aldana showed me a lot she recently sold for $180,000. At that moment it was nothing more than a pile of iron rods, and as I peaked over the mess, it occurred to me that it really wasn't much of a lot—it was a piece of steep hillside. Then, again, the homes are built vertically to get the most living space from what earth there is. The Beverly Hills that I knew didn't look like this, but maybe Aldana was talking about the clientele because as she mentioned, one of the people in her office had shown Tom Cruise some properties—this was in his pre-Katie Holmes days.

North Americans buying real estate in Mexico have traditionally paid in cash. Mostly that's because mortgage financing, when it could be found, was very expensive. By 2006, a number of large U.S. financial institutions began entering Mexico with terms acceptable to American (and Canadian) investors. While I was in Puerto Vallarta, I picked up a local real estate magazine to read about the largest residential loan in Mexico, which was closed through a joint venture of GE Capital and a local lender. The story didn't mention the size of the loan, but it was for a house in the Conchas Chinas district. I did learn, though, that the home in question once belonged to the Wilson family (of Wilson tennis) and was a getaway for President Nixon.

Despite the name, Los Muertos was perhaps the most pleasant neighborhood I saw in Puerto Vallarta. It was obvious that residents experienced a real sense of community living there. Maybe that was because this section of town has a large gay population. A lot of American gay men had bought second homes in the neighborhood and many of them were from the San Francisco area, Aldana said. Two things to remember about Los Muertos are that condos here are expensive—a two-bedroom might go for $600,000 in an older building—and the buyers almost always pay in cash.

Aldana was an interesting woman. She was married and had three young girls when she came to Puerto Vallarta. When the marriage collapsed in 1990 and her husband left, she decided to try selling real estate because she could do that and look after her girls. At first, her sales were to Mexicans, but she quickly realized the new wave of buyers was coming from North America, and she strived to improve her English.

After starting at RE/MAX, she moved to the company that became Coldwell Banker. In 1997, she met the owner of the Century 21 operation in Mexico, and he offered her the Century 21 franchise for Puerto Vallarta. By 2006, she had two offices in the region, two partners, and 20 people working under her *banderas.*

In 2006, her company had a record year in terms of properties sold (her record revenue year was 1999, and that was due to the sale of some very high priced, oceanfront properties). In 2006, Century 21 sold 120 properties and had such a strong pipeline that Aldana had no doubt 2007 would be even better. Of those 120 homes, 80 percent went to foreigners. "Right now we are getting the middle class as our average sale is in the $250,000 price range," she said. "They come from everywhere in North America—California, Arizona, Chicago, British Columbia, Toronto."

Aldana estimates some 20,000 North Americans live full-time in Puerto Vallarta even though sales today are going to buyers 45 to 50 years old, who will either rent the new acquisition or use it part-time until the day when they might eventually retire to Mexico.

It's hard to get a true picture of the number of Americans living in Mexico. One publication quoted the American Embassy in Mexico City, saying 340,000 Americans lived in Mexico at the time of the last census in 2000. A recent newspaper counted 600,000, while a *Wall Street Journal* writer used the figure 1 million.

To write about buying second homes in Mexico I could have chosen a number of hot locations: Cabo San Lucas, San Miguel de Allende, Guadalajara, or Puerto Penasco, an old fishing village at the northern end of Baja, California, popular with Arizonans. I chose Puerto Vallarta because it had a history of Americans living there, it was still relatively small (about 350,000 people in the entire region), and it was poised for rapid growth. No matter where I chose, however, the same conditions and regulations apply to noncitizens looking to acquire a second home in Mexico.

Investment Safety

One of the key questions investors face when investing outside their own country is whether targeted rules and regulations governing land ownership by foreigners exist and if investors can rely on those rules to be protective and not eventually punitive.

I took those questions to an American attorney living in Phoenix, who is solely licensed to practice law in Mexico. As Vernon Penner of Penner & Associates stressed to me when I met him for lunch in Scottsdale, "I do not practice U.S. law or Arizona law."

Penner lived in Mexico City where he worked for a number of international law firms. He met his wife there and when they started to raise a family, they moved back to the United States. That was 20 years ago. His practice mostly consists of investors looking to do business or invest in Mexico and had been steady until one month in 2004. It seems a bit weird, he told me, but "I can pinpoint to the month when things changed." In November 2004, his phone started ringing off the hook. Through 2006, his practice grew by leaps and bounds.

The question I posed to Penner was this: How secure should Americans be about investing in Mexican real estate? The problem for Americans, he responded, is that they are dealing with a system with which they are unfamiliar. If they knew the system, how it worked, and what to expect of the seller, there would be no problem.

Fraud does happen, he added, "but that is because Americans don't do their homework. They just go down to the beach in Puerto Vallarta, look at the sea, look at the sun, like the breeze and say, 'I've got to have a house here.' They are looking for someone to take their money and there is always someone who would do that. If you don't invest the right way, it can be scary. But, if you do it right, you end with good title and ownership."

If one knows the rules, investments in Mexico are safe, Penner assured me. "And every day it gets safer. The rules are changing for the betterment of investments and security."

A Matter of Trust

As Penner noted, it's important to understand the rules and regulations in regard to buying property in Mexico because it is complicated. Much of the complexity derives from seventeenth-century rules preventing foreigners from direct ownership in what are now called "restricted zones." When the Mexican Constitution was written, these limitations were codified.

To make the country more accessible to foreign investment, however, a presidential resolution in 1971 sought to address this issue by creating the *Fideicomiso* as a vehicle for foreigners to acquire real estate property rights in restricted zones, essentially the perimeter of Mexico, 100 kilometers in width from the borders and 50 kilometers from the coastal shores.

The *Fideicomiso*, or trust system, was implemented two years later. Basically, this means a privately held Mexican bank holds title to the property in trust, and the buyer is the beneficiary. In 1993, as a result of the North American Free Trade Agreement, a new foreign investment law was created, which liberalized the *Fideicomiso*, extending the term of the trust from 30 years to 50 years and making it renewable.

So how does all this work? A few simple points:

1. Any foreigner can establish a *Fideicomiso* (the equivalent of an American beneficial trust) through a Mexican Bank in order to purchase real estate anywhere in Mexico, including the restricted zones. To do so, the buyer requests a Mexican bank to act as trustee.
2. The Mexican bank, as a matter of course, obtains the permit from the Ministry of Foreign Affairs to acquire the chosen real estate in trust. With a *Fideicomiso*, the foreign investor has the right to transfer title of the real estate to any other party, including a family member.
3. The Mexican bank becomes the legal owner of the real estate for the exclusive use of the buyer, who has all the benefits of direct ownership: the ability to sell, lease, mortgage, improve, or pass on as an inheritance.
4. The trustee is responsible to the buyer to ensure precise fulfillment of the trust in accordance with Mexican law, assuming full technical, legal, and administrative supervision in order to protect the interests of the buyer.

"The trust can be trusted," Penner said. In other words, the system, although alien to us in the United States, works and works well.

How to Buy Property in Mexico

In practice, the actual acquisition is relatively simple, except for a few quirks. According to Century 21's Adana, this is the way a home-buying venture should transpire:

- Most real estate transactions are opened after the seller accepts a written purchase offer and when both parties sign a purchase-sale agreement (promissory contract). In most cases, the broker requires a deposit from the buyer in order to transmit the offer to the seller. (If the transaction is trans-mitted directly to the seller, it is highly recommended that the buyer consult with a real estate broker or a lawyer before signing any papers or handing over money.)
- In some areas, it is common practice to deliver to the seller, as an advance payment, the equivalent of 20 to 50 percent (including initial deposit) of the total price upon signing the purchase-sale agreement, which should contain a penalty clause applicable in case of a breach of contract by either party.
- Normally, when signing the *escritura*, or official deed, which must be certified by a *notario publico*, or notary public, the balance is paid and the property delivered. This should not take more than 45 days. In certain resort areas the custom of using escrows is catching on.

What confuses most Americans is the term *notario publico*. In Mexico, a notary public is not the same thing as in the States. A *notario publico* is a government-appointed lawyer who processes and certi-fies real estate transactions, including the creation and review of all real estate closing documents. In connection to real estate transac-tions, the *notario publico*, upon request, receives the following offi-cial documents, which by law are required for any transfer: a no-lien certificate from the public property registry based on a complete title search; a statement from the Treasury or municipality regard-ing property assessments, water bills, and other pertinent taxes that might be due; and an appraisal of the property for tax purposes.

Since Brian Porter had been investing in Mexican real estate, I asked him how this worked. His biggest surprise, he said, were the closing costs. "The transaction costs are significantly higher than they are in the United States. People told me closing costs can be as high as 5 to 6 percent of the purchase price and they were. For our home, we paid $140,000—in cash—and our closing costs were $10,000," he said.

Why so high? Generally, the buyer pays the transfer or acquisition tax as well as all other closing costs including notario fees and expenses. That doesn't include the fees to set up a trust, which in Porter's case came to $2,000.

At the back end, the investor doesn't get away so easily either. There is no such thing as a capital gains tax, but in a similar way, the seller gets taxed on the income the investment has made. Penner broke it down for me into easy numbers: you either get taxed at 29 percent of net or 25 percent of gross. I was told when I was in Mexico that there were a variety of ways to ameliorate the pain of taxes through deductions, but being an upright lawyer, Penner said to count on the basic tax rates.

While mulling all that over, there are two very positive factors to consider when investing in Mexican real estate. First, property taxes are very low, at a rate of 0.01 percent, which means on a $200,000 investment, the taxes are just $200. Second, after the turn of the millennium, appreciation on real estate vaulted, not even slowing down when property markets flattened across the border to the north. According to one Mexican real estate publication, in the last six years (2001–2006), the price of condominiums has increased by 14 percent annually and that of single-family residences by 11 percent.

Fraud Factor

Before you start counting your profits, there are some quirks in regard to investing in Mexican real estate about which you must be cognizant, because there have been some fabulous investment blowups, not to say outright acts of fraud, that have been inflicted on unwary Americans.

The most infamous real estate scandal involving Americans occurred at a beachfront development called Punta Banda about 85 miles south of the California border in Baja, California. In the mid-1980s, about 150 property owners, mostly Americans, acquired what they perceived to be valid lease agreements for lots. After building homes and living a life of leisure at the Baja Beach and Tennis Club, all the property owners faced eviction by 1999.

The problem was that the properties were built on an *eijido*, which is a land grant made by the Mexican government to peasant farmers and indigenous groups in the 1970s. This is communal property and it cannot be sold by individuals. According to Porter, "Americans are not allowed to own *eijido* land—period!"

There have been some attempts to privatize *eijido* lands, but any Realtor with integrity will not deal in *eijido* lands, especially in regard to Americans. As a National Association of Realtors' report on Mexico summed up, "these land properties all have serious questions surrounding the validity of land title, because of fraudulent transactions, inadequate registrations, or collective claims. Difficulties in determining true legal title to *eijido* land, and fraudulent transactions related to these uncertainties, are a problem for Mexicans and foreigners alike."

In Punta Banda, the property was given in communal ownership to 80 individuals, who leased the land to developers. Later, a small group of the 80 original landowners challenged the right to development. Their claim was upheld by the Mexican Supreme Court, which found the developers who sold the home sites never had proper legal title. Punta Bunda has been an ongoing legal mess ever since.

When asked about real estate fraud, Christine Chin was surprisingly frank. "Fraud does happen," she told me.

I liked Chin, who was funny in a very irreverent way. When I sent her an e-mail confirming I would meet her in the lobby of my hotel and asked how would I recognize her, she responded, that it would be easy because "I'm Chinese."

A native of San Francisco, Chin, in the mid-1990s, took a job teaching at the American School in Puerto Vallarta. Like others, she fell in love with the area and stayed on. When Prudential Real Estate wanted to open offices in town they looked for someone fluent in Spanish and English and hired Chin who opened the office for the company and was now a sales associate.

Fraud in Mexico occurs, she said, because real estate brokers and agents aren't licensed. The Mexican government does offer a sanctioned exam for real estate agents, but it is not required.

"Anyone can go ahead and sell real estate. And they do," said Chin. "There are a lot of discrepancies as to how people work. Problems arise."

The best way to avoid a problem with a shaky Realtor, said Chin, is to work with a reputable agent and agency. The agent should be a member of the Associacion Mexicana de Profesionales Inmobiliarios (Mexican Association of Real Estate Professionals) or, as it is better known, the AMPI. The organization is similar to the National Association of Realtors in the United States.

There are multiple listing services in Mexico, and I was told title has to be secured to be listed, but that would probably only be the case with the main listing service, Metro Cubicos.

Also, a couple of American title companies are now working in Mexico, but title insurance is not a requirement.

"I'm not concerned about real estate fraud," Porter said. "One reason is, if you buy a property through a real estate company, the possibility of fraud is extremely low. That's because in order for us to list a property, we have to have copies of the deed and copies of the seller's identification. In the United States, if someone says, 'I want to list my house,' you don't ask for a deed, you let the title company worry about that. But here, people were selling property that didn't belong to them, so policies have been established that require a copy of the deed and identification in order to list the property. That is a first screen and it is a good one."

A second screen also exists. In order for a property to be sold, a *notario* has to provide a no-lien certificate, which is used in Mexico in lieu of title insurance.

The Little Things

Although Puerto Vallarta I'm told is about the safest city in Mexico, Porter told me while he was traveling in the United States, his home was burglarized. The problem, he surmised, is that he lives in a new development with a lot of construction going on. Although new projects are secured, during the development stages construction gangs come in and out at leisure. "If you are gone for a period of time, someone will notice," Porter said.

The other problem with buying a home, he noted, is getting services hooked up such as phone, electricity, and cable. To do that in the United States, all it takes is a phone call but in bureaucracy-mad Mexico, you have to go to an office, get on a line (always long and slow), and fill out a form.

Unless, you are planning to live in Mexico full-time, Porter recommends second homeowners invest in a condominium, where there is usually someone on the property around the clock for security purposes.

"Condos are appealing because you can lock up and leave and know that someone will be watching the property," added Chin. The other reason to consider condos is that, as noted, appreciation has been greater with this type of property in places like Puerto Vallarta than with single-family residences. In 2003, Chin sold her first property, a two-bedroom, two-bath condo in an older building in the busy area south of the central city. The American buyer paid $280,000. Today, said Chin, that same unit could be sold for $425,000.

Finally, a third reason to consider condos is that when it comes to beachfront property in Puerto Vallarta, it is still possible to find a unit in a beachfront development, or at the very least something with an ocean view. As for single-family residential, it's already too late. Said Chin, "If you come down here and tell a Realtor you want beachfront property, you'll be out of luck. There isn't any."

10 Things to Know about Buying Property in Mexico

1. In popular locales such as Puerto Vallarta, beachfront property has become rare and expensive. The next, best option is ocean view.
2. Investments in residential real estate are generally very trustworthy.
3. In coastal areas (restricted zones) of Mexico, land is acquired through a long-term trust (*Fideicomiso*) and not owned directly.
4. North Americans buying in Mexico should consult with a real estate broker or lawyer.
5. Title insurance is new to Mexico, but a transaction should include a no-lien certificate, which is based on a complete title search.
6. The *notario publico* is an important person in the acquisition process. Do not confuse the title or the job with that of a notary public in the United States.
7. Avoid *ejido* lands.
8. Closing costs are much higher in Mexico than in the United States.
9. Property taxes in Mexico are extremely low.
10. Stick with a reputable real estate agency as real estate agents are not licensed in Mexico. If you are uncertain, a number of U.S.-based chains such as Prudential, Century 21, RE/MAX, and Coldwell Banker operate throughout the country.

COSTA RICA

SALUBRIOUS CLIMATE, BEAUTIFUL TOPOGRAPHY CREATES COUNTRYWIDE MARKET; LACK OF REGULATION MEANS BUYER BEWARE

My hotel in Costa Rica was located along a highway in Escazu, the sprawling, wealthy suburb west of San Jose, the capital city and major metropolitan area in the country.

There was a lot of development around me, from major shopping malls to office buildings and a small group of car dealers—Maserati, Jaguar, and Ferrari. I quickly surmised there were people with lots of money somewhere around me. Next to my hotel someone had built a pleasant little neighborhood shopping center filled with boutiques, excellent local cuisine, a coffee shop, and even a couple of familiar names: Outback Steakhouse and Hooters.

What struck me as curious, or brilliant, was that among the stores and restaurants in this little shopping center were at least one developer's office and a minimum of three residential real estate offices. Two of the companies, Century 21 and Coldwell Banker faced my hotel, which, considering it was a Marriott Courtyard, probably saw a lot of American business.

I arrived in San Jose at night and the next morning after breakfast I took a short walk through the shopping center. It was about 9:30 and one of the real estate offices had just opened. It was a local company called Bienes Raices Costa Rica Property Sales. As I walked by the storefront, I noticed a young woman sitting at one of the forward desks. I strolled in and she nodded in my direction.

From the back of the office, Latin hip-hop was blaring from a radio, and the young lady, who had probably not expected to see anyone so early, realized it was a bit loud and got up to lower the volume. She looked about 20 years old, her slimness accentuated by very tight faded jeans and high heels. Actually, I admit to doing a double take when she stood as her blouse was open to her midsection, showing off a black push-up bra with exposed breasts rising above.

"They really know how to sell real estate in this country," I thought to myself.

I couldn't quite make out her name, I think she said Naomi, and when I asked her about real estate, she apologized demurely, saying her English wasn't very good. I was guessing she wasn't an agent but an office manager, because she handed me a card with the name of her boss, who she said spoke excellent English—a necessity in the Costa Rican real estate business. Costa Rica is crazy with real estate investment, and much of it is a gringo market.

The country, which sits on the narrows of the North American continent between Nicaragua to the north and Panama to the south, has been a very popular vacation getaway for Canadians, Americans, and Europeans for going on two decades. Squeezed between the Pacific Ocean and the Caribbean Sea, Costa Rica offers an amazing variety of topography, from vast rainforests to tropical beaches to high volcanic mountains. I first arrived in Costa Rica in the mid-1990s for an unusual vacation. Two friends, my wife, and I were to take a small boat down the Pacific Coast of the country, stopping along the way for excursions into the rainforest. Howler monkeys, poisonous snakes, tapirs, sloths, and an unbelievable cornucopia of unique wildlife crossed paths with us. It was an unforgettable experience.

Later on that trip, in San Jose, we met other tourists who had equally remarkable experiences visiting the volcanoes, many still active, which string the country's center like a jagged wall. Costa Rica has so much to offer and people from all over the world want to visit.

Apparently many of those tourists concluded, "Hey, life in this country isn't so bad," and they decided to return and live, eventually to buy property. First came the young and the adventurous, but they were soon overlapped by the older and moneyed looking for a pleasant place to either build a second home or buy land for retirement, which as they looked ahead, wasn't so far away anymore.

Of all the Latin American countries that are now being considered as potential second home markets, a swath of countries stretching from Mexico to Argentina, Costa Rica was one of the first to attract buzz. In the 1990s came the first slow wave of buyers, but when the northwest coast of the country opened up, investment hell descended.

Time on the central Pacific coast can be measured as BM (before Marriott) and along the northern Pacific coast as BFS (before the Four Seasons), joked Alfredo Benchoam, a San Jose restaurateur and dabbler in real estate. The comment was made with levity, but it is really the case that two big lodging chains pioneered new tourism markets. In December 1999, the Los Suenos Marriott

Ocean & Golf Resort opened in Playa Herradura near Jaco and that area began to blossom. The same thing happened further north when the Four Seasons Costa Rica at Peninsula Papagayo opened in February 2004.

Real estate booms have a chain effect, observed Edwin Sanchez, regional director of Central America for the Century 21 real estate organization. "First is the exploration stage where people test the locality and some buyers emerge. Then comes the second stage when big companies, such as major hotel chains, become investors. That gives credibility to the market and leads to the third stage when all other types of investors rush in."

That was a very good explanation of what was happening on the Pacific Coast, although Sanchez works out of San Jose. Oddly, Benchoam doesn't live along the coast, either. He resides in the upscale San Jose metro area community of Escazu, where his restaurant, Tre Fratelli, is located. He also works with his friend Alvaro Riba, a Coldwell Banker franchise owner in the area.

"Every broker in the area goes to Tre Fratelli," exclaimed Riba. "It is the place to go eat, meet developers and brokers, and make deals. It is the hot spot for real estate in Escazu and the Central Valley."

When I stopped by the restaurant, I asked Benchoam if there were any real estate people of importance hanging about. It was after the lunch hour and the restaurant wasn't very busy. Benchoam turned around and then nodded in the direction of two men in animated discussion at an outdoor table. One of the men was the largest retail developer in Venezuela. My guess was he was looking to plant some money outside of his home country.

Weather: The Best in the World

The online page for real estate company Costa Rica Land & Property welcomes readers with this promotional paragraph: "You can live here for less than you might expect. The people are friendly and helpful and a true delight. The country is amazingly diverse. The landscape will never bore you, and of course, the climate is probably the best in the world."

Costa Ricans always say there are two seasons in their country, rainy and not rainy, but it all depends on where one lives. I was told that in the Central Valley, the rainy season stretches from May to

November with the heaviest rains usually arriving in October—but that mostly means expect a daily, quick, afternoon shower.

The northern Pacific coast is more developed than the Caribbean coast because it is generally considered drier. In fact, the knock on the absolutely gorgeous and mostly undeveloped Caribbean coast is that in the rainy season things get washed away.

When I met with Benchoam, he had just received a brochure from a new development on the Caribbean coast called IslaMoin. I scanned the information he had received and noticed resort residences of just under 1,000 square feet were to sell at $232,750. This was presale price, which meant after project completion, they would probably resell in the $300,000 range. At the top end, the development would be selling 4,500- to 5,500-square-foot waterfront homes starting at $1.6 million.

The most interesting aspect of the development was that it was to have a state-of-the-art marina with 380 slips.

The Costa Rican government has plans for 4,000 boat slips in Costa Rica, Benchoam said. "Right now there are just 280 spaces for boats in the entire country. By having 4,000 spaces we are hoping to attract some of those people who don't want to be in Florida anymore. They can transport themselves by boat to Costa Rica where the costs of docking at a marina and buying a condo are half that of the United States."

One of the major problems for those yachtsmen who reside in Florida has been the protection of their boats during the hurricane season. The Costa Rican government is saying its country is a safer bet. One of the more interesting pages in the IslaMoin brochure was a charting of hurricane paths over the last 40 years, none of which directly hit Costa Rica. Some hurricanes have done ancillary damage to the country, such as mudslides caused by heavy rains, but Costa Rica has been spared direct hits.

The plains of Costa Rica are generally the driest areas with some places going months without precipitation. In the Central Valley, the average annual temperature is in the 80-degree range during the day and the 60-degree range at night.

One of the people I was looking forward to meeting while in San Jose was Scott Oliver, who wrote a helpful little book called, *How to Buy Costa Rica Real Estate Without Losing Your Camisa* (shirt). We met over lunch one afternoon and I could tell by the accent he wasn't from North America. He was British but had been living the ex-pat life in 11 different countries. Before coming to Costa Rica he had worked in the field of offshore wealth management in the Cayman Islands. He came to Costa Rica with the thought there might be some business opportunity in the country, and, as he said, "I fell in love with the country the first time I came. It has a perfect climate."

Considering that he wrote a book about real estate, Oliver wasn't much of an investor. He built a second home in the Zona de Los Santos, the country's famed coffee growing region, but for his primary residence he rented a series of condos in Escazu. Finally, he's settling down, building a 3,229-square-foot home in Santa Ana, just west of Escazu. "I didn't buy because I move around too much and didn't want to get locked into a home, but I've been dating the same lady for four years, and yes, there are certain pressures being put upon me," he said with a gleam in his eye.

Asked why he didn't buy a beach property, Oliver shakes his head. "I love walking the beach, swimming, and surfing, but I don't want to live at the beach. I would not live in a beach community. Besides, he added, "some Costa Rica beach communities are over-sold and prices are inflated."

Not wanting to come across as too negative, he added, "Sure, you are paying higher prices than a couple of years ago in places like Tamarindo, but compared to the Cayman Islands and places in the States things are cheap. We've got plenty of people coming down from California buying ocean view condominiums in the $300,000 to $1 million range because they can't get anything near ocean view for that price at home."

Escazu and the Central Valley

My first inclination was to spend all my Costa Rican time along the coast. It's not hard to get to anymore as there is an international airport at Liberia with direct flights to North America. However, just as Costa Rica exhibits a diversity of topography, its second home market is equally as varied. For every person who wants to be by a beach, there are others who would prefer mountain beauty or simply a pleasant spot with a serendipitous climate relatively near civilization.

Since this book is also about diversity in second home markets, I decided to include Costa Rica's Central Valley, which is very close to the capital city and urban populace. The Central Valley is one of the few very popular second home markets on this continent that exists solely because of climate and not because of water.

The Central Valley is just well located: mountains (every day the newer developments climb higher and higher) surround it; an hour away (when the highway gets finished the ride will be quicker) lies the coast; the international airport is just a cab ride away; and down the road just a short commute away lies the big city.

The heart of the Central Valley is the capital city of San Jose, but the wealth has migrated west to a place called Escazu, often called the Beverly Hills of Costa Rica. Obviously, the town has earned its appellation because of the people who live there including the mercantile elite, doctors, wealthy foreigners, embassy folk, and even the president of country, who pops up sans bodyguards in places as mundane as the local Pizza Hut.

As one local real estate guide reports: "This is an extremely popular neighborhood with foreign residents and, in fact, as you go down the main road in Escazu and see the variety of restaurants such as Tony Roma's, TGI Friday's, McDonald's, and Kentucky Fried Chicken you have to blink twice to make sure you're not back in the USA. Here you find palatial estates, high-rise penthouses, luxury accommodations, ambassador's homes, and mixed, right in you will also find simple local homes."

Ten years ago, Escazu was mostly farms. The boom has come because of the high-end infrastructure that was built here, including a huge shopping mall, hotels, upscale restaurants, office parks, modern office buildings (home to a wealth of U.S. companies such as Microsoft, Citibank, and Cisco Systems) and a new hospital (affiliated with Baylor University in Texas) that is considered one of the best in Central America.

"I have been in this country for 10 years," exclaimed Benchoam, who hails from Guatemala, "and now I feel like a grandfather because anywhere in Escazu I stand, I tell people, 'when I first came here there was nothing.'"

The Beverly Hills nickname also comes from the location of the town. It spreads from the valley up the neighboring mountains. The higher in elevation the residences, the better the views.

One of the first people I met in Costa Rica was Alvaro Riba, an investor in Escazu real estate and the owner of the Coldwell Banker franchise in the area.

Riba was born in Spain, but spent part of his early years in Costa Rica. As a young man, Riba lived for a while in Montana and ended up as a ranger in Yellowstone National Park. Then 20 years ago he returned to Costa Rica and began building homes and running a tour business. One of his early investments was 400 acres of land high on the mountainside overlooking Escazu. "It's my own little Yellowstone Park, this project," he said to me as we were driving around Escazu. "I develop 10 percent of the property, leaving 90 percent as primary forest. It has beautiful trails and it is just 50 minutes from San Jose."

Riba wistfully continued his tale: "Twenty years ago, when I began developing, Escazu was far away from the city. I used to take people on horseback riding tours in the area. There were no roads, no electricity, and visitors would fall in the love with the land and views. I would tell them, 'I will sell you a lot and 20 years from now when you retire you could have a home here.' They believed me."

Twenty years ago, Riba was selling lots on his mountain at $4 a square meter. Today, the land is a little more expensive—$75 a square meter.

"The average cost of raw land in Costa Rica was up 68 percent in 2006," Riba said. "But in some areas, it was up 300 percent."

Traditionally, Escazu had been one of the hottest locations for foreigners buying Costa Rican real estate, but it is rapidly being replaced by development along the coast. The problem for Escazu is that it is somewhat overbuilt. When I was there in the spring of 2007, there were 5,000 condo units on the market and a nice, 3,000-square-foot condo on the third floor of a building overlooking the Central Valley could have been had for $230,000. I was told that same unit had been originally listed for $280,000. That was the first hint of any price depreciation anywhere in Costa Rica.

The road to the higher elevations, which forms the border of Escazu, loops to the far side of the mountain overlooking the town of Santa Ana and another valley. The popularity enjoyed by Escazu has spilled further west and Santa Ana is the next frontier of development. The old, small core of the town retains its colonial past, but in the surrounding valley, signs of progress are everywhere, from office buildings to the ever-popular gated communities.

I had thought Santa Ana defined the limits of growth for the Central Valley until I met Terry Mills and Jeffrey Hickcox, who, along with Rodrigo Mendez, formed Costa Rica Land & Property

Company. Whereas Mendez was from Costa Rica, Mills and Hickcox were ex-pats; Mills emigrating in 2001 from Missouri, and Hickcox in 2006 from Connecticut. They operated out of a small town called Atenas, still considered part of the Central Valley, although it sat high in the mountains in an area known for its coffee and sugar cane farms.

"My father was in the timber industry and I lived here as a child," Mill said. "When they took me home, I didn't want to leave. I loved it here, so when I was adult and had the funds, I came back."

Hickcox had a different story. He was involved in real estate investments in Connecticut and was savvy enough to see that capital was leaving the market, so after doing some investigating he realized a number of international markets were still doing well, one of which was Costa Rica. "My wife and I wanted to come to a place where we could live a simpler life, have a cheaper lifestyle, and where there was a better real estate market," said Hickcox, who had two young children with a third on the way.

Hickcox chose Atenas because it was centrally located: 40 minutes to the beaches and an hour to Escazu. "The Pacific Coast is hot and humid, but in the Central Valley you don't need air conditioning or a heater. In Costa Rica, 70 percent of the population lives in the Central Valley because of the infrastructure, hospitals, high-speed Internet, solid electricity, good roads, and Americanized stores. In Escazu, you can get anything you want that's American."

Both Hickcox and Mills also chose Atenas because it was less expensive than some other areas. Said Mills, "I rent a four-bedroom home, where I have my office, on an acre of ground for $135 a month."

At first, the mountains and lush valleys around Atenas looked rural and untouched by the frantic pace of real estate development that could be seen almost anywhere else in the country, but Mills and Hickcox assured me it wasn't so and to prove it drove me to three gated-community projects in the mountains around Atenas, mostly designed for foreign investors. All of the projects were built in higher elevations on the sides of mountains and the views of the surrounding countryside were outstanding. The models were impressive as well with top-of-the-line build-outs in the kitchens and bathrooms, wood ceilings, tile floors, and small swim or infinity pools.

The only disconcerting aspect of these projects were the roads, which were narrow and that wouldn't have been so bad, but the grades were unusually steep. Costa Rica doesn't go overboard with guardrails either, so driving around these new communities was an adventure in and of itself.

There are four new gated communities in the Atenas area, plus a couple of older developments that are sold out. In 2006, Costa Rica Land & Property sold about a dozen properties. In the first three months of 2007, it had already transacted the same amount of business, and on the day Mills and Hickcox met me, they were closing two more deals.

The land is still inexpensive around Atenas. Mills told me it sells for $5 to $7 a square meter (in some places you can buy it for $2 a square meter), but the area is seeing a good deal of price appreciation. Costa Rica Land & Property, for example, listed a 2,500-square-foot home in one of the new developments for $175,000 a year ago, and now it is selling for $350,000.

Resale figures indicate homes on the outskirts of the Central Valley had appreciated 86 percent last year, which is good, but nowhere near the numbers being pulled in on the Pacific Coast, where appreciation averaged 125 percent along the central Pacific Coast and 175 percent on the northern Pacific Coast.

The Pacific Coast

Driving in Costa Rica is not necessarily a whole lot of fun once you leave the San Jose area. To get to the beautiful beaches along the Pacific Coast is still a long, tough ride. Then an international airport was opened in Liberia, which began receiving international traffic just a few years ago. In 2006, 351,515 passengers passed through Daniel Oduber Quiros International Airport, up 18 percent over 2005. In January 2006, passengers coming through the airport increased 24 percent over the same period the year before. Estimates hold that 1 million passengers could be coming through the Liberia Airport gates 10 years from now.

The advantage of the Liberia airport is that it sits only 20 minutes to a one-hour drive from what are sometimes called the Gold Coast beaches in the northeast province of Guanacaste. These would include Playa Hermosa, Playa Flamingo, Playa Brasilito, Playa Tamarindo, and numerous smaller beaches in between.

This is all Chris Simmons' territory. In 1992, the Canadian chartered accountant was looking for a better climate and decided to move with his family to Costa Rica. He had a small family construction company in Vancouver and essentially transported it to a new life on the Gold Coast. Realizing, however, that the real estate markets were on the verge of a boom, around 1999 he and his wife Bonnie opened RE/MAX Ocean Surf Realty in Tamarindo, and they have been expanding it ever since.

"This will be the second year in a row we were the number one international RE/MAX in the world," Simmons told me. "In Costa Rica, we get North Americans, South Americans, and Europeans. Canadians are huge here, considering the size of the country."

The range of projects along the Gold Coast is immense, Simmons said. Just in Tamarindo, going up are a huge golf course resort and an eco-development project that will be erected on 600 acres of jungle, but the build-out will only be on about 8 percent of the land.

Simmons said his strategy is to stick to the high-end traffic, so he only deals in properties in the $150,000 to $3 million range. As he was telling me this, he confessed, "we just got an offer of $3 million for a beachfront property.

"Here you get a two-bedroom, very nice townhome in a gated community, just five minutes from the beach," he said. "The average condo ranges from $350,000 to $600,000. That would be 2,200 square feet, one block from the beach and with spectacular views."

The market has been so crazy along the Gold Coast, Simmons has seen numerous flips (own for short-term and then sell). Obviously, property appreciation is hot—probably hotter than the weather during the summer months.

"I sold a beachfront property in a gated community located about a half-hour south of Tamarindo for $548,000," he said. "The buyers were a couple, about 40-plus years of age from Vancouver. They wanted to obtain the property now because they knew by the time they retired there would be no beachfront property left. I originally sold that same property three years ago. In that period of time, the price more than doubled."

Early in 2007, Simmons said he sold a 1,500-square-foot Tamarindo condo in preconstruction for $300,000. "That was a good deal because when the project is finished, it will sell for $450,000."

Simmons expanded his RE/MAX Ocean Surf Realty to four offices along the coast, hiring a wide mix of Costa Ricans and ex-pats, including Americans, Canadians, and Columbians—and within the past year—an agronomist who was managing farms for the British in Africa. People come to visit Costa Rica, said Simmons, and they want to stay.

Guanacasta isn't the only booming coastal area in the country. The province of Puntarenas dominates the remainder of Costa Rica's Pacific Coast and the core of that is a relatively short driving distance from the capital city. The beaches here are generally just as spectacular as the Gold Coast and the roads connect the important cities, with the concentration of beachfront communities mostly between the city of Puntarenas to the north and Quepos to the south. The center of it all is the city of Jaco and the surrounding communities of Playa Hermosa, Playa Jaco, and Playa Herradura.

"There's so much activity in Jaco, they are beginning to call the place Jacopulco," joked Karen England from her office in Tamarindo. "I've been told 26 permits have been issued for high-rise buildings and condos on the beach. It is crazy with so many cranes on the beach."

England, a native of Kentucky, likes the ex-pat life. She was living in the Cayman Islands selling real estate when a friend told her about Costa Rica's Pacific Coast, where the rainforest came down to the beaches and where hotels were cheap. She moved to Costa Rica in 1989 and established Karen Real Estate. She's been selling properties all over the country, with numerous listings in the hot spots of Escazu, Tamarindo, and Jaco.

"Costa Rica's real estate market was boiling for a while, but over the last three years, it just exploded," she said. Why? "Because life is affordable here," she answered. Things have been so busy, England is now opening a second office in Tamarindo.

The Pacific coast is still affordable, but it used to be more affordable. She recently listed a two-bedroom, 1,000-square-foot townhome for sale at $160,000, but three years ago it was $80,000. That's nothing, she noted, "many properties have gone up three-fold over the same period of time." Over in Jaco, the newer, beachfront condos start at $300,000 but go up to $1 million. Her web site was showing condos in Jaco from $225,000 to $250,000—that was at a site under construction. The online blurb shouted, "BEST deal in Jaco!"

"People who buy in Jaco are from larger cities," she explained. "They like the activity, there's a casino in town and a nice marina. The people who move to Tamarindo are a little more laid back."

Asked if she ever thought about moving back to the States, England replied, "I go to visit. I don't like the cold weather. I cannot understand why anybody lives where it is cold. It is the perfect climate here."

How to Buy Property in Costa Rica

The most important thing to know is that foreigners have the same rights when purchasing property as the citizens of Costa Rica, except in one case, when purchasing beachfront concession property, but more on that later. Here are some key points to understand when buying property in Costa Rica.

Personal or corporate. Although foreign buyers can own property in their own names, most professional Realtors in Costa Rica recommend buying through a corporation. There are a number of reasons for this suggestion, with the top three being: the structure allows the buyer flexibility and more predictability in areas ranging from estate planning (if share ownership is properly structured the investor can avoid passing to heirs a lengthy, long-distance probate procedure); tax management (rules on corporate expenses are more flexible); and when selling, one can avoid paying property transfer taxes a second time by transferring shares of the corporation to the new owner.[1]

Title. When purchasing property in Costa Rica, proper registration of the property, and not the deed itself, is of the utmost importance, according to Costa Rica Land & Property. Simply because an individual may have a seemingly legal title to a property in his name, does not necessarily mean that individual is the legal owner. In fact, Terry Mills warns, there are scam artists who try to sell the same property numerous times. In Costa Rica, most land is titled and registered at the Public Registry in San Jose. Most titles are computerized through the Folio Real.[2]

Deed. Property transfers require the buyer and seller to sign a deed, or *escritura*, before a Costa Rican notary public, who is also an attorney, and for such a deed to be recorded at the *Registro Nacional*, or Public Register. Basically, the notary will draft an *escritura*, register the sale in the Public Register, and handle the closing. The trick to buying property in Costa Rica, said Mills, is to reconcile the actual property with the two documents that legally define a property. The first of these is the *escritura* and the second, the *catastro* map, which is the plat map of the property that is on file. "The problem with defining a property arises from the fact that the *escritura* may not correspond with either the *catastro* or a physical survey of the property," she said.

Attorney/notary. You will need to use a Costa Rican lawyer, especially in regard to title transfers. The attorney should be able to clear title for the buyer. As noted, property titles are registered at the *Registro Nacional* and have a folio real, or titled registration number. Through this number, the attorney can find all the required information on the property, including the landholder's name, any existing liens, mortgages or easements, and the tax appraisal. Obviously, it is recommended the attorney search this database and perform an independent title search before the closing to ensure a clear title.[3] "The hardest thing about finding a lawyer in Costa Rica is finding one that is honest," Mills warned. "If an attorney speaks English, he or she starts working only with foreigners and prices go through the roof. There are a lot of good attorneys who speak English, but their prices are outrageous."

Closing. A sale can be closed if three things have happened: a title search has been done on the property in the *Registro Nacional* (not just the online version), the *escritura* has been prepared, and fees paid. At closing the following items need to be present: a copy of the tax receipt (*impuesto territorial*) proving all taxes and registration fees have been paid as of the date of purchase (this is a certificate issued by the municipality where the property is located); funds to pay all necessary taxes and fees; and evidence that all prior mortgages, liens, and judgments have been lifted.[4] (Some liens and/or mortgages will be lifted during closing by the attorney.)

Post-Closing. After closing, your attorney will have to present the deed and have it registered with the *Registro Nacional,* which will verify the title is clear and that all fees have been paid and encumbrances removed. Only then is the deed actually registered and the buyer deemed the free and clear owner. The *Registro Nacional* will return the original document with proper stamps and seals in about 45 to 60 days—if there are no problems.[5]

Fees. Closing costs will include the notary fee, which is 1.5 percent of the first one million colones of the sales price. Don't be scared off; as of spring 2007 that amounted to about $2,000. The real estate transfer fee totals 1.5 percent of the registered value of the property, plus there is a registry tax of 0.5 percent. Consult your attorney as to whether government taxes and fees should be based on tax appraisal property value or actual sales price.

Establish residency. For those who would use their Costa Rican property as a vacation home, it's important to note that North Americans can stay in Costa Rica legally for three months then must leave for a period of 72 hours, before returning for another three months. If someone overstays the three months, a small fine is levied. For those who want to retire to Costa Rica, requirements maintain that aspiring residents need to prove at least $600 per month pension or $1,200 per month investment income or an investment of between $50,000 and $200,000 in an approved sector of the economy (on these plans, regular unrestricted residency can be applied for after two years).

Beachfront land. Private ownership of beachfront is not allowed. In 1977, Costa Rica passed the Maritime Zone Law for one specific purpose, to keep all beachfront property public, that is, no one can exclusively own a beach. The regulations cover the first 200 meters of shore land (as measured at low tide). However, there is some ambiguity here. While the first 50 meters are inalienable public property, the next 150 meters can be leased from the local governing bodies to private individuals or corporations. The leasing of this land is called *concesiones,* literally, concessions. This division seems clear, but it is actually as murky as tidewater as there are a number of variances (for example, a potential foreign investor must have resided in Costa Rica for at least five years).[6] As one real estate guide noted, "this type of transaction should be avoided if pieces of land with similar conditions and title can be found; otherwise, additional caution must be exerted."

Title guaranty. A number of North American title insurance companies now operate in Costa Rica. Although it is not mandatory, there is some local regulation. The Fidelity Insurance Law, which consists of a contract of indemnification, covers risky situations or laws associated with the loss of title of a property that is related to hidden defects in the chain of title. As one local underwriter wrote, "The undeniable and actual fact that frauds are happening with properties registered at the Public Registry raises even more the level of risk in real estate transactions. This is not only due to possible mistakes and omissions, but also because of fraudulent actions of others."[7]

Caveat Emptor

The real estate investment market in Costa Rica remains wide open—perhaps too unregulated for its own good. Where there are few legal necessities governing investment practices, those with criminal intent, or at the very least, individuals with more greed than piety, target the unwary.

What you still won't find in Costa Rica is an MLS listing, although Century 21's Sanchez told me that his company, which has almost 25 branches throughout Costa Rica, has hired a consultant to try to get one organized.

Probably the biggest problem in regard to real estate in the country is the fact that there is, as many have complained, a lack of licensing requirements and regulations in the sector. Basically, anyone can call himself a real estate agent or broker.

Costa Rica has been trying to pass legislation since 1976, Hickcox said. "The government has refused to regulate the real estate industry."

A number of theories circulate as to why this is so, but the one that makes sense is that it is a cultural phenomenon. Traditionally, business has been done by word of mouth, where one person tells another that a house is for sale and something gets worked out casually between the buyer and seller.

Hickcox thinks eventually the government will have to do something, but "right now it is so unregulated and there are so many twists and turns when it comes to brokers and commissions, you really have to be careful. No question, there are a lot of scams."

In Costa Rica, it's buyer beware, said Oliver. "There is no legislation to protect buyers from unscrupulous real estate brokers; there are no licensing requirements and frankly, there are a lot of real estate agents from other countries down here who are not working legally, they don't speak the local language, know nothing about local business, and don't know much about the Costa Rican legal system, which is Napoleonic and not common law-based as in the United States."

As can be expected this has led to some unsavory business practices. One local newspaper complained: "The lack of mandatory licensing has meant that anybody in Costa Rica can act as a realtor, and many say this has resulted in an influx of foreigners, particularly from the United States and Canada, working in Costa Rica illegally and with little experience. Licensing proponents worry that many of these foreigners may not fully understand Costa Rican property law."[8]

It was convenient of the local press to blame outsiders, but the truth is, many Costa Ricans who call themselves real estate agents are equally unknowledgeable about the real estate laws and equally unscrupulous. That same newspaper article mentioned two big scams: overpricing (when a real estate agent induces a buyer to pay more than the seller is asking and pockets the difference); and selling national park and coastlands to unsuspecting foreigners.

The accessibility of Costa Rica, a wonderful tourism experience for millions of North Americans, and the attractiveness of the land has induced a number of fast-talking promoters to create what are essentially boiler-room marketing operations aimed at North Americans.

Hickcox told me about a friend of his in the States who was invited on a free Las Vegas trip to listen to a seminar about buying lots in Costa Rica. "If the company you are investing with eventually gets it together, you can make money," said Hickcox, "but the problem with these investments is that you have no control, you have no idea which lot you are buying, no idea when the project will be completed, or when the infrastructure is going in. It is all speculation."

Mills added, "several companies have started these projects and not one has been completed. In Atenas, we have three developments that have all the infrastructure, the roads, water, electric, and the lots are legally divided. They have more or less sold out in the time these people have built a gate. They are promoters, not developers."

These kinds of marketing schemes upset guys like Oliver. "There are people buying land in Costa Rica from boiler-room salespeople working in the States, who have never lived in Costa Rica. Many of these operations are out of Florida. These are American-owned companies that have bought land here and then create a whole lot of corporations. The buyers won't own land, they will own pieces of the corporation. These companies buy raw land at 10 cents and sell to the unwary at 7 dollars."

Promoters are not on Oliver's list of the top 10 cautions when buying real estate in Costa Rica, but maybe they should be at number 11. Oliver's list:

1. Remember, real estate brokers are not regulated.
2. There is no MLS system of any kind.
3. The legal system is Napoleonic and not like that of other countries in North America.
4. Spanish is the official language and legal contracts are in Spanish.
5. Work with your own attorney and not the seller's attorney.
6. Be careful with oceanfront property as the laws are very complicated.
7. Be careful when building, permits may be required for such things as removing trees.
8. On the Pacific Coast, a lot of speculative buying is pushing prices higher at a very accelerated pace.
9. Just because you see it on someone's Costa Rica web site, it doesn't mean its accurate or even legal.
10. Whenever possible work with people who have been personally referred to you by other people you know and trust.

10 Things to Know about Buying
Property in Costa Rica

1. Important second home markets for North Americans stretch from the Pacific Coast to the suburbs of San Jose. The Caribbean Coast remains undeveloped, but developments are coming.
2. Many people live inland near the capital city or in the mountains where the weather is much more comfortable than on the coast.
3. The advent of an international airport in the northern city of Liberia has meant direct flights to the United States. This has opened up the northern coastal area to intense development.
4. Condos, townhomes, and gated communities are being developed rapidly all along the Pacific Coast; prices have risen considerably over the past few years and are expected to keep climbing in the near future.
5. Foreigners have the same rights as Costa Ricans in regard to buying property except along the actual shoreline. Rules are very complicated, so investors might be better off with ocean view.
6. While the real estate acquisition process is fairly routine and similar to places elsewhere in Latin America, remember real estate agents are not licensed.
7. Use a local attorney, preferably one that has been referred to you by someone you trust. Do not use an attorney who is working for the seller.
8. Don't buy Costa Rican land from boiler-room or telemarketing operations in the States. Actually, you should never buy land without seeing it first.
9. Use title insurance. A number of North American companies now operate in Costa Rica.
10. A lot of business is done through the who-you-know process. That's not a bad thing, because recommendations from acquaintances are probably the best way to secure needed services.

CHAPTER 11

PANAMA

HIGH-RISE CONDOMINIUM MARKET IN THE TROPICS; CHEAP LIVING, SENIOR DISCOUNTS ATTRACT RETIREES

My last swing through Panama was in the mid-1990s. I had cobbled together a bunch of assignments, some travel and some business, and had the good fortune to spend about five days in Panama City. Part of this work was to see how Panama had been redeveloping the U.S. military structures leftover from our almost century-long stewardship of what used to be called the Canal Zone.

Ironically, the recollection of that trip came back very quickly on the first leg of my journey back to Central America when a fellow sat next to me on the plane who was an avid birder. He was headed to the Amazon for a week of birding, and when I told him I was headed to Panama, which had a pretty good claim to a vast multitude of bird species, he began to jabber about a former military silo that had been transformed into a canopy bird site. "I was at that place," I exclaimed. The birder was very excited because he had wanted to make that trip himself.

When I was there, the canopy birding site had just been completed, but now I'm told the place is an inn, called the Canopy Tower. In a prior life it had been the Semaphore Hill Radar tower, built in 1965 by the U.S. Air Force to monitor the skies for drug-smuggling planes.

Back then, the old silo wasn't my only stop. I visited the forts and residential areas built for U.S. military personnel during the country's many decades of protecting the Panama Canal. At the time, all the locations were vacated but well maintained as if everyone who once lived there had just left an hour before. Some locations were in the heart of Panama City, others in remote areas, but I was impressed by the infrastructure and also by Panama's attempt to maintain everything so as to sell or develop the land and buildings later.

One of my guides at the time casually mentioned that many former Canal Zone personnel often came back to Panama at retirement and even then there were many inquiries about acquiring some of the old military properties for use as a retirement home.

It was very obvious to me that a posting in the Canal Zone was just about the best you would get in the military service. The land was tropically gorgeous and, seriously, how difficult could one's duties have been as there was no enemy to fight. So old hands had fond memories of their days in the Canal Zone. When the time came to retire and these same ex-military personnel set about to consider where in the world to go where the dollar still has some heft, Panama quickly came to mind.

When Jimmy Carter decided to give back the Panama Canal to the Panamanians in 1977 (actual handover was in 1999), there was tremendous consternation in the U.S. press about the ability of local people to manage such a great waterway. (They've done just fine, thank you.) What the U.S. press failed to consider at the time was that after decades of trade coming through their country, the Panamanians had a considerable history of international commerce and were quite adept at managing the mechanisms. Panama City over the last 30 years has transformed itself into a considerable financial center serving Latin America with banking and the world with offshore investment opportunities.

Retirement Benefits

Panamanians understand commercial opportunity and when they saw that a certain, very slim slice of the U.S. population had come to Panama to retire and was very happy in the country, they looked for ways to exploit that phenomenon. So in June 1987, Law No. 6 was passed by the country of Panama. In effect, the law created the retirement discount program (certain restrictions apply):

- **Medical.** 20 percent discount on general, specialist, and surgical doctor fees; 15 percent on hospital and private clinic bills; 15 percent on dental and optometry services; 10 percent on prescription drugs.
- **Food and recreation.** 25 percent discount on airfare and restaurant, 15 percent on fast-food dining; 50 percent on movies and theater; 30 percent on public transport.
- **Services.** 20 percent discount on technical and professional services; 50 percent closing costs for personal loans; 15 percent interest rate for personal loans; 1 percent mortgage interest rate; 25 percent utility bills.

To qualify for all of that, a person needs to get a retiree visa for which the only requirements are a health certificate, a clean background report from the police, and proven monthly income of $500 ($600 for a couple), which must be a pension from a company or government agency source such as Social Security or disability. Slackers probably don't need to know this, but the lower age limit for these discounts is just 18 years.

Combine all that with import tax exemption on household goods and/or cars and no property taxes for 15, 10, or 5 years depending on the property, and the Panamanians have cooked up what they often boast is the "best retiree incentive program in the world."

It's said that when Panama finally took control of the Panama Canal in 1999, 50,000 Americans lived in the country. In 2006, the *New York Times* reported 25,000 to 30,000 Americans have retired to Panama.

"The discounts work," exclaimed Marcel Segui, a real estate consultant with Prime Realtors in Panama City. "When you obtain a retiree card, you get full benefits such as discounts in supermarkets, restaurants, special rates on health insurance and hospitals. That alone probably wasn't enough to attract retirees, but the climate here is very similar to Florida."

To which, Segui added, "in Florida, the prices are exorbitant. Here, for $120,000 you can build yourself a home on a nice plot of ground. Panama is one of the cheapest places in the Western Hemisphere to retire right now."

Peculiarities of Panama City

Segui was, at the time of this discourse, driving me through some new condominium developments in Panama City. The area of the city was called Costa del Este, and a smattering of high-rise condo projects had already begun to sprout from the cleared landscape like weeds in an abandoned lot.

Segui had fascinating insight into Panama City, probably because he was able to see the city from an outsider's point of view. He was born and raised in London, met his wife, who was Panamanian, in London and eventually came to live full-time in Panama City, which his wife called home. Even before moving to Central America, Segui worked in real estate, which, considering that his wife's family was a major real estate owner and developer in Panama City, was both a good and bad thing. The good thing was they both understood property, investment, property values, and property management. The bad thing was they tried working together. The couple had been separated for 10 years, but as Segui told me, "she's still my best friend."

His wife now manages the real estate holdings in Panama accumulated by her family, and Segui has been a successful investor and property agent in Panama City. When he spoke of property he owned, he generally used the pronoun *we,* which I assumed meant he and his wife still owned investments together.

Despite years in Central America, Segui's British upbringing showed brightly. He spoke with a mild London accent and he dressed crisply for the tropics. No sports jacket, but a cleanly pressed, striped shirt highlighted by a crimson-accented tie.

Segui, who still returns to London often during the year, would never move back there. He absolutely loves living in Panama City. I'm not sure if it's the climate or the lifestyle that has seduced him, but as he admitted to me, "When I'm gone from here for a long time, I miss the place."

This doesn't mean that he isn't a realist. There are places in Panama City that are still fairly rough, infrastructure problems remain, traffic can be a nightmare, and customer service is nonexistent.

After driving over a causeway connecting a series of islands to what was once the American Beach, we decided to sit for a sandwich and cup of cappuccino at an outdoor café. Like most restaurants in the city, it appeared overstaffed. And like most restaurants in the city, nothing happens. "The biggest gripe I have with Panama City," said Segui, "is that you absolutely cannot get service in a restaurant". Sure enough, after placing our order, we didn't see another person come to our table for 20 minutes. In fact, we had to wave down a waiter and order all over again. It was no better at the end of the meal, when we were trying to get a bill.

Fortunately for the restaurants, most Panamanians are fairly laid back and are used to the terrible service, but it seemed to drive Europeans and Americans nuts, including Segui.

I thought of that café the next day when I was visiting the shopping mall near my hotel and I went to the food court for a light lunch. There were the usual fast-food eateries one would see in any mall in the U.S., plus a number of local offerings. I opted for the latter and assumed the meal would be prepared and served relatively quickly. It came down to two customers, three working staff, and a wait of 20 minutes. It's a good thing I wasn't very hungry.

Segui believed the problem at restaurants, and I suppose elsewhere, were the low wages.

If he was correct, then living in Panama is clearly a case of getting the good with the bad when it comes to affordability.

Over in Costa del Este, Segui showed me a handsome, high-rise condo project where a two bedroom at presale had been $99,000. Early in 2007, it was selling at $140,000 to $150,000. In one of the older, affluent areas of the city, Segui had recently closed a deal with a couple from the old Canal Zone days, who now live in New York. They bought a two-bedroom condominium for $89,000, which they were going to rent out until future retirement. Even in a super hot market of the city such as along Balboa Avenue, a one bedroom could still be found for $240,000.

Dollars & Sense

Second home and retirement markets are similar and often overlap. However, the economic drivers sometimes diverge.

The original, and still today predominant buyers of second homes are people who are looking for recreational or luxury locations. That is why most second home markets can be found at waterfronts or on mountainsides. Whether people live in a suburban tract home, a large manse in the exurbs, or an apartment in the city, they typically see the second home as an escape retreat— preferably near an ocean or lakeside beach, accessible to remote wilderness, or close to a ski resort.

After the turn of the century, investors began to invade second home markets, not so much because they wanted to spend time at the beach, but because they understood that space in second home markets was limited due to geographical factors and baby boomer demand was strong and getting stronger—two important factors for someone looking for rapid residential home appreciation. A result of the influx of capital not tied to the actual use of property was a sudden and precipitous rise in property values. Second home markets everywhere in the United States became even more expensive.

Retirement markets can be a second home market. Select areas of Florida and Arizona seem to operate along both economic patterns; others work differently, and that's because one of the drivers of retirement areas is cost of living. If you face your retirement years with a steady but fixed income, it would behoove you to retire to a place where your dollar goes a longer way. It costs a lot less money to live in Mesa, Arizona, than Chicago, Illinois. It takes less money to live in Delray Beach, Florida, than New York, New York.

For the world beyond Panama, the desire to live in Panama was at first driven by the retirement market. It was, and still is, much cheaper to live in Panama City as per the average daily dollar expense to maintain a certain standard of living compared with almost anywhere else in North America or Europe. As a result, while the country boasts great beaches, wild and remote villages, and even high mountain peaks, most people chose to live in Panama City.

"Restaurants are cheap here. I can go out to a good place with my wife and three children and the bill is $40 to $45 for five people," Segui said. "I'm a smoker and pack of cigarettes is $1.20, when I'm in the U.K., it's close to $11. Cars are cheaper and insurance is cheaper."

The cost of living in Panama is lower than in the U.S. and much lower than in Western Europe, reiterated Juan Francisco Pardini, president of the Business Panama Group in Panama City. His company's web site comments: "Electricity costs approximately 10 cents to 12 cents per kilowatt hour depending on the area, water and trash collection around $7 per month. Direct TV, telephone, and Internet services vary according to the plans chosen. Direct TV, with a wide choice of English language channels, is approximately $50 per month. Locally produced vegetables, meat, and fish are priced considerably lower than in the USA although imported items may be slightly higher. The minimum wage for housemaids or gardeners is 88 cents per hour. Local beer at the supermarket costs 30 cents per can, and a coffee in a restaurant may be as little as 30 cents."

The information must be good, because Business Panama's web site has become one of the busiest, if not the busiest web site for information on business investment, real estate, and trade in Panama. Not bad, considering Pardini didn't get his company started until 2002.

When buying property in a foreign country, one nagging concern is always the movement of the local currency against the dollar. Panama has eliminated that particular worry as the local currency is the dollar. Actually, the dollar has been legal tender in Panama since 1904 when the governments of both countries signed a treaty, still in effect today, although the official currency is called the balboa for historical reasons.

The other benefit to buying in Panama is that Panama City is an international banking center. There are about 100 local banks, plus a smattering of international banks such as Canada's ScotiaBank, the U.K.'s HSBC and while I was in the city, the talk was that Citicorp had bought up a number of local banks and was reentering the market.

Since banking services are extremely good, as are real estate services, a number of local banks now offer mortgages at rates comparable to those in the United States.

"There are more than 90 banks in Panama City from all parts of the world," Pardini said. "They pay good rates of interest on deposits and here interest income is tax-free. There is good synergy with the real estate finance community. The local banks offering mortgages are competitive, have money to lend, and pricing is good."

In addition, Segui told me that one of his U.S. clients was able to buy a condominium in the city with a mortgage from his local bank in his hometown—which is a testament to the stability and reputation of this local market.

If one is interested in getting a mortgage through a Panamanian bank, here are some things to know:

- Panamanian banks typically only finance titled properties where improvements have been made, infrastructure is in place, or in an urban area. Purchasing, for example, a custom-built home in a planned community would be no problem.
- Panamanian banks generally will not provide financing for raw land.
- Down payments are about 30 percent of purchase prices.
- Applying for a mortgage in Panama is a lengthy process.
- In North America, financing is about credit history; in Panama, it's your ability to pay and the property's loan-to-value ratio.
- The amount of documentation is substantial, requiring at least 13 different papers, such as passport (photocopy); additional photo ID (photocopy); bank statements (photocopy); utility bill (showing name and address); work resume; two original bank reference letters; two professional reference letters; two years of tax returns; income source letter; mortgage application; and property papers including appraisal, purchase contract, and deed of property.
- Terms and rates by international banks in Panama are similar to North American terms and rates.[1]

How to Buy Property in Panama City

Pardini treated me to a delicious lunch while I was in Panama City. He was an interesting fellow, patching together a different kind of business for Panama, a kind of one-stop-shop for investment services. So Business Panama Group offers such lines as real estate; insurance brokerage; capital, title and escrow; legal services; and advisory services. Pardini has always promoted the positive fundamentals of his country abroad and continues to do so from the incredible amount of freely accessible information on Business Panama's web site. He used to be president of the American Chamber of Commerce in Panama, and remains very close to U.S. investors, but Canadian investment in the country has climbed so steadily, he now presides at the Panamanian-Canadian Chamber of Commerce.

"Americans have been coming for the past five years, but in the last two years, the Canadians have discovered Panama," Pardini said. "People are looking for opportunities that they can't find in the United States or Canada in terms of providing profit and return. So, they are looking to Panama, a country with strong economic fundamentals. North Americans feel at home here, and on top of that the whole area is 100 percent open to foreign investors. You can own a house or a condo."

To encourage long-term foreign investment, Panama does not require special permits, authorization, or registration for qualified investors. The 1998 Investment Stability Law protects foreign investors for 10 years following the registration of an investment, thus shielding the investments from changes in tax, customs, municipal, and labor laws.

As Segui noted, there are also a few benefits for foreigners: If you purchase a new property, you are exempt from any duty or property tax for 20 years. It gets better; if you buy a property that was bought by a foreigner 5 years before, you still get 15 years of tax-free benefits.

Okay, how do you buy property in Panama? Checking in with the U.S. Embassy web site, we get this information:

- **Step One.** The Promise to Purchase Agreement is a preliminary contract between the buyer and seller, and gives the buyer time to work out financing and due diligence before committing to buy. It also can be used to get the seller to meet certain commitments and conditions before the sale occurs, and lists contingencies under which the buyer can be released from obligation to buy if questions are not resolved, or if hidden defects are later found.

- **Step Two.** If the buyer is satisfied, a Purchase and Sale Agreement (contract) is made in the form of a public deed and registered at the Public Registry of Panama, at which time the buyer becomes the owner.

Pardini holds to a whole other set of rules. It is important, he stresses, that before purchasing any kind of property in the Republic of Panama that an investor follow these four steps:

1. Make sure to contact a real estate broker who has a license for that business. There are many rogue brokers without licenses and without scruples, who will sell anything.
2. Perform a complete due diligence of the property, including a complete title search, review of cadastral maps, verification of tax good standing of the land, verification of good standing in utility bills, as well as verification of any other special characteristic of the property.
3. Enter into a Promise to Purchase Agreement in order to have enough time to properly execute the due diligence regarding the property. For titled properties this agreement should be recorded in the Public Registry in order to affect third parties.
4. Purchase and Sale Agreement. It is important to include an indemnification clause in the event of hidden defects. Payment should not be made to the owner/seller until the proper transfer of ownership or possession right is undertaken.

Things to know when buying property in Panama:

- You will need to work with a local attorney.
- All judicial processes in Panama are conducted in Spanish. For any real estate transaction in Panama, a contract written solely in English carries no legal weight and is generally not recognized.
- New construction condominium purchases are done in stages. By the time the building is erected, but the interior not built out, you will probably have paid three 10 percent installments.

- Titles are centrally registered at The Public Registry system, which maintains a record of all titled properties throughout most of Panama. Due diligence is fairly routine. The first thing a good realtor will find out is if the land is titled. In addition, the Registry can issue you in writing an abstract title of the land, along with any and all liens, mortgages, encumbrances, and so forth.
- Title insurance is not mandatory, but it is available. "If you go to a bank in Panama, it will not require title insurance as in the United States," explained Pardini. "Here it is an option." Because so many of Pardini's American customers have asked about title insurance, the Business Panama Group has partnered with a U.S. company, Lawyers Title Insurance Corp., now the only title insurer legally licensed to sell title insurance in Panama.
- Realtors have to be licensed, although there are a lot of rogue agents without licenses in the market. If in doubt, work with a company you're familiar with such as RE/MAX, Century 21, or Coldwell Banker.
- There are limitations on real estate purchases by foreigners. For example, foreigners cannot purchase property located less than 10 kilometers from borders or on most islands. Also, there are three main types of property: titled, possession rights, and concession rights. Basically, it comes down to this: titled is when you own the property in your name; possession rights mean you are given the rights to live on the property but you don't actually own it; and concession rights say while the government owns the land, it can grant you the right to live there for an extended period of time, say 50 years, just like a lease.[2]
- Sellers of real estate must pay a Real Estate Transfer Tax of 2 percent on the greater value between that declared in the Contract of Sale and the registered value of the property if it is higher. The annual real estate tax is 2.10 percent, directly proportional to the value of the property.[3] If the seller of the property is not in the real estate business, he pays capital gains taxes over profit on a fixed and definitive rate of 5 percent.
- Realtor commissions are usually from 3 percent to 5 percent of the selling price, although this varies depending on the location and developer. In Panama, the general rule is the seller pays the real estate commission. The buyer must pay the transaction expenses including the registration of title and lawyer fees.

What to Buy

Unlike in most other second home markets, in Panama most people buy in the city, which means, of course, Panama City, and the demand for property there is like a tsunami. Buyers have been flooding into Panama City from all parts of the globe, and high-rise condominium construction has been relentless.

Casey Halloran, a young man from a small town in Pennsylvania, is an economic adventurer and a seat-of-the-pants entrepreneur. He rolled into Costa Rica and started up an Internet consulting company that worked primarily with hotels, travel firms, and real estate companies. Around the year 2000, he parlayed that into one of Costa Rica's largest travel agencies, Costa Rican Vacations. He came down to Panama City on a banking trip, because as he observed, "banking is so much better here than in Costa Rica," and then stayed to do business. "Instantly, I was blown away by the development and within six months I was doing business here with my travel agency," he said.

It was obvious the big play was in real estate, and with a Panamanian partner, he opened a real estate company called New World Real Estate.

Panama City is the Dubai of Central America, Halloran told me and having been to Dubai just the year before I could understand his analogy. Nowhere in the world can touch Dubai for the shear amount of construction going on. When I was there, 25 percent of all the high-rise building cranes in the world were concentrated in that singular place. Thankfully, there are some high-rise cranes leftover and many can be found in Panama City. The city is awash in new construction, almost all of which is high-rise condominiums. Although Donald Trump has not done *The Apprentice* television show in Panama City, he has attached his name to a new project, which will be called the Trump Ocean Club International Hotel & Tower. And just to maintain the Dubai analogy, the Trump Ocean Club mimics the famed sailboat-shaped Burj Al Arab Hotel.

If that doesn't impress, try this: a 102-story, five-star hotel and condominium tower, called ICE, is planned. It's being billed as "the tallest residential building in the world." When I went by the site, it appeared excavation work had started, so maybe it will come to fruition, although there is some concern that the earth, or rock, underneath won't be stable enough for such a tower.

Near my hotel was a spit of landfill called Punta Pacifica, which will be home to the densest collection of condominiums in the city. When I visited, the forest of condominium development going on was almost as impressive as Dubai. Every building stood around 60 stories and was beautifully modern in design. I took a look at the model for a building called Grand Tower and I couldn't believe the size—or the price tag. Size: large; price tag: lower but consistently increasing.

"The last count is 50 cranes in the city," Halloran exclaimed, "and there is an absurd amount of projects in the approval process. Assuming everything gets built that people intend to build it would add 50 new buildings in three years. It almost defies logic—actually it does."

Panama City is a boomtown and real estate investors have flooded into the city for the past five years. Through 2007, price appreciation was enviable. Two years ago, Halloran bought himself a 3-bedroom, 2.5-bath condo unit (he renovated it into a 2-bedroom) of about 1,100 square feet for $93,000 in a district called El Cangrejo near the center of the city. Similar units in his building are now selling for $140,000. "I got in two years ago during preconstruction and before the mayhem started," he laughed. "I could sell my condo fully furnished to a gringo for $160,000."

The assumption is every foreigner wants a half-million dollar condo, Halloran added, but he feels the $200,000 unit is an easier sell because it can be rented very cheaply until the owner feels it's time to retire. And there are plenty of those for sale. When I was in the city, a two-bedroom condo with maid's quarters could still be found for $120,000, and a three-bedroom with 2,300 square feet was going for $220,000. Of course, at presale the same unit was $190,000.

On the day Segui met me, he had just sold a two-bedroom condo to a New York couple for $89,000. Of course, for those with more expensive tastes, a wide variety of penthouses could be found for prices in the $1.6 million to $3.2 million range.

I picked up a copy of the Panama Real Estate magazine from the prior year. The cover story read, "Homes of Panama Present the World's Greatest Address Trump Ocean Club." That looked boring, so I just began to scan the ads, every one of which showed a gorgeously designed high-rise building.

Brief sample of ad copy:

- Vistadesol, Punta Paitilla. Upscale condo city living in the heart of Panama. Three- and four-bedroom apartments beginning at about 2,500 square feet.
- Bayside Condominium, Costa del Este. Penthouses from 5,500 square feet.
- Torre 200, Punta Pacifica. Apartment sizes ranging from over 4,000 square feet. Three bedrooms, each with private bathroom and optional fourth bedroom, kitchen with breakfast nook, terraces with ocean view.

The best of all:

- ICE. Imagine living in a luxurious, five-star hotel condominium with breathtaking oceanfront views, spa, fitness center, infinity pool, ballrooms, restaurants, lounge, basketball court, racquetball court, squash courts, putting green, driving range, in the tallest tower in Panama and Latin America.

So, who is buying all this wonderful property? In addition to the folks from the United States and Canada, there has been a tremendous influx of Europeans and South Americans, the latter of which have come in waves of Argentinians and Columbians and Venezuelans looking to park their money outside their own countries before their governments permanently wreck their economies. Segui told me his most recent sale was to a South African.

When I met Halloran he brought with him a young woman who worked in his office by the name Rebecca Tyre. She was from London, Ontario, and first came to Panama City two and a half years before. "From the very first time I came here on vacation, I fell in love with the country, people, climate, city, everything," she gushed.

After about a year, she finally made her move on a permanent basis. "I met two of Casey's partners when I came down here on one of my trips and they offered me a job," she recalled. "Four weeks after the interview, I sold everything at home, packed a couple of suitcases, and arrived here in October 2005. I have no plans to go back to Canada."

To illustrate how her life has changed from her old Ontario world, Tyre not only rents a condo in the city, but also rents a house at a beach. "In certain areas rents are very affordable," she said.

But what about buying into the boom? "I'm torn because there are so many areas of the country I like, even on a peninsula on the Pacific Ocean in the center of the country," she sighed. "I love so many places, I don't have enough money to buy 17 condos, so I'm trying to figure out where I want to buy."

Halloran had watched the Costa Rican real estate market explode especially along the northern Pacific Coast, and he's become a big advocate of coastal investing—and Panama has a lot of coast. "Right now developers in Panama are making so much money in the city they are not doing anything at the beaches," he said. "The beaches are within an hour-and-a-half drive from the city."

Panama City sits on the Pacific Coast but the tides are so radical that when they ebb, extensive mud flats sit baking in the sun. It's not a very pretty coast and the waters around the city are very polluted, although I'm told the city has contracted with the same British firm that cleaned up the Thames to work the same magic along the city's beachfront.

A lot of the coastal land within driving distance of Panama City is dry, tropical rainforest, Halloran explained to me. "It is no good for cattle ranching or farming, so traditionally it has been undervalued. It's a dry climate, which means infrastructure is easy to manage, easy to develop." It's Halloran's belief that sometime in the next three to five years, tourism will take off there. "Panama City is nice, but you can duplicate it anywhere. There is only so much coastline in the world," he said, sounding like a true real estate junkie. "We bought a few plots here and there, but we are trying to find one large area for development."

I can't remember if it was Pardini or Segui who told me this bizarre story of three Indian families who lived on the coast in the most rudimentary buildings—structures with no electricity and barely out of the stone age—but who were offered millions for their land.

One of the strangest sites to see in Panama City is the occasional tribesman walking about the streets dressed completely in native garb, no shoes and ornaments penetrating the facial skin. It's as if the person just walked into the modern world from a pre-Clovis life deep in the rainforest.

"It's only large tracks of land out there," Halloran continued with big dreams dancing in his head. "No one has divided it up yet. Everyone is buying the huge tracks and waiting to sell to a hotel or a developer, because they know prices are doubling, so you just need to sit and wait."

Most of the land Halloran was referring to is undeveloped with no infrastructure and few, if any, good roads to get to your property even if you were lucky enough to find the right plot of land. That's the key though, said Segui, "when legislators start investing in that land, roads will go in very quickly." And then all investment hell will break loose, just like in Panama City.

10 Things to Know about Buying Property in Panama

1. Panama wants retirees and offers a handsome program of incentives.
2. Most investors buy in Panama City, which, unlike most other second home markets, is really a market of high-rise condominiums.
3. Prices for condos are very affordable, but have been rising because of the demand.
4. Foreigners can own property with the same rights as Panamanians.
5. The cost of living in Panama City is generally much cheaper than elsewhere in North America or Europe.
6. Mortgages are available from Panama City banks. However, your own bank in North America might do a mortgage on a condo in Panama City.
7. Title insurance can be gotten in Panama.
8. If your intention is to rent out your condominium, better to buy in the cheaper range because local salaries aren't that high.
9. While the purchase process is not very complicated, you will still need to use the services of a local attorney.
10. For the investor who doesn't mind risk, there is plenty of opportunity outside Panama City.

CHAPTER

HONDURAS

THE ISLAND OF ROATAN BOASTS CARIBBEAN LIFESTYLE; INVESTORS ENJOY FULL OWNERSHIP RIGHTS TO BEACHFRONT PROPERTY

The old airport in Hong Kong offered the most dramatic approach for a major city. The planes seemed to do a Luke Skywalker down a corridor lined with high-rise apartment buildings. You could almost see what the locales were eating for dinner as the plane descended for a landing.

Well, the old airport is gone so that probably leaves Tegucigalpa as the city with the most exciting approach to its airline runways.

The capital city of Honduras oozes through canyons and valleys of a mountain bowl and as the plane comes in over the sprawling urbanity, it banks left, doing a complete 360 at what looks to be rooftop level before finding the runway dead center in the sprawl. To make its landing, the plane flies over a last rise before the edge of the airport and as I looked out the window I felt the urge to reach out and pluck the antenna off the roof of the house below me.

The driver who met me at the airport, exclaimed Tegucigalpa landings were "very heroic."

This was my first trip to Honduras and for some reason I had visions of rainforest, but the mountain highlands appeared dry and a dusty pallor hung about the city, which hadn't yet overcome a grindingly poor economic history. After the gleaming modernity of Panama City, where I had been prior to coming to Tegucigalpa, the capital looked squalid with pockets of bright Western urban forms emerging. On my ride from the airport, I passed a very large and handsomely designed shopping mall, while new restaurants and fast-food eateries dotted some of the major thoroughfares, a testimony, I suppose, to a rising middle class. My hotel, a Marriott, was as good as any Marriott I've stayed in around the world, and from my window, I could see a few other new structures.

Roatan Action

I was flying into Tegucigalpa because, as I mentioned, I was coming from Panama. Most Americans coming to Honduras never see the capital city. They come for the beach life of the Bay Islands, whether for a simple vacation or because they want to buy a piece of a Caribbean paradise and somewhere, somehow they heard that could best and most inexpensively be done on the largest Bay Island, Roatan.

You can fly directly from Miami, Houston, and a few other U.S. cities to Roatan, which is a real advantage. When I was scheduled to fly to the islands, in that season of an abnormally dry winter, the Tegucigalpa airport was socked in by fog and drizzle. Needless to say, I was looking forward to sunshine and beach. While sitting around the surprisingly modern Tegucigalpa Airport, I scanned some of the information I downloaded from the web site of Steve Hasz, a real estate agent at RoatanLife Real Estate, who I would be visiting later that day. A number of carriers fly directly to Roatan, including Continental, Taca, and Delta Airlines. In addition, charters fly from Ontario, Canada, and there's also a direct flight from Milan, Italy.

Having traveled extensively through the Caribbean, I know there are some islands that would wage war for that kind of frequent airlift. Roatan, with its big runway, was drawing the tourist crowds— within limits. Most flights were available solely on the weekends; folks in the tourist trade on Roatan were hoping to see midweek flights as well.

Most people who come to the Bay Islands simply want to stay put and enjoy the surf and sand, but there are a lot of interesting things to see in Honduras, including some amazing Mayan ruins at Copan. For that intra-Honduras excursion, there is a small group of entre-preneurial airlines including Sosa and Islena Air. I flew the latter from Tegucigalpa to Roatan with a scheduled stop in La Ceiba.

After two hours of waiting for the fog to lift, my flight was cleared for take off. Hmm! A two-engine, propeller-driven, small aircraft taking off in a dense fog from a city surrounded by mountains—for a moment there I wasn't sure how fortunate I was. I got to talking to Hasz, who, with his father, has restored an old Contra plane in Tegucigalpa, and he said my plane was actually Russian built. That didn't make me feel any better.

My flight was supposed to be an indirect flight with a quick stop in La Ceiba, but the weather was truly awful, and we were never out of the cloudy muck the whole way. It was apparently too inclement in La Ceiba as well so landing there was out, and we flew straight on to Roatan. Finally, a break for me.

We got underneath the clouds and I saw below the deep verdure of a tropical island stretched against an azure sea. I looked for the other Bay Islands, but could not see far enough into the horizon and then the plane went low along the coast, and we were quickly dipping into the same elevation as the island's mountainous spine.

Roatan is the largest of the six Bay Islands (there is growing investor excitement on Guanaja and Utila). All the islands are located about 35 miles off the north coast of the mainland and are surrounded by the second largest reef in the world, the Mayan Barrier Reef. Hence, diving, snorkeling, sailing, and fishing are accessible, facilities extensive, and the experience absolutely world-class.

The modern history of the islands unfolds in this manner: In 1502, Christopher Columbus arrived looking for fresh, drinkable water. He eventually found some natural springs on Guanaja. Later, the Spanish colonized the mainland, but the British came to control the populace of Roatan and did so until the 1860s. So although Spanish is the language of Honduras, the most common language on Roatan remains Caribbean English. As Hasz noted, the island "has yet to adopt to mainland ways."

Roatan is a long, skinny slice of land stretching 32 miles east–west and is just three miles wide at a maximum point. There are a couple of larger townships, the largest being Coxen Hole, which sits directly west of the airport. Further west to the end of the island sits West Bay, West End, and Sandy Bay, traditionally the most popular with tourists and the first choice of foreign investors looking for real estate. I spent a fine evening in West End, the night spot on the island for ex-pats and tourists, first dining in a place called the Argentinian Grill, because it was owned by Argentinians, and then at a local bar, Sundowners. It was late winter in North America, but here the restaurant was full and the bar crowded, mainly with a lot of folks who knew each other.

An Instant Attraction

When I arrived on the island, I had scheduled time with John Edwards, one of the pioneer real estate professionals on Roatan and owner of Century 21/J. Edwards Real Estate and numerous entrepreneurial investments. Since my plane was late, I had to quickly scramble to meet him, which wasn't easy because my hotel, the Mayan Princess (developed by Edwards), was in West Bay and he was at a new resort property he was developing called Parrot Tree Plantation that sat near the middle of the island. It wasn't a far distance, maybe 10 miles, but it would take almost an hour to get there. The roads in Roatan are two lanes with no shoulders. Drivers often stop in the right lane, usually for no important reason—maybe to talk with friends—forcing traffic to wait until the left lane is clear before they can move forward. This doesn't even take into account the massive foot traffic that often spills over into the streets, which also must be avoided.

When I eventually arrived at Parrot Tree, an hour later, John Edwards was sitting quietly with a couple, who were seriously considering buying a second condo at his development. Edwards excused himself from the couple, shook my hand, and asked if I would mind waiting as he had to deal with two sets of potential buyers.

After talking with the first couple, Edwards quietly moved on to a second couple, from Alberta, Canada, who also were interested in buying a Parrot Tree condominium.

I slipped into the coffee shop for some lunch and met another couple, these two from Seattle, and they were on the verge of buying two condo units with an approximate total purchase price of $700,000.

The Seattle man and wife were retired and quite chatty. They gave me the first insight into the lure of Roatan.

"I had never gone anyplace, where I said, 'gee, wouldn't it be wonderful to live here,'" the wife said to me. That is, until they came to Roatan.

They had initially come on an investment tour to Latin America, including stops in places like Argentina, but it was the few days in Roatan that turned their heads. The plan was to buy a two-bedroom unit where they would live for four or five months of the year, basically the cold weather months in the United States. They would also keep their place in Seattle as they liked to summer there.

The Seattle couple had children of college age. Their plan was to keep the family vacationing together even as the children got married and had kids of their own. For that reason, the couple also intended to buy a second unit that would be part of the hotel rental pool. "When the kids come down, we would have the other unit," the wife explained. "It would be like an extra bedroom."

Price Points

This was the Seattle couple's first investment outside the United States and the husband had a competitive view of where his dollars were going. "Roatan is less developed, but it is much more affordable than other places in the Caribbean," he told me.

The Parrot Tree product is much more affordable than other developed Caribbean areas like the Cayman Islands, Edwards later repeated. "We sell here an 1,800-square-foot, two-bedroom, two-bath, nicely appointed, solid concrete, built to withstand a San Francisco earthquake unit that can be had for $489,000. The same product on the Grand Caymans would go for $1.5 million."

Parrot Tree boasted cheaper units such as a condo efficiency that was selling at $269,900. There was also a four-bedroom, 2,500-square-foot unit selling for $750,000.

I also asked Hasz about Roatan compared to other Latin American second home markets. His comment was that people compare prices on Roatan to Mexico and for comparable units, the island was about one-third the price points. That kind of discount for Roatan would hold up when compared to what one would pay for decent land elsewhere in the Caribbean.

Edwards, who has been on the island since 1991, had a lot of interesting stories to tell about the island's aggressive price appreciation, such as a piece of property he bought in West Bay for $90,000, sold for $200,000, and then bought back for $345,000. He still owns that land.

Just out of curiosity, I asked Edwards what the $269,900 condo efficiency unit sold for originally. The answer: six years ago it could be had for $215,000.

When I asked the husband from Seattle what he expects in the way of appreciation for his investments, he told me, "We missed the first bounce, but the market is still on the way up. The infrastructure is getting better. We anticipate a lot of appreciation once the Parrot Tree hotel here gets built."

Later, I would see Edwards work his charm on the Seattle couple, getting two contracts signed as I observed from a nearby table.

Edwards was an interesting personality. Born in London, Ontario, his family moved to San Diego and then to Iowa. To this day, Edwards still owns a farm in the state. However, wanderlust struck him just at about the time he should have been settling down with his family. He was working in the home improvement business around the

Des Moines area when someone told him about Belize. Some of his friends had already moved there and in 1979 he did so as well. He and his partners caught the original Central American land rush for North Americans, getting involved in property speculation before developing two lodging properties on Ambergris Cay—the Belize Yacht Club and Edwards' first hotel called the Mayan Princess.

In 1991, Edwards read an article about Roatan opening up property to foreign investment. Sensing opportunity once more, he moved from Belize to Roatan. He became the second real estate agent on the island, but the first to open a real estate office.

"There were no requirements for being a Realtor at the time," Edwards recalled. "It didn't even require a trade license. But the business has become more sophisticated. Now there is a Roatan Realtors Association, 16 to 17 real estate brokerage firms, and about 65 agents. We are associated with the National Association of Realtors in the United States."

As of 2005, Realtors have had to be licensed in Roatan.

Nascent Condo Market

Besides owning the Century 21 franchise for the island, Edwards has become the Donald Trump of Roatan. He is one of the largest, if not the largest developer on the island. Among his many holdings and developments are his second Mayan Princess in West Bay, Parrot Tree Resort, and now a third resort being readied for development.

It wasn't easy—especially at the beginning. His first big development, the Mayan Princess Resort, took about 10 years to develop. "It was a labor of love," Edwards said wistfully. There were a couple of problems, the first being physical. The resort sits on a beautiful stretch of beach, but to get to it the road climbs a steep mountain spine, then declines, not always gracefully, to sea level. When Edwards decided to build the Mayan Princess, there was no macadamized road, just a dirt track.

"The road was long and nasty," he laughed. "Sometimes you couldn't even get out of here because of the mud. It was after the road was paved that sales took off. In the few months after the paving, we sold as many units as we had in all the years before."

The biggest obstacle wasn't the adventure in getting there, but being too early for the market. Edwards' big innovation for the island was to sell the individual resort units as condominiums and letting owners put them into the resort's rental pool when they were not using them. "In the early days, we didn't have the North American traffic and what there was at the time was mostly the diving crowd," he explained. "And they were not the same divers you see today, the doctors and lawyers with thousands of dollars worth of gear. They were dive bums and backpackers."

"We started the Mayan Princess ahead of the market," Edwards continued. "No one caught onto the condo market until we started selling some real volume. That was about four years ago."

Where is the condo market today on Roatan?

Very healthy, Edwards responded. "Today, raw land in good locations is appreciating about 20 percent annually and so are condominiums—maybe a little more. There are probably 10 condo projects that are currently under construction on Roatan. That is not a tremendous number, but for a small island like this, it is a good start."

Not everyone is so sanguine about the Roatan condo market.

There are probably fewer than 500 condo units total on the island, Hasz estimated, but there were 3,200 permits issued from 2005 through 2007. "The condo market might be getting overbuilt," he said. "It could slump a little bit."

Single-Family Residential

Hasz doesn't sell many condos, doing a much better business in single-family homes and raw land. One of the problems he has with condos is that many are in the condo-hotel category where an investor buys a condo property and when the owner is not using it, it can be rented out as a hotel room to tourists. "I noticed that in almost all of the condo-hotel developments, people are not making money on operations," he told me. "They might make something on appreciation if they get a preconstruction purchase. For a condo-hotel unit, there are a lot of management fees."

Although, he added, "if you pick your property carefully, there are some that are giving a significant rental return; Half Moon Bay that are bringing in over $75,000 a year in rentals."

And in some condo-hotels projects there is an extra fee if you want to live in your unit and not put it into the rental pool, said Jaime Stathis, who now works with RoatanLife Real Estate.

Stathis was raised in Connecticut, but was living in Montana when she made her first trip to Roatan. "A friend of mine made a visit, came back, and said to me, 'you would like this place.' I visited in March, stayed for a week, stayed for another week, and then another week. Everything fell into place. I got rid of my house, and five weeks later I was back."

This is the way it works, she said, "people come for a vacation and end up staying."

Stathis likes to say when she came to Roatan she was a massage therapist and an aspiring novelist. The first part of that didn't work out well in Roatan, because the island is somewhat spread out and it was difficult to lug her massage table and equipment about. Then she saw an ad Steve Hasz put in the local paper and decided to go into the real estate business.

Although she hadn't been in the business for very long, she noticed a lot of the North Americans coming through Roatan had first considered Mexico and Costa Rica. They had moved on from Mexico because of the fact you couldn't directly own beachfront property there, and those that had visited Costa Rica found prices were already very high. Now they were considering Roatan.

Upon arrival, Stathis quickly bought into the real estate market. Like most ex-pats she was attracted to the vibrancy of the West End and acquired a small house that needed a bit of fixing up. The price was a very affordable $128,000. Because she was in the real estate business, I asked what she would sell that house for in the current market (about one year after acquisition). Without blinking an eye, she answered $180,000.

Hasz likes the single-family home market, but Edwards frankly admits he is just not sure about single-family homes. "We are in the business of building and selling condominiums primarily. That is what we market. We probably sell 10 times as many condos as single-family homes. There is a shortage of single-family homes and those that are constructed are built for someone. There is not a lot of product available."

Wide Selection of Product

It was midafternoon on my first day on the island and the sun had finally broken through. A strong breeze blew onshore. Edwards conducted all his business, three couples in the afternoon when I was there, on the patio of the coffee shop. It's my office, he joked.

He looked younger than his 60-plus years with well-trimmed, graying hair surrounding a boyish face now a bit lined with age.

His movements were minimum and patience eternal. All his Roatan developments from the first—the Mayan Princess—to his current, Parrot Tree—were built out over many years. Sales, as I could see from watching him, took a long time to play out as even those very willing to buy wanted to sit and chat away I could see he never cut off the chatter, although he has listened to the same types of stories from a thousand different people.

An advertisement for Parrot Tree Plantation often took the back cover of the local magazine, *Bay Island Voice*. I noticed in a 2006 ad, Parrot Tree was offering beachfront condos for $259,900 with an asterisk. The key on the asterisk read "price subject to increases." (Honduran currency is the lempira, but all big purchases are in dollars. In Roatan, dollars are widely accepted.)

Although you don't really see it as you drive around the island, real estate is a major business here. In my hotel room was a copy of *The Bay Islands Breeze*, officially called the *Bay Islands Real Estate & Community Magazine*. It was stuffed silly with advertisements for property such as:

- Large Cay (island) just off French Harbor. With beautiful views all around and surrounded by tropical tress. Perfect for just about anything. $1.5 million.
- West End Beachfront. White sand! Only waterfront property available in West End with 2.2 acres and 75 feet on the beach. $495,000.
- Casa Portofino in West Bay Beach. Private, 2-bathroom villa. Only 400 feet from best beach on Roatan. $359,000.
- New home. 3-bedroom, 3bath. Located in Turtling Bay with fabulous views of the north shore's turquoise waters. $219,000.
- West Bay Road. At the very top of the hill where everyone stops to view the south and north coasts of the island is a 12-acre development lot with acre and half-acre parcels starting at $75,000.

Almost makes one want to move there.

Price Points

Hasz figures about 30 percent of his clients are buying long-term, perhaps to eventually retire to the island; about 30 percent expect to either live on Roatan forever or off and on for at least four years and then will probably sell; 30 percent are trying to build quickly and will sell when construction ends; and 10 percent will just buy land, not build, then flip on the rapid appreciation.

For those who are thinking of buying land and building on Roatan, the average cost to build out interior space is about $100 per square foot, and that includes what Hasz calls "luxury construction" of granite counters, hardwood floors, stainless steel appliances, and so forth. However, decks are important and new homes boast 20 to 25 percent deck space as compared to house size and that drops the construction costs down into the $75 per square foot range. As a comparison, construction costs in New York and South Africa are closer to the $300 a square foot range.

Both Duane Thoreson and Barb Wastart, a couple from Seattle, had recently retired. They came to Roatan on a vacation swing through Central America and when it was all over decided to pick up stakes and move down. "We fell in love with the island," said Wastart. "We said, 'life is short, let's do it.'"

Actually, the couple had considered moving to the warmer climates south of the U.S. border even before their vacation. Their first consideration was Mexico, but the ownership laws were not as favorable as Roatan. They even tossed about really going to the edge by buying in Nicaragua. Then the Sandinistas were returned to power and that squelched that idea.

Initially, Thoreson and Wastart wanted to buy a beach house, but they quickly learned it is not so desirable to have a house on the beach if you intend to live on the island all year round. As a beachfront homeowner, there are a couple of issues like salt spray and sand fleas. "If you are going to do the beach, it is best to find a lot on the south shore, because the tradewinds keep the bugs down," Thoreson noted.

Like most ex-pats, the couple wanted to buy in West End and they found a lovely little house about 900 feet from the beach. It was a traditional Roatan home, constructed on stilts above a ground floor, cement slab. Living space is one flight above with access by stairs. There are several theories as to why Roatans live one flight up: flooding is always a possibility (less of a possibility if not on the beach); it is above many of the flying insects; air circulates under the home keeping it cool; and the slab is a good place for storage. After purchasing their 1,000-square-foot house for $220,000, Thoreson and Wastart, two handy people, built a guest suite on half the ground floor, thus adding 450 square feet to the house.

The couple has long-range plans to build a wellness retreat on the island, but in the short term they intend to erect a couple of spec homes. When I visited with them, they had bought their first piece of land for that project.

I asked if there was a savings between building here and in Seattle. As far as Thoreson could tell, the cost of materials was the same because everything had to be shipped. In fact, some people simply order a container from Home Depot in Tampa and have everything shipped in at once. The big savings, he added, was in labor costs. "You can get laborers for about $10 a day," he noted.

Labor is still relatively inexpensive in Roatan. For example, a full-time maid/cook costs about $160 a month, a full-time gardener $180 a month, and if you just wanted to splurge and go out for a lobster dinner, that might cost $11 (including tip!).[1]

How to Buy Property in Honduras

So how does one buy property in the Bay Islands?

Ownership. First and foremost, it's important to know that non-Hondurans can absolutely own land in the Bay Islands, with limitations. Foreigners may own up to 3,000 square meters or approximately three-quarters of an acre in their own name. Another popular option is to create a Honduran corporation to hold title to larger parcels, hold multiple properties, or simplify the selling of a property. Stock certificates to the corporations are then held by the foreign owner in a bearer form. The owner becomes president, *administrador unico*, of the corporation—meaning you have 100 percent control and ownership.

Residency. Okay, you know you can own land, but what about residency? Honduran law states that if you plan to live in Honduras for more than three months, you must establish residency. There are several types of residency, including retirement status, so it's best to consult an attorney on this matter. Getting the residency issue settled takes time, expect to wait at least six months before it becomes final.[2]

"There are about 65,000 Hondurans in the Bay Islands, plus another 5,000 foreigners," said Cesar Gonzalez Jr., a young Honduran attorney who met me for dinner one night in West Bay. "Most of the foreigners are tourists with extended stays and coming in and out because of immigration procedures."

Legal Matters. You will need to contract with a local attorney to complete the residential purchase. As a column in *The Bay Island Breeze* noted: "The most important way to protect your new investment is to choose a reputable and thorough attorney. All of the protections offered through the Property Laws of Honduras come through the *Escritura Publica*, which is the recorded legal transfer document prepared by an attorney." "For foreigners, every important matter, whether it is immigration, purchasing property, or establishing a business while in Honduras requires legal assistance," Gonzalez emphasized.

The Acquisition Process. Basically, your engagement with the seller involves a purchase agreement with money put in escrow. An attorney will do the due diligence including checking to make sure the land is clear of any liens and mortgages. The initial paperwork obviously involves this purchase contract and according to a Honduras real estate web site, this document will be prepared by a broker and an attorney and on The Bay Islands will probably be in English, although it may ultimately be in Spanish to maintain enforceability, because for a property transfer to be valid and recorded in Honduras, the documentation (*escritura*) must be written in Spanish.[3] The purchase contract will establish time frames, purchase price, financing terms (most acquisitions are still cash purchases), escrow agent, and such important items as a new survey with a Honduran engineer's stamp, inspections, and title opinion.

Title Insurance. Although not required, North Americans are comfortable with title insurance and a couple of U.S. title insurers now operate on Roatan. *The Bay Island Breeze* recommends title insurance with this proviso: The most important documents binding at title insurance policy are an Attorney's Title Opinion, provided by an approved Honduran-licensed attorney and the payment of a fee (ranges from 0.5 percent to 1.5 percent dependent upon the services required).

Documents. The list of documents needed to close on a property include: a copy of current title (*escritura*); original, signed and stamped survey in the seller's name, which must match the title's description and area; original *catastral* certificate in the seller's name, which is a type of satellite survey (the area on the *catastral* certificate must be the same as the title states); and a copy of paid property tax receipt for the current year. (The attorney will check for a clean title history and a lack of liens on the property.)

Taxes. Depending on the cost of the property, there are numerous attorney and notary fees. Taxes on the acquisition amount to 2.5 percent of the closing price, with 1 percent going to the local municipality and 1.5 percent to the federal government. "The 1.5 percent has to be paid to the central government within three days of closing otherwise it's a 20 percent fine," Gonzalez said. "As soon as that tax is paid, we issue the first copy of the protocol of the notary, which includes a certification of the receipt of the tax. That is then photocopied and taken to the municipality, where, along with the survey of property, it is booked into the system. Then a certificate is issued and stamped by the registrar. This is the point where the 1 percent tax to the municipality is paid. After about two to three months, the buyer has the title."

On the Mainland

The rush to invest in real estate on the island of Roatan appeared to be building, but I was curious whether a similar demand by foreigners also existed on the mainland. On coming back to Tegucigalpa, I stopped by to see Jessica Cerrato, a young woman who headed the RE/MAX office in the capital city.

I already heard many negative stories about Tegucigalpa, that crime was rampant and life was dangerous. Maybe the stories were correct as the entrance to my hotel often looked like an armed camp; people in uniform with serious weaponry making sure no riff-raff got into the hotel. Well, I've been to other cities where hotels also had armed guards on the premises, so I still wasn't sure that was an accurate indicator of crime statistics.

To help me get to the RE/MAX office, Cerrato sent a driver to my hotel. The driver, who spoke passable English, was happy to chat. Apropos of really nothing I said, the driver launched into a harsh critique of life in Tegucigalpa, the gist of which was it wasn't safe to go out at night. The risk of bodily harm or robbery was such a serious problem that social life in the city was restricted.

Well, Tegucigalpa wasn't Panama City, but Cerrato told me she had seen an increasing number of Americans make inquiries about Honduras. "Americans are coming here for second homes," she said. "Mostly they like the beach areas, although we had an older couple who was looking for something in the mountains. We found a place for them in a picturesque little town, Valle de Angeles, about 30 minutes from Tegucigalpa."

Honduras boasts a wild and wonderful Caribbean coastline and it appeared from my conversation with Cerrato that the next frontier of tourism and vacation home markets was already underway at the shoreline.

For those folks who go to Roatan by boat from the mainland, the jumping off point is the small city of La Ceiba. It's also a popular tourist destination and the country's eco-tourism capital because of its proximity to Bonito Peak National Park, a mountainous area of highlands, canyons, and steep cliffs.

The coastal region near La Ceiba is marked by brackish lagoons and mangroves, but going west about 40 miles is the coastal town Tela, which boasts very fine beaches. It's here where the next vacation paradise is slowly evolving. "In Tela, they're building two big resorts, La Ensenada Beach Villas and Bahia de Tela, with wonderful villas," Cerrato said. "The villas are for sale, as well as second homes and condo-hotels."

In the first project to get underway, La Ensenada Beach Villas, about 40 percent of the units have been taken in presale, Cerrato said. "This is a very nice project with American-style details and the condos are bigger than in Roatan, with three bedrooms, three baths, and fully equipped kitchens."

Cerrato said four of her clients have bought there. All were from colder climates: New York, Boston, Colorado, and Canada. "I have another client from Colorado who wanted to be in La Ceiba because they assumed the beaches would be good there. I offered them instead properties in Tela," Cerrato told me. "They will come back later in the year to see for themselves."

I didn't know the Tela projects, but I knew the Honduras Shores Plantation development in Tela offered lot and home sales. I checked online and saw the development was selling 240 lots for future vacation or retirement homes; a variety of house plans were available at prices in the $50,000 to $80,000 range.

Cerrato was not in the real estate business when she was selected to manage the first RE/MAX office in Tegucigalpa about five months before I met her, but she was smart, attractive, well organized, and bilingual.

"There's a RE/MAX on the Bay Islands and that is American style," she laughed. "Here it is Honduran style." I'm not sure what that meant, and I hoped it was a good thing.

The office was getting busier, she said. "About 30 percent of our clients come from other RE/MAX offices around the world. The first foreign client we had was someone from Toronto who had seen us on the Web. Investors are finding us."

10 Things to Know about Buying Property in Honduras

1. When real estate investors talk about buying in Honduras, they generally mean Roatan, and to a lesser extent the other Bay Islands.
2. Although not well-known, Roatan has good airlift for the Caribbean, with direct flights from numerous cities in North America and Europe.
3. Most North Americans heading to Roatan opt for the western tip of the island. Here one finds the major concentration of restaurants, bars, and what passes for ex-pat nightlife.
4. Foreigners can directly buy property in Roatan, and prices are generally cheaper than Mexico or elsewhere in the Caribbean.
5. The condo market is new, but growing. However, much of the new product will fall into the condo-hotel category, where the unit, when not in use, will be put in the rental pool of the hotel.
6. The single-family home market is limited by a lack of existing structures. Most investors buy land and then build.
7. Some handsome new developments are being created in the center and eastern end of the island.
8. The purchasing process is not complicated, but it is different. It will be necessary to use a local attorney.
9. It's possible to attain Honduran residency. However, there are different categories of residency so it's important to know the laws. Again, an attorney will be necessary.
10. Honduras' next big vacation market will be along the Caribbean coastline west of La Ceiba. Tela has great beaches and North American investors are already buying.

CHAPTER 13

DOMINICAN REPUBLIC

PUNTA CANA SECOND HOME MARKET HOT, HOT, HOT; PRICES REMAIN MODERATE EXCEPT IN UPSCALE PROJECTS LIKE CAP CANA

'm mostly known as a financial and real estate journalist, but I have a whole other life as a travel writer. It's an interesting gig as about six times a year I find myself in a wonderfully strange port of call that I never in my life imagined I would have visited. Mostly I travel by myself or with my wife, but once a year my friend Edward Moss, who I have known since I was 16 and who is an avid photographer, meets me where I'm headed. He does this because (a) he likes to travel and (b) he jumps at the chance to take photographs in exotic locals.

Moss has shot pictures for me from Jakarta to Dubai, from game parks in South Africa to rainforests in Costa Rica. My favorite photos, two of which have been blown up and hang in my den, were from an early trip he and I made to Cuba. So, when I was organizing my journeys for this book, I sent him my itinerary with a note that Wendy, my wife, was joining me in Mexico and Newfoundland, and he could take any of the other locations. He decided he would meet me in the Dominican Republic. I said that's great and left him with the task of finding us a place to stay in the destination, Punta Cana.

This wasn't going to be very difficult as Punta Cana has become one of the great resort locations in the Caribbean. Moss dithered for a few days. His problem was, as he researched each mega-resort on the Internet, that most were very family-oriented. Moss, like me is an empty nester, our kids are young adults and out of the home, and wherever we were to stay, he didn't want to be inundated by hundreds of kids belonging to other people. His choice was a property called the Excellence Punta Cana that billed itself as an adult resort. When he pitched the idea to me, I agreed, and Moss got online and billed four nights to his credit card.

About two weeks before I was beginning my Caribbean jaunt, a trip that would include Puerto Rico, Virgin Islands, and Dominican Republic, Moss called me and said he had to back out because he was busy at work and was selling his home. Because the room was already paid for, I asked my wife if she wanted to go. She checked to see that she had some frequent flyer miles, booked a flight, and planned to arrive in Punta Cana a day before me as she was coming directly—more or less—from Phoenix.

When I finally arrived at Excellence, a splendid, all-inclusive resort, I realized immediately that this was a couples kind of place and that if Moss had made the trip it would have been difficult to arrange for two beds in a room instead of the large four-poster, romance-inducing king bed that sits in probably every unit. Moreover, others at the resort would have assumed he and I were that other type of couple. Not that the resort cared, numerous other types of couples, mostly of the female persuasion, were enjoying the resort when I was there.

Although I was quite glad my wife decided to make the journey saving me from being at a couples' resort by myself, I felt bad for my buddy because he missed an opportunity to take the kind of photos he loves, local society on the brink of modernity.

Despite its reputation as the up-and-coming resort location in the Caribbean, Punta Cana is a long stretch of resort and condominium development in an otherwise very undeveloped part of the Dominican Republic. While the hotels are up and the privately owned airport is fully functioning, a lot of the infrastructure such as decent housing and roads are still being built. The Excellence was one of the resorts furthest from the airport, a good 20 miles north on the coast, but to get there one has to travel a slim, local road, badly potholed, unmarked, and still subject to occasional horse traffic. For someone who had never driven that road before, it was a leap of faith that I was heading in the right direction, and if I was, that I would reach my destination without the car disappearing into a deep hole, the bush, or the many construction sites where new condominiums and resorts were being erected.

Origins and History

If you look at a map of the Dominican Republic, you'll see the country is shaped like a triangle with the apex pointing eastward at the island of Puerto Rico. This extreme eastern end of the country was largely virgin forest right to the edge of the ocean. Then in 1969, an unlikely quartet of investors got together to buy 58 million square meters of land on the coast. The four investors were Dominican financier Frank Raineri, U.S. labor mediator Ted Kheel, fashion designer Oscar de la Renta, and singer Julio Iglesias. Eventually, they began building the megadevelopment Puntacana Resort & Club. The group was also responsible for building the local airport, which is the largest private airport in the Caribbean. This is no small affair as the Punta Cana airport saw 1.7 million tourists pass through its portals in 2006. That's three times more than any other airport in the country, including the country's other major tourist location, Puerto Plata, and the capital city, Santo Domingo.

Besides the undeveloped land, what drew investors to Punta Cana (actually a stretch of seacoast running from Cap Cana through Punta Cana and Bavaro to Uverto Alto) was 43 kilometers of white sand beaches, or as Karl Lober, owner of Trust Realty in Bavaro said, "on the east coast of the Dominican Republic stretches the longest array of powder white, coconut strewn beaches in the Caribbean."

Over the last 25 years, steady growth has ensued with the region now boasting 50 hotels and resorts and more than 25,000 hotel rooms. Where once there were no golf courses, now they are blooming like native vegetation with a host of famous golfers from Jack Nicholas to Nick Price signing off on new properties.

Along with the hotels have come condominium developments and huge megadevelopments, the latter of which include myriad individual projects such as villas, condos, hotels, sports facilities, golf developments, and a host of other amenities.

The Market

When I was in staying in Puerto Rico, I always ate dinner at my hotel, and after seeing me there a few nights, Patricia Martinez, the hotel's food and beverage supervisor, stopped by my table to chat. When I told her I was working on a book about second home markets and that I would eventually end up in Punta Cana, she got very excited. It turns out that her family for five years running went there for vacation. They liked the area so much, she and her husband were looking to buy a condo and, in fact, had their eye on a small development near the Bavaro Princess resort. This was a new project and one-bedroom units were going for $120,000.

When Lober first visited Punta Cana a dozen years ago, a considerable number of the area's hotels had already been built, but there was not much civilization beyond the beach. Now, he says, there's a lot of infrastructure development going on to catch up with the popularity of the region as a tourist mecca and second home venue. Restaurants, businesses, offices, and roads are all going up in a crazy quilt mess of spontaneous brick-and-mortar eruptions.

After living in Santo Domingo for 10 years, Lober moved to Punta Cana, eventually opening his own real estate brokerage and service company. Lober grew up in Germany, but 15 years ago he left seeking warmer climates. He tried Spain and Majorca, finally immigrating to the Dominican Republic. He seems to have settled down happily in Punta Cana. Anyway, business is booming for him, so it doesn't appear he'll be going anywhere else too soon.

"What people are looking for is access to the beach," he said, and since the big resorts have taken big chunks of the good beach sites, a new generation of smaller developments was being built in walking distance to the white sands along the shore.

"We have a new project called Palm Suites that is going up right next to our office and just 300 meters from the beach," he said. "We have a beach club called Palma Sands and condo owners can use the facilities at a 20 percent discount."

I checked Lober's web site and it was touting Palm Suites condos at a starting price of $119,500 for a two-bedroom, two-bath, 1,800-square-foot unit and penthouses with rooftop terraces were listed at $179,500.

That seemed cheap and it was compared with other prices in the Caribbean, yet it wasn't out of line with prices at other developments in the area. I couldn't write as fast as he was rattling off condo and villa projects nearby, many of which were in the $100,000 to $200,000 range. Of course, he said, you can start working your way up to grander developments and he mentioned the nearby Cocotal Golf & Country Club. One of his listings was a villa (duplex) of 3,229 square feet with three bedrooms and three and a half baths that was selling for $475,000.

Back in the mid-1990s, Rico Pester visited Punta Cana and made an investment. He bought a million square meters of land, paying just $1 a meter. He has since brought in partners and expanded the holdings to 5 million square meters. The property, which is not on the ocean, is now worth $28 a square meter.

Pester, also a native of Germany, has lived in the Dominican Republic for 14 years and besides being an investor also owns the RE/MAX franchise for the area, which he calls Island Realty.

He was kind enough to drive out to my resort for a chat. Although it was not a short trip, he often made the journey because he was selling land in the Uvero Alto area. Whenever I commuted back into Bavaro, I could see a poster with his name on it.

When I asked him why there were three isolated resorts in Uvero Alto and then nothing on the coast for many miles before hitting the clutter of resorts in Bavaro, he responded: "Some of the oceanfront has no beach. It's still all farmland. Although cows are on the property it's very expensive farmland for sale in large plots of 200,000 square meters. That's at $75 a square meter, which means you need $15 million to buy the land."

"I have many billboards," Pester said, laughing. I suppose he could make fun of himself because he was representing some very large plots of land: 270,000 square meters for a resort, 185,000 square meters for a resort, 500,000 square meters for a resort, and 3.3 million square meters for a future development.

"In late spring [2007] I met with three or four general managers of hotel chains from the United States, Costa Rica, and Mexico who were looking to buy properties," he said. "For example, the U.S. buyer wanted property to build a hotel, large residential area, and golf course. It's always a long process before someone comes in and puts $15 million to $20 million down for land."

This is not to say there isn't real estate for the everyday investor. Close to my resort, Pester was building a 60-unit condo with access to the beach and a private beach club. A 1,702-square-foot condo in preconstruction was billed at $275,000. Not such a bad deal because in comparison, Pester was representing another project going up in Bavaro where a 900-square-foot condo was selling in preconstruction for $200,000. "When it is complete, it will sell for $250,000," he told me.

It's not all beach in Punta Cana. As noted, there are a fast-growing number of golf properties, and to see what's going on with them I checked in with Emma Espinal Inoa, an attractive young woman who is a rookie broker at PCR Punta Cana Realty S.A. In her opinion, the best golf course in the area at that moment was Cocotal Golf & Country Club, a gated community. "This is a high-class area," she began. "A one-bedroom condominium starts at $180,000 and a two-bedroom at $290,000. Of course prices rise from that starting point and there are a few single-family homes that are in the $500,000 price range."

Inoa told me of an American retiree friend who bought a town-house at Cocotal two years ago, paying about $170,000. "Now," she said, "he wants to buy a bigger property and is selling the property, which he bought brand new, for $290,000."

Another property Inoa touts is White Sands, a beach and golf development that was under construction when I was there and is targeted to open in 2008. The development was not very large with 81 beach-view apartments, 90 percent were gone in presale. The first ones to sell were at $178,000 for a one bedroom. Currently, she noted, a one-bedroom unit carried a $190,000 price tag. "We expect to see about 35 percent appreciation annually."

Home Values Rising

Although prices are very reasonable as compared to most of the Caribbean, property values have been climbing steadily, especially as North Americans began coming down in big numbers starting around 2004.

Lober told me about an older development called Los Corales, where about a dozen years ago, condos cost less than $50,000. Now they were $300,000 with some on the beach up to $600,000. Empty lots that used to cost $60 a square meter were now $200 a square meter.

In three years, he said, some condo prices have tripled.

"We have very high appreciation here," Pester affirmed, and a lot of it appears to be juiced by speculators flipping newly built properties. "For condos under development, we sell during construction and sometimes we resell for the individual owner after construction. Appreciation is 50 percent in the 12 months it takes to complete a unit." That would be for a condo on the beach, because appreciation on a presale price for a condo near the beach is running at 25 percent to 30 percent.

There is not much land available for apartments on the beach, so most new construction is close to the beach but not on the water. Nevertheless, Pester estimated in summer 2007 there were a couple of thousand condo (villas and townhouses) units under construction.

If demand doesn't meet the supply, that could lead to over-building and, inevitably, a quick end to appreciation. Pester didn't think that would be happening in the near future. "You cannot imagine all the resorts that are coming in. That creates demand for business, infrastructure, people. They need apartments, houses, buildings." Resorts also attract tourists who are introduced to the area for the first time and suddenly think, "Maybe I should own a property here."

The boom in Punta Cana is just starting, Pester said. "This will be a hot market for the next 15 years."

Pester, who built a successful insurance business in Germany, eventually sold it because he wanted to slow down his life. If anything, he's a bit more frantic. When he opened his RE/MAX office in 2002, it was doing 15 to 20 transactions a year. In 2007, with three offices and 10 sales associates, he guesses his franchise will end up doing 200 to 300 deals. "We are on fire," he said excitedly. "I need more associates."

Cap Cana

After I interviewed Karl Lober, he recommended that I see what was going on at the famous Cap Cana megaproject being developed south of the Bavaro near the airport. My eyes opened wide. Cap Cana is probably the most well-known development in all of the Dominican Republic, a fact surely heightened by the vast self-promotion of Donald Trump who has his own project there called Farallon Trump at Cap Cana.

When I expressed interest in Cap Cana, Lober was kind enough to make some calls on my behalf, because access to the development was tightly controlled. As most individual residences in Cap Cana will cost seven figures or more, one doesn't want tourists and other types of *hoi polloi* wandering about.

Although my Spanish is extremely weak, I heard Lober explain that I was a writer working on a book about vacation home markets, and that was good enough to get us a tour of the place. When Wendy and I arrived at the big information center outside the gates of Cap Cana we were cordially met by Gabriel Prado, one of the project's sales executives, who, after some brief chit-chat, handed us off to a "hostess," Dana Dominguez, who would be our guide for the day.

We spent three hours, including a break for lunch, touring the megaproject, which totals 31,000 acres and is 10 miles long north to south—a small county back in the States. In between, when all is completed, will be at least six golf courses, a marina, a fountain and waterfall feature, roadways, a town for locals who will work at the resort, swimming pools, tennis courts, hotels, stores, private beach and golf clubs, an ecological habitat, and numerous individual developments with names like Villas Las Lagunas, Green Village, Punta Espada Golf Club, Racquet Village, Marina Cap Cana, and more on the way.

Dominguez, our guide, was an absolutely gorgeous young woman from Santo Domingo, who had a marketing degree from a Dominican university and spoke three languages fluently. This was her first big job (the entry-level position in the Cap Cana marketing team) and she was very happy to be there. Obviously, if she worked hard and well, then she could start her climb up the organizational ladder and perhaps garner some of the riches that were being made at Cap Cana. This was going to be a tremendously successful development and by the time all was said and done, the sales team here could end up wealthy enough to buy their own homes in the development.

A tremendous amount of construction was going on when we toured Cap Cana and a lot had already been completed, but it was still just a small part of the complete picture. Whenever we drove by a project under construction and I would see, for example, 60 villas being erected, I would ask Dominguez about prices. She quickly responded with the appropriate number along with the comment, "sold out." This happened more often than not.

"What's that over there?" I asked.

"That's the beach club with 18 villas and five bungalows," she answered.

"When were they developed?" "Three years ago. They sold out right away at about $500,000 for a three-bedroom villa. Today they would cost over a million."

"And that development over there?"

"That's the Golden Bear Lodge, developed by Jack Nicklaus, and the Villas Back Nine, which have views of the golf course."

"How much do they cost?"

"They all sold out at $2 million a piece."

We went to the Punta Espada Golf Club for lunch (the first signature course by Jack Nicklaus at Cap Cana and soon to be a PGA tour stop) and as we were leaving I pointed out what looked to be empty land. Dominguez gazed in the direction I was pointing. "Those are land sites. They were over a million dollars also and sold out."

I did come across one development that wasn't sold out yet. It was a hotel property called the Altabella Fishing Lodge Suites and Apartments. The five-star project was still under construction alongside the marina of Cap Cana when I visited. The Fishing Lodge's suites and apartments were sold like condos, but when not in use would be put back into the rental pool for guests. They were selling for $370,000 to $1.8 million. "Most are sold," said Dominguez. "I think there are 15 or 20 left."

What's ironic about the success and notoriety of Cap Cana is that it was the Britney Spears of the local press, which could not write enough bad things about it, commenting regularly that it was a busted project, a failure where the investors and developers were in trouble. Every week it seemed the project would go down in flames.

"The major newspaper here published a large, front-page story that Cap Cana was a broken project and investors were in trouble," Inoa recalled. "The article predicted the project would not happen and that was the last word for many years."

Today, in Marina Cap Cana reside the first 61 investors in the massive project. They were all Dominican and all plunked down $1 million to live in the new development. Perhaps things were tenuous in the early years because as a reward for their faith, all the early investors were given either a plot on a beach development or along one of the signature Jack Nicklaus golf courses (he designed the first three courses at Cap Cana). Although I didn't get to view it, the shore development on a small bay is supposed to have the most beautiful, white-sand beach in the project, and has since become known as *Solares de Playa Fundadores*, literally founder's beach lots. Today those gifts of land sell for $6 million.

Marina Cap Cana is a massive dockside project that will not only be the densest development in the megaproject, but also, in effect, the city center. It will be home to yachts and mega-yachts and constructed with interior waterways so it will be like a little Venice in the Caribbean, even boasting its own water taxis. From one of the boardwalks along the seaward inlet to the project I noticed on the far side of the land, about a hundred yards away, an older building that looked like a condominium structure. "Is that part of Cap Cana?" I asked with some surprise. The answer was no, it was Puntacana Resort. The word was, the older and first megadevelopment in Punta Cana, in comparison with the new Cap Cana, was not up to snuff. It was pretty obvious to me as I looked at the Puntacana Resort building across the landscape that Cap Cana was light-years into the future.

No matter where you stand in Cap Cana, your attention naturally gets drawn to a dramatic ridge to the south, where a long cliff line of grey rock rises out of the green jungle (soon to be villas and golf courses). "What's that?" I asked Dominguez, expecting some lengthy explanation of geographic formations and ancestral peoples committing dramatic acts of worship. Instead, she answered very matter-of-factly, "that's Farallon."

It was Donald Trump's project. I have to admit I was a little shocked somehow that The Donald had managed to gain control of the land above the cliffs, the most exciting site in all of Punta Cana. Actually, my jaw dropped not in awe of Trump's ability to find the right spot (I'm told his son Eric actually discovered the site and convinced his father to invest), but in disappointment. Something that geologically dramatic should have been a national park.

As a lover of the outdoors, I was especially disappointed to see Cap Cana had cut down a section of the ridge line and built a land bridge so a road could be built directly from the lowlands to the top of the rise. As a real estate writer, on the other hand, I could see Trump's vision, especially as I drove up the new land bridge to the top of the cliffs and looked out over Cap Cana, the coastline, undeveloped jungle, and everything else in the world to the north.

Trump divided the land above the cliffs into 68 rectangular plots. To accentuate the view, he built small observation platforms on each site, then he put it all up for sale at prices from $3 million to $7 million for the lots. Within four hours, 64 of the 68 lots sold. The buyers were 35 percent from the Dominican Republic, 30 percent from the United States and Puerto Rico, and 30 percent from Venezuela (flight money), Spain, and Latin America.[1]

Trump crowed at the time, "We are truly surprised at the speed at which these sales were achieved. Never has $300 million been sold in such a short time in the Dominican Republic and the Caribbean."[2]

I'm told the lots now sell for $7 million to $10 million, but Dominguez said there were probably some speculators amongst the buyers, which is not always such a good thing for future appreciation.

Puerta Plata

I was supposed to meet Dean Brown in Bavaro as his Century 21 agency was opening an office there, but we couldn't coordinate.

Brown lives and works on the north coast of the country near Puerto Plata, the other major vacation spot in the Dominican Republic.

Brown, a native of North Carolina, moved to the Dominican Republic late in 2000 looking to retire, but he got a little bored and decided to sell real estate. When he joined Century 21, the local office had just three agents and he was working part-time selling a couple of properties a year. Now the office has almost 30 agents and he works full-time averaging 25 sales a year.

Punta Cana seems to get all the publicity these days, yet the Puerta Plata area has been in the resort business for at least four decades and continues to be a good market for second homebuyers.

"This area has gone through a number of cycles," Brown explained. "In the 1980s, Canadians and Americans were coming here and buying. Then in the 1990s, we were getting a lot of German-speaking people from Central Europe and starting around 2000, the English speakers came back including the British, especially because their pound is so strong against the dollar."

What also has pumped up the market is a new round of building. Beginning around 2004, gated communities and luxury condos were being erected and this has been a real draw. Like elsewhere, prices vary in these newer, gated communities with individual homes that can cost $2 million to $3 million, but condominiums are still affordable for most in the $200,000 to $250,000 range.

There's cheaper stuff, Brown said. Condos that are not on the water but have an ocean view can still be gotten for $150,000 and the older product, say a circa 1989 condo, sells for $180,000.

The big action now, Brown added, is outside of Puerto Plata in an area stretching from Cabarete to Sosua (called the Acapulco of the Dominican Republic; mass tourism on the island first began here). "There are some developers here that have been building pretty strong for the last couple of years and many of their projects are coming to a close. Also, in the past year a number of developers from the States have come down, bought quite a bit of property and are beginning to break ground."

The good news in the Puerto Plata area is that beachfront properties still can be had fairly cheaply. Brown said he had a home listed at $700,000. If one wanted to go even further out into the country-side, a small, basic house can be acquired for around $150,000.

Like everywhere else, prices of vacation home properties have been appreciating steeply over the past few years. Beachfront lots that Brown sold in 2005 for $130,000 are now going for $260,000.

"I bought some land in 2004 and sold it a year later with a 100 percent increase in price," Brown told me. He had more examples. "I bought a house for $83,000 and sold it three years later for $155,000, and I bought condos at $75,000 and nine months later sold them for $105,000."

Most of Brown's clients are from the northeast United States. "Think about it," he said. "You can board a plane in New York and be here three and a half hours later. It can take you that long to drive from New York to the Jersey shore on a Friday afternoon in the summer."

How to Buy Property in Punta Cana

In 1998, Dominican Republic President Leonel Fernandez signed into law a decree ending restrictions on real estate ownership by foreigners. Before the decree, buying real estate was complicated, but since then foreign real estate investors have the same rights as Dominicans.[3] Otherwise, real estate transactions in the country are governed by the Land Registry Law of 1947 and its amendments, which essentially means ownership of property is documented by Certificates of Title, which are issued by Title Registry offices.

On the Trust Realty web site, Lober includes an article from a local attorney, who writes on the subject of buying Dominican Republic real estate. The key steps to transfer ownership or real estate from a seller to a buyer are the following:

- Buyer and seller must sign a "contract of sale" before a notary will authenticate it. If the buyer is married, the spouse must also sign the contract of sale (contains legal description of property, price, and other conditions of sale).
- The authenticated contract of sale is then taken to the nearest Internal Revenue Office to request the appraisal of the property, to check that the seller is in compliance with tax obligations, and to pay the transfer taxes.
- The contract of sale and Certificate of Title of the seller are deposited, along with the documentation provided by the Internal Revenue office, at the Title Registry office for the jurisdiction where the property is located.
- The Title Registry office issues a new Certificate of Title in the name of the buyer and cancels the old certificate issued to the seller.

- Taxes must be paid before filing the purchase at the Title Registry Office, and they include a 3 percent transfer tax (based on the market value of the property as determined by the tax authorities, not on the price of purchase stated in the deed of sale) and 1.3 percent Dominican Stamp Tax and a few other minor expenses such as a tax on certified check, sundry stamps and tips at the Registry.[4]
- In the Dominican Republic, it's a common practice to create a local corporation that will buy the property. Due to a loophole in the tax law, by going this route, all transfer taxes are avoided (there are other benefits as well so consider this as a good option).

According to Pester, there are number of fees involved in the closing process and they can be broken down into four groups: lender fees (charges for loan processing, underwriting, preparation and establishing an escrow account); third-party fees (insurance, title search, termite inspection, and so on); government fees (deed recording and state and local mortgage taxes); and escrow and interest fees (homeowner's insurance, loan interest, real estate taxes, and occasionally private mortgage insurance). Even with all that, Pester maintains the process is not very complicated and relatively inexpensive. He guesses closing costs usually end up to be about 7 percent to 7.5 percent of purchase price.

The one difficulty in Punta Cana is getting a mortgage. "Ninety-five percent of the condo and home deals are all cash," he cautioned. "Financing is still difficult here because everything that is sold in Punta Cana is in U.S. dollars. If you can find financing, it would take a couple of weeks to get approvals and by that time the property would be sold."

Pester's recommendation: Have your money available.

One of the local title insurance companies offers its own 10 steps to what it calls a "smart purchase" of Dominican real estate. The company recommends:

1. Buyer, or buyer's legal representation, research the authenticity of the Certificate of Title.
2. Check with the Title Registration offices, Land Court, and General Internal Revenue Directorate to make sure there are no embargoes or outstanding tax issues on the property.

3. The office in charge of the property's legal procedures and investigations will vary depending on location, so one needs to find the right place to go.
4. Given the complexity of processes and the land jurisdiction system, hire an attorney.
5. Research the local zoning laws.
6. Understand what ancillary costs (water, electricity, maintenance, garbage collection, etc.) will run.
7. Inspect the property.
8. Keep current with the transfer process time line.
9. Verify that all information on the contract of sale is accurate.
10. Register the purchase immediately after closing so as to avoid fraud or other hassles.[5]

10 Things to Know about Buying Property in the Dominican Republic

1. Punta Cana has gotten very popular as a resort and second home market, but the infrastructure in the area is just beginning to catch up.
2. Prices for condominiums are still relatively inexpensive compared to elsewhere in the Caribbean.
3. The rise in home values is expected to continue into the near future; Realtors believe the boom in Punta Cana is just beginning.
4. Center of Punta Cana market is in Bavaro, but development stretches 20 miles along the coast from Cap Cana to Uvero Alto.
5. Cap Cana represents the upscale market; individual developments have been selling out rather quickly.
6. Puerto Plata market on the north coast remains popular.
7. Beachfront property can still be found in the Puerto Plata region.
8. Most North Americans buying second homes in Dominican Republic pay cash.
9. One way to reduce tax burden is to buy second home through a local corporation.
10. An attorney will be needed for a home purchase.

CHAPTER

NEWFOUNDLAND

AN UNLIKELY CANADIAN SUCCESS STORY; EUROPEANS REDISCOVER NEW WORLD AND CREATE A SECOND HOME MARKET ON SHORES OF MOUNTAIN LAKES

In the first week of March 2007, my wife and I made a trip to Isle de la Madeleine, an island in the middle of the Gulf of St. Lawrence that is the starting point for seeing newborn seal cubs. The mother seals give birth to cubs on the ice flows in the gulf and the helicopters that fly to the ice flows leave from Isle de la Madeleine. After a wonderful trip, our plane was flying back to Montreal via Gaspe. As we approached the small Quebec town, the pilot of the plane announced "mechanical problems" and after we safely landed we weren't sure if we were going to be leaving again that day. Fortunately, the problem was minor and the plane was off again a few hours later heading to Quebec City.

Now, it was mid-May. My plane was flying over Isle de la Madeleine heading for Deer Lake, Newfoundland, when the pilot announced, "mechanical problems," and we were diverted to Halifax, Nova Scotia. When the time came for us to return from Deer Lake via Montreal to the United States, Air Canada dispensed with any announcement of mechanical problems and simply canceled our flight, once again diverting us to Halifax so we could resume our journey.

I'm now sure there is a Gulf of St. Lawrence Triangle that disrupts Air Canada flights over the eastern part of the nation. The Triangle seems to be just a minor disturbance in the Force because in the first two instances the mechanical problems surrounding my flights were not serious enough to hamper the plane landing. However, we did have to change planes in Halifax before heading into Deer Lake and then when we were leaving we had to do another change of planes to get out of Deer Lake.

My wife and I began our trip to Newfoundland from Arizona, which was, in May, already experiencing triple-digit temperatures. We had a couple of stops along the way, the last of which was in Toronto, where the last flight originated. As the plane filled, I thought everyone for the most part looked like my wife and I, traveling in comfortable clothes. No one wore shorts, but there were plenty of sandals, t-shirts, and tank tops. Then the plane landed in Deer Lake and out of nowhere jackets, windbreakers, and sweaters appeared. I looked at my wife with an uh-oh expression because we were going to have to walk across the tarmac to the terminal and all our cool weather gear was packed in our baggage.

Scanning the Internet for Newfoundland weather every day before the trip, we knew we were not going to be in Arizona anymore, but when our plane began its descent over Newfoundland, I could see snow on the ground. Suddenly I was consumed with worry, wondering as I watched the snow-covered earth pass by below, just how warm was my cold weather clothing tightly squeezed into my luggage? It was almost June. Haven't they heard of the word "spring" in Newfoundland?

Most folks down in the Lower 48 have a passing knowledge of Newfoundland. I should say they have at least heard of the place, but I would wager to guess, 9 out of 10 Americans couldn't locate it on a map. The island sits higher up than you first thought on that globe you might now be spinning, and certainly further east as it pokes into the chilly North Atlantic, which, of course, accounts for the long winters.

The first time my wife and I came to Newfoundland was almost a decade earlier. Then, we flew into St. John's on the East Coast and spent a few days there looking at whales and puffins before flying to Deer Lake, where we drove north to the very end of the island. There, like something out of a James Bond movie, we donned wet suits, hopped into a kayak, and paddled around the headlands into the North Atlantic before eventually alighting on rough beach, stripping off the wet suits, and hiking for what seemed like an hour across a bog to a lighthouse where we would be staying the night.

It was one of the best vacations we ever had, so when I said to my wife she could go on any trip that I was making for this book, she nixed Panama City, Costa Rica, Virgin Islands, and Puerto Rico. Been there, done that. She also decided against taking the Pacific Ocean journeys. No, she would go with me to Newfoundland. That was her first choice.

In the course of researching this book, many of the people I have interviewed asked me, "Well, where would you buy a second home?" It's always a surprise to them when I answer, "Not on a beach." I live in Arizona, which is obviously a hot weather state, so I don't have to escape to a warm weather location. I already live in one. And secondly, the Bergsman family vacation has traditionally been to a ski area.

Skiing and snowboarding have always been my boys' favorite vacation sports. If my interrogator forces me to choose an exact location, I would say in the Banff area of the Canadian Rocky Mountains, a truly wondrous spot in North America, and when I was researching places to write about for this book, Canmore, outside of Banff, was one of the places I visited.

I knew I wanted to include a Canadian location in this book and I not only visited my favorite spot, Canmore/Banff but also Whistler and other locations in British Columbia, where the skiing is always great. The problem was, these were very expensive locations to buy a second home, equal in prices to the great ski venues (Aspen, Park City, Tahoe, and the like) in the United States.

Sadly for me, Canmore (Banff is in a national park and one can't actually develop new property there) was too pricey for consideration. Alberta, the home of the oil sands industry was going through a boom and folks from Calgary, which was just one hour to the east, were madly buying up properties there. The oil boom in Alberta and the population boom in British Columbia were pushing up prices too quickly in Canada's far western provinces.

So, after doing some more research, I came across a five-year-old Royal LePage study, which reported the least expensive vacation market in Canada was Newfoundland, where the price for a standard cottage in 2002 averaged just $31,500. As a comparison, the equivalent cottage, in say, British Columbia, cost $275,000.[1]

My first thought was, well that's understandable because, who the hell wants to buy a vacation home in Newfoundland? However, as I began looking into Canadian real estate trends I noticed a surprising pattern. In the first quarter of 2006, sales activity in Alberta and (big surprise!) Newfoundland was at record levels.[2] Things didn't look too bad in 2007 either. A spring 2007 report by the Royal LePage was encouraging, although it cautioned: "The continued loss of workers to Alberta has led to a shortage of skilled tradesmen in St. John's and delays in new construction are common, leading some buyers to turn to resale homes instead."[3]

I called the office of Royal LePage in the St. John's area to ask about cottages and vacation homes and I was surprised when the broker I spoke to told me that the market for vacation homes really wasn't in St. John's, located on the far eastern peninsula of the province, but in the Deer Lake/Corner Brook area on the far western shore where I would find a lot of second home action.

After hanging up the phone, I checked in with my wife, and we had our flights booked almost immediately. We were going back to Newfoundland.

Humber Valley Pioneers

Many families in Newfoundland own a second home, usually a cabin or a cottage on a lake, but the concept of a "vacation home," or a property owned by someone who lived off the island and would visit a second residence a couple of times a year didn't exist on the island until very recently—2004 to be exact. And the fact that this type of property exists at all in Newfoundland is really due to just one person, a Canadian businessman named Brian Dobbin.

Newfoundland is a very large island, 43,200 square miles, with a very small population, about 500,000 souls, mostly located along the eastern and northeastern shores. In Canada, they often talk in economic terms of have and have-not provinces and Newfoundland was, indeed, a have-not province. If, on the island itself, there was a have and have-not location, then the have-not location (other than the sparsely populated interior) was the western coast.

While the western coast didn't have population mass, the largest city being Corner Brook with a population of about 20,000 people, it was geographically dramatic with rugged coastlines, deep forests, rolling mountain ranges, fjords, and glacial lakes. In the center of the western coast, just beyond the municipality of Deer Lake, sits Gros Morne National Park, a stunningly beautiful region with all the topographic features I just mentioned concentrated in a relatively small area. After doing my research for this book, my wife and I spent three days in the park, hiking, sightseeing, and avoiding moose, which were as plentiful as dogs in a Disney movie.

Due to the park itself and beautiful scenery up and down the western coast, the region evolved into a popular summer tourist destination. Locals also loved it because of the lakes and mountains and the wide variety of outdoor activities there—lake fishing, ocean fishing, sailing, hunting, hiking, and so on. The Humber River, which flows through western Newfoundland, is considered one of the best salmon fishing rivers in the world. And the local lakes are trout fishermen favorites.

Route 1 of the Trans-Canada Highway runs north–south along the west coast and for miles along the eastern shore of a large body of water called Deer Lake. As a result, most of the development in the western region of the province occurred east of Humber River and Deer Lake, but Brian Dobbin looked at the heavily forested hill-side rising on the western shore of Deer Lake near where it empties into the lower Humber River and saw potential.

Dobbin, who was from the East Coast of the island, used to come to the Deer Lake area to vacation and realized what the place lacked was quality accommodations. The location he spotted was good for a couple of reasons. First, the river was at a narrow point here and he knew that to develop on the western shore he would need to build a bridge (which he did) and second, there was already a bit of residential history here.

The great Canadian timber magnate, Sir Eric Bowater, built a large home near here in 1954, which he called Strawberry Hill because of the wild strawberries that grew on the surrounding hills. On two visits to Newfoundland, Queen Elizabeth and her husband Philip, resided at Strawberry Hill and rumor has it that their son Prince Edward was conceived on one of these visits. Other notable visitors include such politicians as Canadian Prime Minister Pierre Trudeau and U.S. President Dwight Eisenhower.

Dobbin and some investors bought the property, which is now an inn with an excellent restaurant, and close to the main house built six attached dwellings on a hillside and two freestanding chalets near the river. Although the prices were in the $100,000 to $200,000 range, well above the local market, they sold out very quickly.

Just as he suspected, Dobbin concluded there could be a market for vacation homes in the area. The initial dwellings allowed Dobbin and investors to test the "resort" concept, where the chalets, when not in use by the owner could be put back into the rental pool, which is the backbone of the Humber Valley Resort.

"We run a resort operation," said Mike Clewer, managing director of Humber Valley Resort. "We rent the chalets out on behalf of the owners and there is a net rental split, which means we take the rental and remove certain costs associated with renting the property and share the balance."

(There is a tax advantage to this approach. As long as 90 percent of the usage of the residence is for commercial purposes, there is an allowance before the Canadian government starts taxing the property. Owners can effectively use their dwelling for five weeks out of the year before taxes kick in, although contracts with Humber Valley would allow owners to stay for six months if they wanted.)

In 2002, Dobbin and his investors acquired 660 acres of raw land adjoining Strawberry Hill on a moderately sloping mountainside that dropped to the very edge of Deer Lake. The land was earmarked for a golf course, restaurants, clubhouse, spa, and most importantly 321 chalets—each chalet would sit on about 1.5 acres of land.

Dobbin and investors put about $50 million into infrastructure developments including the bridge over the Humber River. Finally in 2003, properties at the brand new Humber Valley Resort came to market.

"The first potential buyers had to be taken across the river by boats," Clewer said. "They stood in the woodlands and we had to sell them the dream."

The concept was that the accommodations, or chalets, would be between 1,800 and 2,000 square feet with three bedrooms and three bathrooms.

Within two years, all the lots were sold. "In January 2003, we had a meeting here and the plan was to sell 70 properties that year," recalled Margaret Budgell, Humber Valley's property sales manager. "By the time December rolled around the sales number was at 200."

Prices for the land were then in the $100,000 range and because construction costs were reasonable at the time, the whole project might have cost an early investor $350,000 to $400,000.

Suddenly, and most surprisingly, western Newfoundland was on the map as a vacation home market.

For Dobbin and his investors, the project was so successful they picked up an additional 1,600 acres. A bigger Humber Valley Resort will be brought along slowly for a number of reasons, Clewer explained. First, when there were just 321 plots, buyers realized they would sell quickly so they had a sense of urgency to acquire. When there is another 1,600 acres to develop, that urgency fades. Second, there was some speculative buying in the first phase and after three to four years, some of the original buyers have decided to put those properties back onto the market. So as to not deflate the resale market, it was also necessary to slow new development.

If you were lucky enough to buy and build in 2003 or 2004, the value of your Humber Valley Resort home would be up about 300 percent in 2007.

Most of the principal buyers in the first phase were Europeans, who enjoyed an incredible bonus on the exchange rate between pound and euros and the Canadian dollar. Many of these buyers wanted to take advantage of the exchange rate by building bigger homes so newer plots of land grew larger and homes were being designed in the 2,500 to 3,500 square foot range with five and six bedrooms.

Today, 400 plots in Humber Valley have been sold, 170 homes already developed, and in spring 2007 another 40 were under construction. Clewer guessed by 2009 all the sold properties will be fully built out.

A Different Buyer

As noted, like similar resort areas, the Humber Valley Resort chalets are individually owned, but when not in use by the homeowner they can be put into the rental pool to be used by other vacationers. My wife and I were typical guests. We stayed two nights at a lakeside chalet and it was a wonderful experience.

The chalet, one of the smaller ones in the resort area, was about 1,800 square feet on two stories with a master bedroom upstairs and two smaller bedrooms downstairs. Since it was a home, there was a full kitchen, dining area, and living room. Decks were constructed at the back of the home so one could sit and look at the lake. There was also a hot tub ready for us to use on a landing constructed at water's edge.

I didn't know who the homeowner actually was, but when I scanned the guestbook, I saw a lot of the vacationers who had come to this property were from Great Britain.

Humber Valley succeeded not only because it is located in a wild, beautiful, and relatively undeveloped part of the world, but because the owners chose an unusual marketing approach. The target group was not wealthy folk in Toronto or Montreal, not successful investment bankers from Boston or New York, but people with excess capital in the United Kingdom.

The original sales push began in the U.K. for a number of reasons: first because there is affinity between the two countries; second, the flying time between Newfoundland and London is only five and a half hours; third, Newfoundland is scenic, undeveloped, and close to nature, which is a strong selling point to those big city dwellers in places like London; and fourth, in the U.K., there is an economic push for people to own property and that has resulted in some of the highest housing prices anywhere in the world. For what one would pay for a tiny, one-bedroom flat in London, a person could buy a huge house on an acre of land with fantastic scenic vistas in Newfoundland.

In 2007, the ownership breakdown at Humber Valley Resort showed 60 percent of the buyers were from the U.K.; 25 percent from Ireland; and the rest from scattered locations in Europe, the United States, and elsewhere in Canada. Homeowners at the resort come from 14 countries.

Charter flights now run twice a week in the winter (for skiing) and in the summer from London directly to Deer Lake airport, which has undergone a considerable renovation. The government investment to expand the airport continues as the province hopes to attract regular flights as well as direct connections to other cities such as Dublin.

When I was in Newfoundland, I kept running into people from Ontario, Canada's most populous province and home to its biggest city, Toronto. Air Canada now runs direct flights between Toronto and Deer Lake.

"We are scratching the surface in regard to marketing in Ontario and the United States," Clewer said.

American hunters and fishing enthusiasts have been coming to Newfoundland for decades, but that hasn't translated into vacation home ownership in the past. Humber Valley Resort is starting to attract Americans, Clewer said, with investors from such diverse states as New Jersey, Florida, and Texas. In the near future, the resort will be marketing to the New York area as well as Boston.

"A lot of places in the United States look similar to Newfoundland," Clewer said. "And there are areas in the U.S. that boast better scenery or wildlife, so it makes it difficult to compete. However, those places are heavily commercialized, promoted, and sold. Newfoundland is a much better value."

Market Changes

Lisa Anthony, the marketing manager at the Humber Valley Resort, told me this story. In 2006, she and her family moved from St. John's to the West Coast of Newfoundland. At the moment they are renting a home, but she and her husband decided they wanted to buy in a small community called Pasadena, a short drive from the resort. Much to her surprise, prices of residential homes had risen so fast, it was tough to find anything affordable to buy. She had been looking at a modest home on a small lot for $250,000. Five years before, just about any home in Pasadena could be had for $80,000 to $100,000.

Beginning in the mid-1990s, residential housing prices began to climb in almost all major Canadian cities from Halifax on the East Coast to Vancouver on the West Coast. Home prices were even climbing in the center of the country, in places like Winnipeg. In Newfoundland, the major city, St. John's, benefited from the rising prices, but on the West Coast, nothing. Not even in Corner Brook.

"The local market had been stagnant for about 10 years or more," Budgell said. "There was no steady appreciation like you saw elsewhere."

That was before Humber Valley Resort came into the picture, which changed people's perception of what homes could be worth. Up until the opening of the resort, western Newfoundland was a local market, but afterward the lands between Corner Brook and Deer Lake entered the global marketplace.

"If you were to talk to me 15 years ago, and asked, 'What is your second home, vacation home, market like?' I would have said, 'What are you talking about?' Everybody in the province owns a house and a cabin," said David Gillard, a veteran real estate broker and owner of Royal LePage NL Realty Ltd. in Corner Brook.

Now, he joked, "we have evolved."

Today, the phrase "vacation home market" is a common expression among locals, Gillard observed, "and we are just realizing what it means in the context of our island. We know this is a special area in the province, and people will pay premium dollars for the opportunity to live here part of the year."

The sudden jump in home prices can be attributed to the aftereffect of people paying $500,000 and more to live nearby, but it was also caused by foreign investors who came to look at Humber Valley Resort, saw what a beautiful area western Newfoundland was, and began traveling about seeing what else was available. In 2003–2004, everything was cheap and European visitors began buying residences, lake cottages, land, even businesses.

Chris Brothers, who owns Island Realty Inc., the Century 21 franchise in Corner Brook, met a couple from England who had bought a chalet at the Humber Valley Resort, but were looking to move to Newfoundland full-time. He found them a restaurant/gas station in the quaint seaside town of Rocky Harbor, which they bought.

The residential home market was slow for so long in western Newfoundland that Century 21 had closed its only office there in the mid-1970s. Brothers, who had been working in the financial services industry, decided he wanted to be his own boss and acquired the franchise. When I met Brothers at his office, which occupied the first floor of an old Corner Brook retail structure, he had been in the residential brokerage business for a year and a half. He seemed to have got in at an opportune time.

"The West Coast of Newfoundland is beautiful. And then there's the national park. In the summer months, tourists from the United States and, in fact, from all over the world visit," Brothers said, wistfully. They visited, toured, but never bought. Then came Humber Valley Resort and with it an influx of Europeans running around buying up real estate.

"A lot of people who owned properties, which had been family land for decades, are now selling," he said. "There is a half-acre lot on Deer Lake, which is selling for $295,000. Before Humber Valley Resort, you could have bought it for $20,000."

Even in Corner Brook, a blue-collar city where the two biggest industries are fishing and timber, prices have jumped. Homes that were selling for $140,000 have changed hands above $200,000, said Brothers. "We had a house sell for $360,000 that five years ago had sold for $190,000."

While the Corner Brook to Deer Valley residential market appears red hot, Gillard said, "a great deal of what we are seeing is actually catch-up. If you had been here 8 to 12 years ago, this was not a very upbeat place. We had gone through eight to nine of years of depressed values; people were selling properties and losing their shirts."

To Gillard, the big price increases, which came suddenly and without warning, simply brought home prices closer to the Canadian average. "My gut feeling is that we have on average enjoyed a 15 percent to 20 percent increase in prices over the last five years," he noted, but that only pushed the average price of a home in the area to $150,000, as compared with the average house price in Canada of $265,000.

The bull market in home prices has finally slowed, said Mel Tessier, proprietor of the Sutton Group Humber Realty Ltd., found on Main Street in Corner Brook. This doesn't mean the market has gone from boom to bust, but said Tessier, "We are at the flat point in a stair climb. The market was flat, went up, is going flat again as it catches its breath, and then will take off again. This area offers everything you can want—sailing, boating, golfing, skiing, cross-country skiing, hiking. It's a great place to have fun," he said. The only thing it could use is a few more days of sunshine. Newfoundland weather can be very wet and very unpredictable.

Other Developments, Other Areas

I briefly mentioned there was skiing in the Deer Lake-Corner Brook corridor. In fact, there is a small but well-regarded ski area called Marble Mountain Resort about halfway between the two population centers. Of course, it isn't Whistler, but some tour books tout Marble Mountain as the best skiing east of the Rockies.

From what I could see from the Trans-Canada Highway, Marble Mountain looked well-designed, making the most of its 1,700-foot summit (a not-too-shabby 1,600-foot vertical drop), 35 trails, 7 mogul runs, Terrain Park, and half-pipe. The longest run is three miles and the annual snowfall averages 16 feet.

Although there is something called the Marble Villa, a ski-in/ski-out condominium-style accommodation, there really wasn't a condo market to piggyback on in the ski trade until the Humber Valley Resort boom. Now there are a host of projects under construction or in the planning stages. "There are condos for sale in Steady Brook (a nearby community), and there might be some units left for sale as I don't think all were sold," Tessier said. "But the thing is, they keep building them. There is one project under construction now, and I just drove by some land where they were tearing down a house and I suspect they'll be putting condos up there, too."

In what I thought was an unusual marketing ploy, small billboards were erected near Marble Mountain advertising prices for condos. If my drive-by scribbles are accurate, one sign advertised condos for $133,000 and another for $239,000.

Of course, with the success of Humber Valley Resort, other developers have quickly moved into the region, scouting different locations. Gillard showed me the plans for a project called Taylor Estates in which his company was involved. Shortly after Humber Valley Resort opened, Gillard's firm sold about 150 acres on the shores of Deer Lake to a developer, who created a master plan for a 60-acre first phase. About 85 percent of the original lots have been sold, Gillard said. "Most of those lots were sold in the first 15 months with a high percentage going to British, Scottish, and Irish investors." The developer is now planning the second phase.

After we chatted in his office, Gillard called in one of his associates, Wayne Smith, who is involved in still another development on Deer Lake called South Brook Point. Smith passed me his plans, which involve a small project on a triangular spit of land totaling 31 acres that juts into the lake. The master plan shows 48 individual lots and 6 condo units on the east and west ends of the footprint. The lots average about one-third of an acre and entry-level costs will be in the $250,000 range. However, some lots on the water will go for $350,000 and one spectacular site will sell for close to a million.

Smith told me the project hasn't even been marketed and he doesn't yet have final drawings, but six lots have sold, and two more are close to the selling point. "These are good investments," Smith said. "Five years ago, if you paid $50,000 for a lot on the water people would say you paid a hell of a lot of money, but not today. The Humber Valley Resort did a fantastic job of marketing in the U.K. and showed us what the value of property is."

In May 2007, Royal LePage issued a report on Canada's cottage market, identifying 10 hidden gems. Number one on its list was George's Lake, about a 20-minute drive south of Corner Brook. The report noted, "George's Lake is an ideal spot for cottage-goers seeking affordable waterfront property. For $75,000 to $90,000, a seasonal, 50-year-old waterfront cottage can be found. George's Lake is renowned for its world-class fishing and wilderness access."[4]

Nearby George's Lake is the smaller Pinchgut Lake, and both were mentioned by Tessier as locations popular with locals that suddenly have been discovered by outsiders. Forget that $75,000 price tag. Tessier said he heard of one property going for $150,000.

Smith told me he'd been working on another development, much further to the south, almost at the southwestern tip of the island in a tiny, coastal community called St. Andrew's. "I'm involved with architects from Ontario and the Caribbean with a project that has a golf course," he said. "It's just a 15-minute drive from the ocean and sits along the International Appalachian Trail."

The Humber River flows south through Deer Lake before emptying into a great inlet called the Humber Arm. Along the southern coast of the inlet sits a string of older, small communities. I didn't visit here, but a number of Realtors told me the coastline here is majestic and it is where smart money will be heading soon. Others predict another coastal town, further south, called Stephenville, merits scrutiny. When I was in Newfoundland, the talk of the day was the closing of a newsprint mill in Stephenville where 300 people lost their jobs. A vacation home development there would be very helpful.

I know when people talk about vacation homes, they mostly think of beach locations. There's plenty of coastline in Newfoundland, but not too many days for sunbathing. No, this is the place to come to get close nature, where land has never been developed, where lakes abound and fishing is plentiful, where mountains roll down to the sea, where the air is crisp and clean, where the forests are thick enough to foil Hansel and Gretel, where moose and caribou are the most dangerous things on the road, and where, despite recent appreciation, it's still a damn cheap place to buy a second home.

How to Buy Property in Newfoundland

The home-buying process in Canada is very similar to that in the United States, so I'm not going to dwell on it very much. Tessier, however, does make some recommendations for investing in Newfoundland real estate.

First and foremost, don't buy property without using a lawyer. "I would not buy a doghouse in Canada without a lawyer investigating the title and deeds," he said frankly. Part of the problem, particularly in Newfoundland, is that many titles are not necessarily legally enforceable because property inheritance in the past has often been an informal process. A father dies and gives each son a parcel of land, but there are no documents to prove this actually happened. "In the rural areas, land titles can really be a problem," he said.

It's possible and fairly easy—depending on your credit history—to get local financing from a Canadian bank, and that process will take no more than 10 days at the most.

Finally, the multiple listing service is fairly new in western Newfoundland and not everyone subscribes to the concept. "There was a big debate about it here," Tessier recalled. At this point, he said, "Everyone else has caved into MLS, but my company does not subscribe to the system. We are the only ones left. Everything we sell is exclusive to us."

10 Things to Know about Buying Property in Newfoundland

1. Most of your neighbors in the dedicated vacation resort areas will be Europeans.
2. The main vacation home property is Humber Valley Resort, but others are being built.
3. The epicenter of Newfoundland's second home market is Deer Lake, but there is no shortage of remarkable lakes throughout the province.
4. The big surprise is that there is good skiing here at Marble Mountain.
5. The condominium market is just beginning to take off; most of the projects are located near Marble Mountain.
6. You should consult an attorney when buying properties in Newfoundland.
7. Home prices have appreciated considerably in recent years but remain far behind the rest of Canada.
8. Western Newfoundland remains virgin territory for second home investors; potentially, the whole western coast is ripe for investment.
9. Newfoundland has miles of coastline and miles of lakeshore.
10. Western Newfoundland is really a market for those folks who want to get close to nature, love the outdoors, enjoy observing wildlife, glory in beautiful and majestic surroundings, and plan on having an active winter and summer.

NOTES

Chapter 1

1. Tracie Rozhon, "Symbols of the Gilded Age, With a 21st-Century Luster," *New York Times,* November 24, 2006.
2. Kimberly Blanton, "Tide Going Out for Cape Home Sellers," *The Boston Globe,* June 10, 2006.
3. Craig Savoye, "Americans Buy Second Homes as a Refuge," *Christian Science Monitor,* November 23, 2001.
4. Les Christie, "Second-Home Sales at an All-Time High," CNNMoney.com, April 24, 2006.
5. "Second Home Survey Released by Resort Developer Centex," www.escape homes.com, June 17, 2004.
6. Les Christie, "Second-Home Sales at an All-Time High," CNNMoney.com, April 24, 2006.
7. Alex Frangos, "Plots & Ploys: Selling Sunshine," *Wall Street Journal,* November 22, 2006.
8. Alex Frangos, "Plots & Ploys: Selling Sunshine," *Wall Street Journal,* November 22, 2006.
9. "A Second Home across the Pond," www.fredricksburg.com, April 1, 2005.
10. Denny Lee, "A Second Home in Bulgaria?" *New York Times,* October 28, 2005.

Chapter 4

1. Blanche Evans, "Puerto Rico Realtors Report Increasing Interest in Homes," *Realty Times,* May 5, 2005.
2. Luis Ramos, "A Trip to Bountiful," *Caribbean Business,* November 27, 2003.
3. Stephen Simpson, "Another Ouster in Puerto Rico, "www.fool.com, October 3, 2005.
4. "In re R&G Financial Corporation Securities Litigation," www.blbglaw.com.
5. Thom Weidlich, "Puerto Rico Bank to Settle Suit for $74.3 Million," *Caribbean News,* March 6, 2007.
6. "Closing Costs," www.vendemossucasa.com.

Chapter 5

1. "Don't Stop the Carnival," www.st-croix.net.
2. "Introduction to St. Thomas, USVI," www.frommers.com.
3. Tom Bolt, "Crime Tops Voters Concern," http://lawblog.vilaw.com, October 7, 2006.

Chapter 6

1. W. Nicholas Captain, "Appraisal Models for Taxation Purposes: A Simplified Approach for a Small Market, Island of Guam," *Real Estate Issues*, Winter 2003.
2. Dr. Leroy O. Laney, "Guam Outlook Brighter than in Several Years," *First Hawaiian Bank Economic Forecast*, Guam Edition 2006–2007.
3. Dr. Leroy O. Laney, "Guam Outlook Brighter than in Several Years," *First Hawaiian Bank Economic Forecast*, Guam Edition 2006–2007.
4. Steve Limtiaco, "Realtor: New Rates Unfair; Proposal Targets Home Buyers, Sellers," *Pacific Daily News*, May 1, 2007.
5. Brenna Lorenz, "What's It Like to Live on Gaum?" www.heptune.com.
6. Brenna Lorenz, "What's It Like to Live on Gaum?" www.heptune.com.
7. Brenna Lorenz, "What's It Like to Live on Gaum?" www.heptune.com.

Chapter 7

1. John Toland, *The Rising Sun: The Decline and Fall of the Japanese Empire 1936–1945*, Random House, 1970.
2. John Toland, *The Rising Sun: The Decline and Fall of the Japanese Empire 1936–1945*, Random House, 1970.
3. John Toland, *The Rising Sun: The Decline and Fall of the Japanese Empire 1936–1945*, Random House, 1970.
4. Agnes Donato, "Cohen Calls for 'Flexible Federalization,'" *Saipan Tribune*, April 20, 2007.
5. John Toland, *The Rising Sun: The Decline and Fall of the Japanese Empire 1936–1945*, Random House, 1970.
6. "CNMI: Only 56 Passengers on JAL's Last Flight," *Pacific Magazine*, October 27, 2005.
7. Liberty Dones, "Chamber President-Elect Backs Article 12 Amendment," *Saipan Tribune*, December 17, 2006.

Chapter 8

1. "American Samoa—Basic Establishment," *411*, March 2007.
2. "American Samoa—Basic Establishment," *411*, March 2007.
3. "American Samoa—Basic Establishment," *411*, March 2007.
4. "Legal System in American Samoa," www.rjvlaw.com.

Chapter 10

1. "Buying Property in Costa Rica," *Costa Rica Real Estate & Tourism Guide*, February–March 2007.

2. "Buying Property in Costa Rica," *Costa Rica Real Estate & Tourism Guide*, February–March 2007.

3. "Buying or Building Your Costa Rican Dream House," www.costaricarealestate service.com.

4. "Property Rights and Foreign Investment in Costa Rica, www.realestatecosta rican.com.

5. Buying or Building Your Costa Rican Dream House," www.costaricarealestate service.com

6. "Property Rights and Foreign Investment in Costa Rica" www.realestatecosta rican.com.

7. Carlos Andres Jimenez Roja, "Buying Property in Costa Rica: The Importance of Title Guaranty," *Costa Rica Real Estate Premiere*, Edition 12.

8. "Real Estate Agents Call for Mandatory Licensing," www.dominicalrealty.com.

Chapter 11

1. "A Foreigner's Guide To Financing Property in Panama," *Panama Real Estate Magazine*, Summer 2006.

2. Panama Real Estate Laws, www.panamarealestatepros.com.

3. "Investment in Panama: What You Should Know," *Business Panama*, November 2006.

Chapter 12

1. "Buying and Living in Honduras," www.honduras-realestate.com.

2. "Buying and Living in Honduras," www.honduras-realestate.com.

3. Laura Moulder, "Top Ten Tips for Buying Property in the Bay Islands," *The Bay Islands Breeze*, Issue 2–2.

Chapter 13

1. "US$300 Million in Just Four Hours," *Dominican Today*, May 20, 2007.

2. "US$300 Million in Just Four Hours," *Dominican Today*, May 20, 2007.

3. "The Dominican Republic," www.totallyproperty.com.

4. "Buying Real Estate in the Dominican Republic: An Overview," www .punta-cana.us.

5. "Ten Easy Steps to a Smart Purchase," Stewart Title Dominicana Realty Guide, 2007.

Chapter 14

1. Jim Adair, "Family Feuds Erupt over Bequeathed Vacation Properties," *Realty Times*, May 23, 2002.

2. "Canadian Real Estate Headed for Record Books," www.inman.com, May 8, 2006.

3. "Canadian Housing Market Exceeds Expectations in First Quarter," www .royallepage.ca.

4. "Hidden Gems, Hot Spots, Top 10 Tips—Cottage Buyers Take Note," www .royallepage.ca.